CATHEDRAL ORGANISTS
PAST AND PRESENT

CATHEDRAL ORGANISTS
PAST AND PRESENT

A RECORD OF THE SUCCESSION OF ORGANISTS

OF THE

CATHEDRALS, CHAPELS ROYAL, AND PRINCIPAL

COLLEGIATE CHURCHES OF THE

UNITED KINGDOM,

FROM ABOUT THE PERIOD OF THE REFORMATION UNTIL THE PRESENT DAY.

WITH BIOGRAPHICAL NOTES, EXTRACTS FROM THE CHAPTER BOOKS, ANECDOTES, &c.

BY

JOHN E. WEST,

FELLOW OF THE ROYAL COLLEGE OF ORGANISTS ; ASSOCIATE OF THE ROYAL ACADEMY OF MUSIC.

KALPAZ

ISBN: 978-93-5128-787-2(HB)

First Published in 1899
Indian Reprint in 2017

Published by

Kalpaz Publications
C-30, Satyawati Nagar,
Delhi – 110052
E-mail: kalpaz@hotmail.com
Website: kalpazpublications.com
Ph.: +91-9212142040

Cataloging in Publication Data—DK
Courtesy: D.K. Agencies (P) Ltd. <docinfo@dkagencies.com>

West, John E. (John Ebenezer), 1863-1929**, author.**
Cathedral organists : past and present : a record of the succession of organists of the cathedrals, chapels royal, and principal collegiate churches of the United Kingdom : from about the period of the reformation until the present day : with biographical notes, extracts from the chapter books, anecdotes, & etc. / by John E. West.
pages cm
"First published in 1899"—Title page verso.
ISBN 9789351287872

1. Organists—England. 2. Church music—England. I. Title.

ML396.W51 2017 DDC 786.50942 23

PREFACE.

No complete or adequate record of past and present Cathedral Organists of the United Kingdom has hitherto been published. The following pages have, therefore, been compiled to supply this want.

The idea of this book originated in a somewhat imperfect list of Cathedral Organists, which I had gathered from various sources for my own private use. It afterwards occurred to me, however, that an amplification of this material, including short biographical notes concerning those Organists of whom any information could be obtained, might, if published, prove useful as a work of reference to Church musicians and to those interested in the history of this branch of the art of music.

The assistance of the majority of the present Cathedral and Collegiate Organists, and, in some cases, that of the Cathedral Clergy and Chapter Clerks, was accordingly asked, in searching their registers and other documents for further information on this subject; and it is greatly owing to the ready and generous manner in which these gentlemen have responded to my inquiries, that I have been enabled to obtain so complete and authentic a record.

It is difficult to state definitely when the office of Organist in our Cathedrals began to assume an independent and personal character; but, speaking approximately, it may be said to date from about the period of the Reformation.

In the early services of the Church very little practical skill was required for the accompaniment of the plain-song upon the primitive organs then in use, and the duties of Organist were apparently shared, in the majority of cases, by certain of the members of the Choral Establishment in turn. So that, although, in the early records, frequent mention is made of the "Organista," "Pulsator Organorum," "Lusor ad Organa," &c., these, and other distinctive titles applied to the player upon the organs, refer merely to the person filling that office for the time being. At Hereford, in the thirteenth century, the Organist was called "Clerk of the Organs"; at Exeter, at one period, he held the title of "Clerk of the Chapel"; and at St. Paul's he was appointed by the Præcentor "to keep the table and instruct the boys."

In tracing the history of Cathedral Organists an important distinction has to be drawn between Cathedrals of the Old Foundation and those of the New Foundation.

Cathedrals of the Old Foundation are those which retained, after the suppression of the Monasteries by Henry VIII., their original constitution; consequently there was no provision in the Statutes for an Organist as a separate and independent officer.

The following are the thirteen Cathedrals known as those of the Old Foundation:—

Bangor	Lincoln	St. Paul's
Chichester	Llandaff	Salisbury
Exeter	St. Asaph	Wells
Hereford	St. David's	York.
Lichfield		

Cathedrals of the New Foundation are those which were re-constituted in the time of Henry VIII. They are fourteen in number. Nine of them—

Canterbury	Durham	Rochester
Carlisle	Ely	Winchester
Dublin (Christ Church)	Norwich	Worcester

had previously been both Monasteries and Cathedrals; the remaining five:—

Bristol	Gloucester	Peterborough
Chester	Oxford	

had been simply Monasteries, and their Sees were then for the first time established.

In the Statutes of Henry VIII. for Cathedrals of the New Foundation, provision was generally made for the office of Organist. Exceptions to this, however, occur at Winchester and at Ely, where the Organist was not recognised as a distinct member of the Foundation until the time of the Statutes of Charles I. and Charles II. respectively.

In cases where no provision was thus made for an Organist, the office continued to be held by one or more of the members of the Choir, or by someone who was *virtually* Organist, but *statutably* a member of the Choral Establishment, receiving his salary, or the greater part of it, as a Vicar Choral or a Lay Clerk. Sometimes he was one of the Minor Canons or Priest Vicars, where such were included in the Choir, as at Exeter, Hereford, &c. Even at the present time the Organists of Exeter, Lichfield, Salisbury, and Winchester are, according to Statute, Lay Vicars; that of Lichfield receiving, as Organist, the annual salary of £4, as ordered by Bishop Hacket's Statutes, which were first put into force by Bishop Lloyd in 1693.

The office of Master of the Choristers has, since the Reformation, generally been united with that of Organist, especially in Cathedrals of the New Foundation; and where exceptions to this arrangement have occurred, they have, as a rule, only been in the case of individual Organists. At Lincoln—a Cathedral of the Old Foundation—however, the appointment of Master of the Choristers was separated from that of Organist in 1595, and, with one or two exceptions, the two posts were not re-united until the year 1850.

It has been impossible to trace a complete list of the earlier Organists in some of the Cathedrals of the Old Foundation from the fact that, the duty being generally allotted to certain members of the Choral Staff in turn, a very imperfect record exists as to which of these members were in the habit of performing the same. For this reason it *may* happen that one or two of the earlier names given under these Cathedrals are not those of Organists, and that, on the other hand, some of those whose names should appear as such have been omitted. At certain Cathedrals other circumstances, of course, have precluded the possibility of tracing a complete succession of the Organists.

In the case of Bristol, for instance, a break of nearly a century (1639-1734) occurs. The Cathedral records corresponding to that period were destroyed when the library was burnt during the riots of 1831, and no information concerning the Organists there during that break has been discovered from any other source.

At Llandaff, also, there was no Organ or Choral Service from 1691 until 1861, and the existing record of Organists there previous to 1691 is very imperfect.

During the search for information at Wells two breaks were discovered in the records, one of them being significantly noted—"Per bella civilia." The period of the Civil Wars has, in fact, produced a *hiatus* in the musical records of many of our Cathedrals and Collegiate Churches, owing to the destruction of the organs and music books by the Parliamentary troops, and the suspension of the Choral Service consequent upon that turbulent period. In 1644, moreover, an Ordinance of Parliament was passed for the entire suppression of Organs and the Choral Service, thereby temporarily depriving Organists and members of the Choir of their appointments. This Ordinance continued in force until the Restoration, when the Choral Service was resumed and Organs were again allowed.

Amongst other Cathedrals from which the information obtained has been somewhat incomplete are Lichfield and Southwell, the latter having no available record of past Organists earlier than 1718, with the exception of one solitary name which occurs at a pre-Reformation period. On the other hand, the lists of Bangor, Durham, Dublin (Christ Church and St. Patrick's Cathedrals), Exeter, Gloucester, Hereford, Norwich, Oxford (Christ Church), Peterborough, Rochester, St. Paul's, Salisbury, Worcester, and King's and Trinity Colleges at Cambridge, will be found nearly complete from a comparatively early date; whilst those of Chester, Ely, Lincoln, Westminster Abbey, the Chapel

Royal, St. George's Chapel at Windsor, and Magdalen College at Oxford may almost be regarded as giving an unbroken succession from about the time of the Reformation.

In the case of the recently established Cathedrals which were previously parish churches, with no endowed musical foundation—viz., Liverpool, Newcastle, St. Alban's, Southwark (St. Saviour's), Truro, and Wakefield, it has not been considered necessary to include the names of the *parochial* Organists who held office before the establishment of the See.

The biographical notes given under the names of the various Organists refer principally to their appointments and work as church musicians, and are not intended as a complete and exhaustive outline of their musical careers. Consequently, the matter devoted to well-known Organists, whose names are to be found in most of the musical biographies, will often appear to be short in proportion to that given under less distinguished names, much of which is recorded for the first time.

Several anecdotes, interesting extracts from Chapter books, &c., are included, many of which have never before been published.

Very little is mentioned concerning *Organs*, the subject being an extensive and peculiar one, and almost beyond the scope of the present book.

I desire to tender my grateful acknowledgments to the following who have kindly rendered me much valuable assistance in the compilation of this work:—

PROFESSOR PHILIP ARMES, M.A., Mus.D., Organist of Durham Cathedral.

IVOR A. ATKINS, Esq., Mus.B., Organist of Worcester Cathedral.

FRANK BATES, Esq., Mus.D., Organist of Norwich Cathedral.

G. GALLOWAY BEALE, Esq., Mus.B., Organist of Llandaff Cathedral.

MRS. JOHN STOCKS BOOTH, St. Alban's.

The REV. E. BRADLEY, M.A., Priest Vicar and Sacrist of Lichfield Cathedral.

A. H. BREWER, Esq., Mus.B., Organist of Gloucester Cathedral.

JOSEPH C. BRIDGE, Esq., M.A., Mus.D., Organist of Chester Cathedral.

PERCY C. BUCK, Esq., M.A., Mus.D., Organist of Bristol Cathedral.

JOHN S. BUMPUS, Esq.

EDWARD BUNNETT, Esq., Mus.D., Organist to the Corporation of Norwich.

The REV. CANON CHURCH, D.D., Sub-Dean of Wells.

C. E. CLARKE, Esq., late Assistant Organist of Gloucester Cathedral.

FREDERICK L. CLARKE, Esq., Bursar's Clerk of King's College, Cambridge.

D. J. D. CODNER, Esq., late Organist of St. David's Cathedral.

Richard Cope, Esq., Chapter Clerk of Windsor, and Clerk to the College, Eton.

J. M. Cowper, Esq., Curator of the Library, Canterbury.

Miss Crawford (daughter of the late Major Crawford), West Hill, Putney, S.W.

Edwin J. Crow, Esq., Mus.D., Organist of Ripon Cathedral.

The Rev. Arnold D. Culley, M.A., Mus.B., Cantab., Deputy Priest Vicar of Exeter Cathedral.

The Very Rev. A. P. Purey-Cust, D.D., Dean of York.

The Rev. Canon W. E. Dickson, M.A., late Precentor of Ely.

F. G. Edwards, Esq., Editor of *The Musical Times.*

The Rev. E. H. Fellowes, M.A., Mus.B., Precentor of Bristol Cathedral.

H. E. Ford, Esq., Mus.D., Organist of Carlisle Cathedral.

George Gaffe, Esq., Organist of St. Alban's Cathedral.

Miss Gunton, Rimmersfield, Chester.

Basil Harwood, Esq., M.A., Mus.D., Organist of Christ Church Cathedral, Oxford.

Frederick Iliffe, Esq., Mus.D., Organist of St. John's College, Oxford.

E. J. Hopkins, Esq., Mus.D., late Organist, and now Hon. Organist of the Temple Church.

John Hopkins, Esq., Organist of Rochester Cathedral.

John Horan, Esq., Organist of Christ Church Cathedral, Dublin.

Walter H. Hughes, Esq., Chapter Clerk of Bristol Cathedral.

William Hutt, Esq., Organist of Winchester College.

Haydn Keeton, Esq., Mus.D., Organist of Peterborough Cathedral.

Henry King, Esq., Late Assistant Vicar Choral of St. Paul's Cathedral.

Charles Harford Lloyd, Esq., M.A., Mus.D., Precentor of Eton.

W. H. Longhurst, Esq., Mus.D., Late Organist of Canterbury Cathedral.

J. B. Lott, Esq., Mus.B., Organist of Lichfield Cathedral.

Donald W. Lott, Esq., Formerly Organist of St. Columba's College, Rathfarnham.

Messrs. Macdonald and Malden, Chapter Clerks of Salisbury Cathedral.

The Rev. Canon A. R. Maddison, M.A., F.S.A., Priest Vicar and Succentor of Lincoln Cathedral.

The Rev. F. T. Madge, Minor Canon and Librarian of Winchester Cathedral.

A. H. Mann, Esq., Mus.D., Organist of King's College, Cambridge.

The Rev. W. Mann, M.A., Late Precentor of Bristol.

J. C. Marks, Esq., Mus.D., Organist of Cork Cathedral.

The Rev. R. T. Marshall, Minor Canon, Precentor, and Sacrist of Winchester Cathedral.

T. Westlake-Morgan, Esq., Organist of Bangor Cathedral.

H. C. Morris, Esq., Organist of St. David's Cathedral.

Sir Walter Parratt, Knt., Mus.D., Organist of St. George's Chapel, Windsor.

H. C. Perrin, Esq., Mus.B., Organist of Canterbury Cathedral.

J. Kendrick Pyne, Esq., Organist of Manchester Cathedral.

F. J. Read, Esq., Mus.D., Organist of Chichester Cathedral.

George Riseley, Esq., late Organist of Bristol Cathedral.

Thomas Shindler, Esq., M.A., LL.B., Registrar of the Royal College of Organists.

G. R. Sinclair, Esq., Organist of Hereford Cathedral.

The Rev. R. F. Smith, Precentor of Southwell Cathedral.

C. F. South, Esq., Organist of Salisbury Cathedral.

The Right Rev. the Lord Bishop of Bangor, D.D., late Dean of St. Asaph.

A. W. Wilson, Esq., B.A., Mus.D., Organist of St. Asaph Cathedral.

D. J. Wood, Esq., Mus.D., Organist of Exeter Cathedral.

The following, now deceased, also afforded me their kind help:—

John Naylor, Esq., Mus.D., Organist of York Minster.

J. M. W. Young, Esq., Organist of Lincoln Cathedral.

I cannot conclude these introductory remarks without expressing my deep sense of gratitude to my friend, Mr. John S. Bumpus, for the ungrudging manner in which he has given me the benefit of his long experience in matters relating to the history of Cathedral music, and, moreover, for so readily and constantly placing at my disposal his most interesting and valuable library. The sound advice, voluminous information, and kind encouragement which he has given me throughout the preparation of this work have enabled me to accomplish that which might otherwise have been an impossible task.

My special thanks are also due to Mr. F. G. Edwards, the Rev. H. O. Mackey, and Dr. A. H. Mann, for having read the proofs and for having offered several valuable suggestions.

JOHN E. WEST.

West Kensington,
September, 1899.

The following are amongst the various printed books, periodicals, catalogues, &c., from which information has been obtained for this work:—

"The Choral Service of the United Church of England and Ireland." John Jebb, D.D. [1843.]

"Cathedralia." A constitutional history of the Cathedrals of the Western Church. Mackenzie E. C. Walcott, B.D. [1865.]

"The Dictionary of National Biography." Edited by Leslie Stephen and Sidney Lee. [1883.]—(*In progress.*)

"A General History of the Science and Practice of Music." Sir John Hawkins. [1776.]

"A General History of Music." Charles Burney, Mus.D. [1776-89.]

"A Dictionary of Music and Musicians." Edited by Sir George Grove, C.B. [1878-85.]

"British Musical Biography." James D. Brown and Stephen S. Stratton. [1897.]

"A Short Historical Account of Degrees in Music." C. F. Abdy Williams, M.A., Mus.B. [1893.]

"Succession of Organists of the Cathedral Churches of Armagh, Christ Church, and St. Patrick's, Dublin," &c. Compiled by Major G. A. Crawford, M.A. [1881.]

"Papers, documents, law proceedings, &c., respecting the maintenance of the Choir of the Cathedral Church of Bangor, as provided for by an Act of Parliament, passed in the reign of King James the Second, A.D. 1685." Collected and arranged by Joseph Pring, Mus.D. [1819.]

"The Old Cheque Book, or Book of Remembrance, of the Chapel Royal." (Camden Society.) Edited by E. F. Rimbault, LL.D. [1872.]

"The History and Antiquities of the Cathedral Church of Canterbury." John Dart. [1726.]

"The Early Statutes of the Cathedral Church of Chichester." Mackenzie E. C. Walcott, B.D. [1877.]

"Annals of St. Fin Barre's Cathedral, Cork." Richard Caulfield, LL.D., F.S.A. [1871.]

"Registers of Durham Cathedral." Transcribed and annotated by Edward Arthur White, F.S.A. Edited for the Harleian Society by George J. Armytage, F.S.A. [1897.]

"History and Antiquities of the Cathedral and Conventual Church of Ely." James Bentham. Addenda by W. Stevenson, F.S.A. [1817.]

"Fasti Herefordensis." Francis T. Havergal, M.A. [1869.]

"A Short Account of the Vicars Choral, &c., of Lincoln Cathedral, from the 12th Century to the Accession of Edward VI." Also four

Papers on the same subject continued to the present time. A. R. Maddison, M.A., F.S.A. [1878.]

"Some account of the Condition of the Fabric of Llandaff Cathedral from 1575 to its re-opening in 1857." Alfred Ollivant, D.D. (Bishop of Llandaff). [1857.]

"A Register of the Presidents, Fellows, Demies, . . . and other Members of St. Mary Magdalen College, Oxford." John Rouse Bloxam, D.D. [1853-76.]

"Memorials of the Church of St. Peter and Wilfred, Ripon." Edited, for the Surtees Society, by J. T. Fowler. [1882-86.]

"Registers of the Cathedral Church of Rochester." Thomas Shindler, M.A., LL.B. [1892.]

"History and Antiquities of the Parish of St. David's." Captain George Manby. [1801.]

"History and Antiquities of St. David's." Jones and Freeman. [1856.]

"The Organists and Composers of St. Paul's Cathedral." John S. Bumpus. [1891.]

"A History of the Antiquities of Southwell." W. Dickenson Rastall, M.A. [1787.]

"A few Notes on the Temple Organ." Edmund Macrory, Q.C. [1861.]

"The Marriage, Baptismal, and Burial Registers of the Collegiate Church or Abbey of St. Peter, Westminster." Edited and annotated by Col. Joseph Lemuel Chester, LL.D., D.C.L., F.R.H.S. [1876.]

"Documents relating to the History of the Cathedral Church of Winchester." Edited, for the Hants Record Society, by R. W. Stephens, B.D., F.S.A. (Dean of Winchester), and F. T. Madge, M.A. (Minor Canon and Librarian of Winchester Cathedral). [1889, &c.]

"Annals of Winchester College." T. F. Kirby, M.A., F.S.A. [1892.]

"Annals of Windsor," &c. Tighe and Davis. [1858.]

"History and Antiquities of the City and Suburbs of Worcester." Valentine Green. [1796.]

"A Survey of the Cathedral Church of Worcester." William Thomas. [1736.]

"Eboracum"; or, the History and Antiquities of the City of York, together with the History of the Cathedral Church, &c. Francis Drake, F.R.S. [1736.]

"A Survey of the Cathedrals of York, Durham," &c., &c. Browne Willis. [1742.]

"Annals of the Three Choirs." Daniel Lysons, M.A., F.R.S., F.S.A., John Amott, C. Lee Williams, Mus.B., and H. Godwin Chance, M.A. [1895.]

"History of the Handel and Haydn Society" (Boston, U.S.A.) Charles C. Perkins.

"English Church Composers." ("The Great Musicians" Series.) William Alexander Barrett, Mus.B. [1882.]

"Purcell." ("The Great Musicians" Series.) William H. Cummings. [1881.]

"An Account of the Musical Performances in Westminster Abbey and the Pantheon . . . 1784, in Commemoration of Handel." Charles Burney, Mus.D. [1785.]

"Sir John Stevenson." A Biographical Sketch. John S. Bumpus [1893.]

"Memoir of Sir Robert Stewart." Olinthus J. Vignoles, M.A. [1898.]

"A Few Words on Cathedral Music and the Musical System of the Church, with a Plan of Reform." Samuel Sebastian Wesley, Mus.D. [1849.]

"Fifty Years of Church Music." W. E. Dickson, M.A. [1895.]

"Musical and Personal Recollections during Half-a-Century." Henry Phillips. [1864.]

"The Musical Haunts of London." F. G. Edwards. [1895.]

"Court and Private Life in the time of Queen Charlotte." Journals of Mrs. Papendiek. Edited by her grand-daughter, Mrs. Vernon Delves Broughton. [1887.]

"A Collection of Anthems as sung at Christ Church and St. Patrick's Cathedrals (&c.), Dublin." John Finlayson, M.A. [1852.]

"Catalogue of Ancient Choral Services and Anthems preserved . . . in the Cathedral Church of Ely." Edited by W. E. Dickson, M.A. [1861.]

English Musical Gazette. [1819.]

Ecclesiologist. [1859.]

Musical Times.
Musical Opinion.
Musical News.
Musical Standard.
Canterbury Press.
&c., &c.
} Various Numbers.

CONTENTS.

CATHEDRALS.

	PAGE
ARMAGH	1
BANGOR...	2
BRISTOL	6
CANTERBURY	8
CARLISLE	11
CHESTER	12
CHICHESTER	16
CORK	18
DUBLIN—	
CHRIST CHURCH	20
ST. PATRICK'S	24
DURHAM	26
EDINBURGH—	
ST. MARY'S	28
ELY	29
EXETER...	32
GLOUCESTER	34
HEREFORD	40
LICHFIELD	44
LINCOLN	46
LIVERPOOL	50
LLANDAFF	51
LONDON—	
ST. PAUL'S	52
SOUTHWARK (ST. SAVIOUR'S)	57
MANCHESTER	58
NEWCASTLE	61
NORWICH	61
OXFORD—	
CHRIST CHURCH	65
PETERBOROUGH	68
RIPON	70
ROCHESTER	71
ST. ALBAN'S	74
ST. ASAPH	75
ST. DAVID'S	76
SALISBURY	78
SOUTHWELL	80
TRURO	82
WAKEFIELD	82
WELLS	83
WINCHESTER	85
WORCESTER	89
YORK	92

COLLEGIATE CHURCHES AND CHAPELS, &c.

	PAGE
CAMBRIDGE—King's College	96
" " St. John's College	98
" " Trinity College	99
ETON COLLEGE	102
LONDON—Chapel Royal (St. James's)	104
" Temple Church	111
" Westminster Abbey	112
OXFORD—Magdalen College	118
" New College	122
" St. John's College	125
RATHFARNHAM—St. Columba's College	126
TENBURY—St. Michael's College...	128
WINCHESTER COLLEGE	130
WINDSOR—St. George's Chapel (Royal)	131
INDEX OF ORGANISTS' NAMES	135

ARMAGH.

	Year of Appointment.	Year of Resignation or Death.
RICHARD GALWAY	1634	——

In his Patent he is described as "Primus et modernus Organista dicti cœnobii."

*

JOHN HAWKSHAW (? Junr.)	1661	1695

(See under Christ Church and St. Patrick's Cathedrals, Dublin.)

ROBERT HODGE (? Junr.)	1695	——

According to the records he succeeded John Hawkshaw. He was therefore probably a son of Robert Hodge, of St. Patrick's Cathedral, Dublin.

*

WILLIAM TOOLE	1711	1722

(See under Cork.)

SAMUEL BETTRIDGE	1722	(?)1752
JOHN WOFFINGTON...	1752	(?)1758

Died 1758.

ROBERT BARNES	1759	1774

He is said to have resigned in 1774, on becoming a Vicar Choral.

LANGRISHE DOYLE, Mus.D., Dub.	1776 (? 1774)	——

(See under Christ Church Cathedral, Dublin.)

*

RICHARD LANGDON, Mus.B., Oxon.	1782	1794

(See under Ely.)

JOHN CLARKE (afterwards CLARKE-WHITFELD), Mus.B., Oxon., Mus.D., Dub.; Cantab. et Oxon.	1794	1797

(See under Hereford.)

JOHN JONES, Mus.D., Dub.	1797	1816

Born 1767. Pupil of Dr. Arnold. Vicar Choral of Armagh Cathedral, 1796; Organist, ditto, 1797. Resigned 1816. Died 1820.

FREDERICK WILLIAM HORNCASTLE	1816	1823

Dismissed in 1823. Afterwards appointed a Gentleman of the Chapel Royal. Composer of Glees, Songs, Pianoforte pieces, &c.

---

* These blank spaces, which occur from time to time throughout the book, indicate either the period of the suppression of Organs during the Commonwealth or a break in the succession of Organists.

B

ROBERT TURLE 1823 1872

Younger brother of James Turle, Organist of Westminster Abbey. Born at Taunton, 1804. Appointed Organist of Armagh Cathedral, in succession to F. W. Horncastle. Retired on a pension, 1872. Died at Salisbury, 1877. Composer of Church Music. Two Double Chants by him are still in use.

THOMAS OSBORNE MARKS, Mus.B., Oxon., 1870; Mus.D., Dub., 1874 ... ... 1872 ——

Brother of Dr. J. C. Marks, Organist of Cork Cathedral. Born at Armagh, 1845. Chorister in the Cathedral and afterwards pupil of Robert Turle and Assistant Organist. Appointed Organist on Turle's resignation. Conductor of the Armagh Philharmonic Society. Composer of Church Music, Organ pieces, Part-songs, Songs, &c.

BANGOR.

From the following it appears that there must have been an Organist at Bangor Cathedral as early as 1360, if not before:—

The celebrated Bard, Dafydd ab Gwilym, who wrote in the fourteenth century, makes particular mention of an organ and choir at Bangor in his time, in a commendatory Ode addressed to Hywel, Dean of Bangor. The Ode, which was in Welsh, has the following: "Whose organ, and harmonious choir, are unrivalled in performance." Hywel was made Dean of Bangor in 1359 and Bishop in 1370. This Ode, therefore, must have been written between 1359 and 1370, and the allusion to an organ renders it obvious there must have been an Organist at that time.*

THOMAS BOLTON ... ... —— 1644

Died January 1, 1644. Buried in the Cathedral.

A VICAR CHORAL (name unknown) was Organist 1689 1691

Chapter order, October, 1689:—"That Hugh Johnson be one of the singing-men in the choir of the said Cathedral *while a Vicar Choral is Organist there and no longer* and that he have a salary of eight pounds per annum payed him during the said time out of the tithe of Llandinam in the County of Montgomery pursuant to a late Act of Parliament in that behalf made and provided."†

THOMAS ROBERTS 1691 1705

Born about 1658. Appointed Organist of Bangor Cathedral at a salary of £14.

From his tombstone, once in the North Transept of the Cathedral, it appears that he was the first "Endowed" Organist since the Restoration, the Organists of Bangor having been paid, from that time down to the present, from the tithes of Llandinam, Montgomeryshire, before mentioned. The

---

* I am indebted for this, and for much of the information regarding the organists of Bangor Cathedral, to Mr. T. Westlake Morgan, the present Organist.

† The Act of King James (1685) for the maintenance of the Bangor Choir and the repair of the Cathedral Church.

following was the inscription on his tombstone:—"Here lies in the hope of a joyful Resurrection the body of Thomas Roberts, the first Endowed Organist of this Cathedral since the Restauration, who died on the 18th of May, in the year of our Lord, 1705, and the 48th year of his age."

Christian names Unknown.

(NATHANIEL?) PRIEST 1705 1708

Was nominated for the post by Mr. Hall, Organist of Hereford. In the event of his giving satisfaction and improving the singing at the end of a twelvemonth he was to receive a gratuity of £5 "to reward and encourage his diligence."

Probably the Composer of a Service in F, in the books of Canterbury, Oxford, and elsewhere.

(See also under Bristol.)

—— SMITH 1708 1710

—— FERRER 1710 1712

JOHN RATHBONE 1713 1721

Elected in 1713, but drew his salary from August, 1712.

THOMAS RATHBONE 1721 1750

Son of the foregoing.

THOMAS LLOYD 1750 1778

RICHARD JARRED (or GERARD) 1778 1782

The record of his appointment says *Jarred;* but in 1779 he was paid as *R. Gerard.* He was probably a relation of the *Gerards* at St. Asaph Cathedral.

WILLIAM SHRUBSOLE 1782 1784

Born at Canterbury, 1760. Chorister in Canterbury Cathedral. Organist of Bangor Cathedral, 1782. Dismissed in 1784 for "frequenting Conventicles." Appointed the same year Organist of Spa Fields Chapel, Clerkenwell, London. Died in London, January 18, 1806. Buried in Bunhill Fields, Finsbury. Composer of the tune "Miles Lane," which is generally associated with Perronet's Hymn "All hail the power of Jesu's name."

The first strain of this tune was cut upon his tombstone, in 1892, when it was restored, at the instigation of Mr. F. G. Edwards, who collected subscriptions for that purpose.

Within a month of his appointment at Bangor, he performed his duties in a manner so satisfactory and promising that the Chapter thought proper for his encouragement to allow him £8 8s. towards the expense of his journey and the removal of his harpsichord and other effects from London to Bangor.

EDMUND OLIVE 1784 1793

Afterwards Organist of the Parish Church, Warrington. Died at Warrington, November 18, 1824. Compiler of "Sixteen Psalm tunes, adapted for three voices."

During his appointment at Bangor, Olive was allowed £4 a year extra for keeping the organ in tune.

JOSEPH PRING, MUS.D., OXON., 1808 ... ... 1793 1842

He was not formally appointed Organist until September 28, 1810, although he had acted since 1793 in place of his relative, Mr. Olive, who had resigned in his favour.

In Dr. W. Hayes' Collection of Anthems (1795) Joseph Pring's name appears amongst the subscribers as "Organist of Bangor Cathedral and Beaumaris."

Born at Kensington, 1776. Chorister in St. Paul's Cathedral. Organist of Bangor Cathedral, 1793. From 1813 to 1819 engaged (together with three of the Vicars Choral) in litigation with the capitular body for the recovery of certain of the tithes belonging to the maintenance of the Cathedral Choir, which had become misappropriated by the Chapter. The suit was heard by Lord Eldon, the eminent Chancellor, whose language is said to have often been more forcible than polite. It was only partially successful, and resulted in a much smaller increase of salary to the musical staff than they were entitled to, under a strict interpretation of the Act.*

Died February 13, 1842. Buried in the Cathedral Yard, Bangor. Composer of Church Music, Songs, &c. Compiler of "A Collection of Anthems used in Bangor Cathedral." Author of a booklet on the opening, construction, &c., of the Menai Suspension Bridge; also of a volume of the proceedings connected with the lawsuit mentioned above.

EPITAPH ON DR. JOSEPH PRING.

Ah! gifted man! his death we all deplore,
The favourite son of Nature, and of Art;
High was his calling, genuine his lore,
With such a genius we felt loth to part.

Dim are the eyes of relatives and friends,
As on the Bangor Choir affection doats;
Delusive fancy from the organ swells
Still to the sorrowing ear his requiem notes!

His master music in the Church below
Is hushed for ever!—Still we hope he plays
Immortal anthems; where the sounds of woe
Shall never damp the sweetness of his lays.

(E. THOMAS, Clynnog.)

[*Translated from the Welsh of R. Williams.*]

The *last stanza only*, in Welsh and English, is engraved on Pring's tombstone in the Cathedral Yard. The whole was printed in Welsh and English at the time of Dr. Pring's death, on a black bordered leaflet.†

Dr. Pring was created a Welsh "Pencerdd" in Bardic circles, and he even became acquainted with the vernacular itself.

JAMES SHARPE PRING 1842 1868

Son of the foregoing. Born about 1811. Chorister in Bangor Cathedral, and afterwards Assistant Organist to his father. Organist, 1842, the appointment, however, being made from year to year, probably owing to the alarm of the Dean and Chapter at Dr. Pring's spirited lawsuit. Died June 3, 1868, aged 57. Buried in Glanadda Cemetery, Bangor. Some Chants by him are to be found in Warren's Collection.

He was musical editor of the "Bangor Collection" of Anthems, adapted from various composers (1848). The English words were fitted to the music chiefly by the Very Rev. James Henry Cotton, Dean of Bangor, and formerly Precentor.

Mr. T. Westlake Morgan has kindly supplied me with the two following anecdotes of J. S. Pring:—

(*a*) When the See of Manchester was founded in 1847 and Bishop Lee was consecrated its first Bishop, Mr. Pring, meeting his attached friend, Dean Cotton, in Bangor one day, alluded to the appointment, and remarked: "I

* It is said that this lawsuit so impoverished Dr. Pring that he and his family were for some time in great need, and could only obtain their necessary sustenance on credit.

† A copy of this, now in the possession of Mr. J. S. Bumpus, was given to Miss Hackett, in 1842, by J. S. Pring, the Doctor's son and successor.

say, Mr. Dean, they ought to have made *you* Bishop of Manchester." "Why, Mr. Pring?" enquired the Dean. "Because Cottonopolis would then have had a *Cotton* Bishop," was the Organist's reply.

(*b*) Mr. J. S. Pring suffered some considerable inconvenience on account of his obesity. A story is told of him in connection with a Choral Festival in Bangor Cathedral. He was presiding at the organ (then on the screen), and Owain Alaw (Mr. John Owen, of Chester) was wielding the baton. Coming out of the Cathedral, Mr. Pring, overcome by the Conductor's somewhat rapid "tempi," walked slowly up the incline towards the iron railings which bounded the Precincts; feeling fatigued, he seized hold of the bars of the gateway with both hands, and, steadying himself, rested awhile. Owain Alaw, on coming up, enquired what he was doing. Mr. Pring, with characteristic humour, replied that he was taking "*a bar's rest.*"

ROBERT ROBERTS 1868 1871

Born in St. Anne's Parish, Llandegai, near Bangor, May 24, 1840. Chorister in St. Anne's Church. Pupil of H. S. Hayden (Organist of St. Mary's, Carnarvon, and son of William Hayden, Organist of St. Asaph Cathedral). Student of the North Wales College for Schoolmasters, Carnarvon, where he became successively Third Master, Third Master and Music Master, and Music Master only. Assistant Organist of Bangor Cathedral, 1866; Organist, 1868 (appointed probationally by the year). Died of pleurisy February 9, 1871. Buried in Glanadda Cemetery, Bangor. Composer of a Welsh Funeral Service, Cantata "The Siege of Harlech Castle," Part-songs, &c.

A window was erected to his memory, and that of the Principal's two children, in the North Wales Training College Chapel at Carnarvon (now removed to Bangor). He was much beloved and respected, and his death, at the age of thirty, was greatly deplored. At the funeral service, held in the Cathedral, Spohr's "Blest are the departed" was sung, when one of the choristers, William Jones (a great favourite of the deceased Organist), became so affected during the singing of one of the solo portions that he completely broke down, and sobbed aloud.

ROLAND ROGERS, Mus.D., Oxon., 1875 ... ... 1871 1892

Born at West Bromwich, 1847. Organist of St. Peter's, West Bromwich, 1858; St. John's, Wolverhampton, 1862; Tettenhall Parish Church, 1867; and Bangor Cathedral, 1871. Resigned the latter post, 1892. Now Organist of St. James's, Bangor, and Lecturer in Music at the University College of North Wales. Composer of Cantatas, "Prayer and Praise," "Florabel," and "The Garden," Church Music, Part-songs, Organ pieces, &c.

TOM WESTLAKE MORGAN ... ... 1892 ——

Born at Congresbury, Somerset, 1869. Chorister in King's College, Cambridge, and afterwards Pupil-Assistant to Dr. Mann and Organist of St. Catharine's College. Student at the Royal College of Music. Organist of St. George's Church, Paris, 1889; St. John's, Wilton Road, London, 1890; St. David's, Merthyr Tydvil, 1891; and Bangor Cathedral, 1892. Appointed Examiner to the Welsh Section of the Incorporated Society of Musicians, 1894. Music Master of the North Wales Training College, Bangor, 1895-1897. Collected funds for, and superintended the building of, the large four-manual organ by Hill in the Cathedral, opened in 1897. Composer and Editor of Welsh and other Church Music, &c.

BRISTOL.

The Organist appointed at the Reformation (according to the statutes of Henry VIII.'s Foundation, dated June 4, 1542) was—

JOHN SENNY... ... ... 1542 ——

At a Salary of £10 per annum.

ELWAY BEVIN ... ... (?)1589 1637

Of Welsh descent. Pupil of Tallis. Gentleman of the Chapel Royal, 1605. He was compelled to forfeit the latter appointment, and that at Bristol, upon its being discovered that he was an adherent to the Romish faith. The exact year of his death is unknown. Composer of Church Music, &c. Author of "A Briefe and Short Introduction to the Art of Music," dedicated to the Bishop of Gloucester, "unto whom" Bevin appears to have "been much bound for many favours." It is a quaint and interesting book, and a useful guide to the solution of the ingenious forms of Canon which were largely practised by composers of that time.

EDWARD GIBBONS, Mus.B., { Cantab. (?) / et Oxon., 1592 } ...(?)1599 (?)1609

Also Minor Canon and Precentor.

Elder brother of Dr. Orlando Gibbons. Born about 1570. Organist of King's College, Cambridge, 1592. Organist, Minor Canon, and Precentor of Bristol Cathedral, (?)1599. Left Bristol, and became Organist and Custos of the College of Priest Vicars of Exeter Cathedral, 1609-1644. Matthew Locke was one of his pupils. An Anthem by him, "How hath the citie sate solitary," is in the Tudway Collection.

It would appear that Bevin and Gibbons were Organists together for some period. Probably, however, Gibbons only took occasional duty at the organ.

At King's College, Cambridge, "Gibbins" (as he was more usually called) received 20s. a quarter as his salary, and 11s. 8d. for the instruction of the Choristers. He had to provide for the making and mending of the Choristers' clothes. At Exeter, in 1634, a complaint was made that he was in the habit of neglecting his duties, and he, with two other Vicars Choral, replied to the charge.

He is said to have assisted Charles I., at the time of the Rebellion, with the loan of £1,000, for which service he was afterwards deprived of his estates and rendered homeless in his eightieth year.

ARTHUR PHILLIPS, Mus.B., Oxon., 1640 ... ... 1638 1639

Born 1605. Clerk of New College, Oxford, 1622. Organist of Bristol Cathedral, 1638. Organist of Magdalen College, Oxford, and University Choragus, 1639. During the Rebellion he went abroad, and was Organist to Queen Henrietta Maria. He subsequently returned to England, where it is supposed that he died. Composer of "The Requiem; or, Liberty of an Imprisoned Royalist," "The Resurrection," &c.

The Bristol Cathedral Records are very imperfect, as they were mostly destroyed in the Riots of 1831, when the Library was burnt. Hence the absence of information, for nearly a century, in regard to the Organists.

NATHANIEL PRIEST was Organist in 1724. Probably the —— Priest mentioned as Organist of Bangor Cathedral, 1705-1708, and Composer of a Service in F.
(See under Bangor.)

JAMES MORLEY 1734 1756

GEORGE COMBES 1756 1759

EDWARD HIGGINS 1759 1765

Without doubt, the same Edward Higgins, "a native of England," who became a Vicar Choral of Christ Church and St. Patrick's Cathedrals, Dublin, 1765.

GEORGE COMBES (Re-appointed) 1765 1769

EDWARD ROOKE 1769 1773

SAMUEL MINEARD 1773 1777

RICHARD LANGDON, Mus.B., Oxon. 1778 1781
(See under Ely.)

RICE WASBROUGH 1781 1802

Buried in the Cathedral. Near his grave is a monument to him, his wife, and eldest son, John.

JOSEPH KEMP, Mus.D., Cantab., 1809 ... ... 1802 1809

Born at Exeter, 1778. Pupil of William Jackson. Appointed Organist of Bristol Cathedral, 1802. Removed to London and became a teacher there. Died in London, 1824. Composer of an Oratorio, "The Crucifixion," Church Music, "Twenty Double Chants," Cantatas, Glees, &c.

JOHN WASBROUGH 1809 1825

Eldest son of Rice Wasbrough, above mentioned. Died 1825. Composer of Church Music. There is a Chant by him in Warren's Collection.

JOHN DAVIS CORFE... ... ... 1825 1876

Son of A. T. Corfe, Organist of Salisbury, and brother of Dr. C. W. Corfe, Organist of Christ Church Cathedral, Oxford. Succeeded John Wasbrough as Organist of Bristol Cathedral, 1825. Conductor for many years of the Bristol Madrigal Society. Died 1876. A memorial window to him was placed in the Cathedral by public subscription, October, 1877.

GEORGE RISELEY 1876 1898

Born at Bristol, August 28, 1845. Chorister in the Cathedral, 1852. Afterwards articled pupil to J. D. Corfe. Assistant Organist of the Cathedral and Organist of various churches in and around Bristol. Organist of the Colston Hall, Bristol, 1870. Organist of the Cathedral, 1876. Resigned 1898. Conductor of the Colston Hall Concerts, and, since Sir Charles Hallé's death, of the Bristol Musical Festival. Conductor of the Bristol Royal Orpheus Glee Society, 1878. Conductor of the Bristol Society of Instrumentalists, 1887. Conductor of the Bristol Choral Society, 1889. Professor of the Organ at the Royal Academy of Music. Conductor of the Queen's Hall Choral Society, and Musical Director of the Alexandra Palace, 1898.

PERCY CARTER BUCK, M.A., Mus.D., Oxon. ... 1899 ——
(See under Wells.)

CANTERBURY.

MATTHEW GODWIN, Mus.B., Oxon. ... ... —— ——
(See under Exeter.)

—— SELBY was Organist, circa 1600.

"In 1660, at the time of the Restoration, one pound (£1) was given to FRANCIS PLOMER as Organist of the Sermon House" (the last four words have been crossed out by a pen). Mr. J. M. Cowper, the Curator of the Library, and a distinguished Canterbury antiquary, to whom I am indebted for much of the information concerning the Organists of Canterbury Cathedral down to the year 1700, is of opinion that Plomer's appointment was Cromwellian, and that he was dismissed with a gratuity of one pound sterling.

THOMAS GIBBES ... ... 1661 (?)1669

Possibly a son of Richard *Gibbs*, Organist of Norwich Cathedral.
According to the registers he was still Organist in 1664. There is no record of his resignation or death. He probably held the office until the appointment of Chomley, in 1669.
(See also under Norwich.)

RICHARD CHOMLEY... ... ... 1669 1675

"In 1675, on December 9, Richard Chomley, the Organist, represented to the Chapter of the Cathedral that 'by reason of age and other infirmities' he was willing to surrender his place, and to remove to London or elsewhere. Thereupon it was agreed to pay him the next quarter's wages, to bestow upon him ten pounds towards his expense of removing, and to allow him a pension of twenty-five shillings a year, to be paid quarterly. The salary attached to the office was then forty pounds a year."*

ROBERT WREN 1675 1691

Probably a son of Charles Wren, Organist of Rochester Cathedral.
"On the same day, December 9, 1675, the Chapter elected Robert Wren, 'a member of this Church,' as Chomley's successor. At the time of his election, Wren was one of the Lay Clerks of the Cathedral."† Died 1691. Buried in the Cloisters.

NICHOLAS WOOTTON 1692 1698

Admitted Organist and Lay Clerk, December 1, 1692.
In April, 1698, he was summoned to appear before the Chapter "to answer to such matters as shall then be objected to him." Wootton seems to have failed to comply with this order, as on June 27 it was resolved that "forasmuch as Nicholas Wootton, Organist of this Church, hath left and deserted that place," and for other misdemeanours, "he be removed, and the place be void."
Died April 16, 1700. Buried in the North Aisle of the Cathedral.

* Article by Mr. J. M. Cowper in the *Canterbury Press*.
† Ibid.

Daniel Henstridge 1699 1736

(Previously Organist of Rochester Cathedral, and also, possibly, of Gloucester Cathedral. The *Daniel Henstridge* at the latter Cathedral was more likely, however, to be the father of the above.) Appointed Organist on probation, December, 1698, one of the conditions being that he should take upon himself to teach not more than ten King's Scholars to sing "Tallis his Service"; another, that the new Organist "shall assist Porter* as far as he is capable in instructing him on the organ." Sworn and admitted Organist and Master of the Choristers, June, 1699. Died 1736. Buried in the Cathedral. The Organ parts to some of his compositions (including a Service in D) are still extant in MS.

William Raylton 1736 1757

Pupil of Dr. Croft. Appointed to Canterbury, 1736. Died 1757. Composer of Church Music. His Service in A is still sung at Canterbury, and a Service in E flat and one or two Anthems are in MS. in the Cathedral books. A setting of the opening Burial Sentences by him is to be found in Vincent Novello's Collection of Purcell's Sacred Music, Vol. IV., and was probably intended to precede the setting by Purcell, in the same key (C minor), of the remaining Sentences, which is contained in the same volume.†

Samuel Porter 1757 1803

Born at Norwich, 1733. Chorister in St. Paul's Cathedral, and pupil of Dr. Greene. Organist of Canterbury Cathedral, 1757. Retired 1803. Died at Canterbury, December 11, 1810. Buried in the Cloisters of the Cathedral. A tablet erected there to his memory has recently been restored. A volume of Cathedral Music was prepared by him and published by his son, William James Porter. His Service in D is issued in octavo form by Messrs. Novello.

Highmore Skeats (Senr.) 1803 1831

Born 1760. Chorister in Exeter Cathedral. Vicar Choral of Salisbury Cathedral. Organist of Ely Cathedral, 1778-1803. Died at Canterbury, June 29, 1831. Buried in St. Martin's Churchyard.

His son (Highmore Skeats, Junr.) succeeded him at Ely, and was subsequently Organist of St. George's Chapel, Windsor.

Composer of Church Music (including a Complete Morning and Evening Service in C, in triple time throughout), Glees, Songs, &c. Editor of Dr. J. Stephens's‡ Cathedral Music and of a Collection of Songs.

His Anthem, "The righteous souls that take their flight," is included in a Collection of Short Anthems by Dr. Longhurst, and has been sung at the burial of several of the Canons, &c., of Canterbury.

In 1825 (or 1826) James Longhurst, father of Dr. W. H. Longhurst, added "German pedals" to the old organ, then standing on the Rood Screen,

---

* This could not be the Samuel Porter mentioned as Organist of Canterbury, 1757-1804.

† It should be remembered that Purcell's familiar music to "Thou knowest, Lord the secrets of our hearts," is *another* setting of the Burial Sentence commencing with those words, and was written as a Funeral Anthem for Queen Mary. Dr. Croft was afterwards so impressed with its beauty that he incorporated it into his setting of the Burial Sentences in preference to attempting to set the same words himself.

No one can deny the deep feeling and solemn simplicity of the now familiar *Croft and Purcell* Sentences; but there are some really beautiful and characteristic touches in Purcell's lesser known and more elaborate settings in C minor (commencing at "Man that is born of a woman"), and they deserve, in conjunction with the opening Sentences by Raylton in the same key, a more frequent hearing.

‡ See *sub voce* Sarum.

and supplied the instrument with seven 16-ft. pedal pipes.* These "German pedals" were supposed to have been the first examples of their kind introduced into Kent. Skeats, then Organist, had a great aversion to them, and would not use them. When anybody wished to hear the pedal pipes he would call his pupil, Jones, saying: "Here, Jones, come and show these *things* off, I never learned to *dance*."

THOMAS EVANCE JONES 1831 1872

Born 1805. Chorister in Canterbury Cathedral. Pupil of Skeats. Lay Clerk of Canterbury Cathedral, 1822; Master of the Choristers, ditto, 1830. Succeeded Skeats as Organist, 1831. Died at Canterbury, 1872. Buried in St. Martin's Churchyard. Composer of Church Music. Only one Anthem by him was published—"Unto Him that loved us."

WILLIAM HENRY LONGHURST, Mus.D., Cantuar., 1875; F.R.C.O. 1873 1898

Born at Lambeth, 1819. Chorister in Canterbury Cathedral (under Skeats). Pupil of Stephen Elvey and T. E. Jones. Lay Clerk and Assistant Organist of Canterbury Cathedral, 1836. Was offered the post of Organist of Carlisle Cathedral, 1842, but declined it. Succeeded Jones as Organist and Master of the Choristers, 1873. Created Mus.D. by the Archbishop of Canterbury, 1875. Retired from post of Organist of Canterbury Cathedral, 1898, after a period of no less than seventy years of active musical service there. Composer of Church Music, Organ pieces, Violin pieces, a Cantata for Female voices, "The Village Fair," and a MS. Oratorio, "David and Absalom."

Dr. Longhurst relates the following anecdote concerning himself and one of the Cathedral vergers:—"Some few years ago, a certain Canon of the Cathedral sent one of the vergers to me while I was playing the opening voluntary, with a message to inform me that, as there was *only one* Minor Canon present that (Sunday) morning, *he* (the Canon) would chant the Litany. "And," said the verger, "would you give him the note?" "Certainly," I replied. To my surprise the verger still lingered on the steps. "All right, A——," I said. He still remained stationary, and at length made the innocent inquiry: "Please, sir, shall I wait for it?"

This was the same verger who, when describing the new organ to some visitors, pointed upwards and told them that "the new *hargin* was put hup in the *Trifolium*"; that "the connection between the console and the hargin was done by helectrics"; and "the whole thing was set in motion by hydraulic water!"—From "Reminiscences" [No. 3, by Dr. W. H. Longhurst], recorded in the Monthly Journal of the Incorporated Society of Musicians.

HARRY CRANE PERRIN, Mus.B., Dub., 1890; F.R.C.O. ... ... 1898 ——

Born at Wellingborough, 1865. Pupil of Sir Robert Stewart. Organist of St. Columba's College, Rathfarnham, 1886; St. John's, Lowestoft, 1888. Conductor of Lowestoft Choral Society. Organist of St. Michael's, Coventry, 1892. Conductor of Coventry Musical Society. Choir Inspector and Conductor to Church Choral Association for the Archdeaconry of Coventry. Organist and Master of the Choristers, Canterbury Cathedral, 1898. Composer of Church Music, Songs, Pianoforte Music, &c.

* At the time of the completion of these large open wood pipes, Dr. Longhurst was a small boy, six or seven years old; he distinctly remembers being made to crawl into one or two of the largest of the pipes and therein sing a little song. It is not every Cathedral Organist who could say that he had sung a song in one of his own organ pipes!

CARLISLE.

JOHN HOWE... ... ... 1677 1693

THOMAS HOWE 1693 1734
Son of the preceding.

ABRAHAM DOBINSON 1734 1749

CHARLES PICK 1749 1781

THOMAS GREATOREX 1781 1784
Son of Anthony Greatorex, Riber Hall, Matlock. Born at North Wingfield, Derbyshire, 1758. Pupil of Dr. B. Cooke. Lived for some time with his patron, the Earl of Sandwich, at Hinchinbrook House, near Huntingdon. Organist of Carlisle Cathedral, 1781. Resigned, 1784, and lived at Newcastle. Afterwards travelled in Italy. On his return to England was appointed Conductor of the Concerts of Ancient Music, in succession to Joah Bates; and, in 1819, Organist of Westminster Abbey. For some years Conductor of the Birmingham and York Festivals. He was also an eminent Mathematician and Astronomer. Fellow of the Royal and Linnæan Societies. Died 1831. Buried in the West Cloister, Westminster Abbey.

At the time of his death (July, 1831), Westminster Abbey was being prepared for the Coronation of William IV.; but, out of respect for Greatorex's memory, the Dean caused the coverings placed over the organ to be temporarily removed. George IV., when Prince Regent, once said to Greatorex: "My Father is Rex, but you are a Greater Rex."

THOMAS HILL 1785 1833
There is a Chant by him in Bennett and Marshall's Collection, 1829.

RICHARD INGHAM 1833 1841
Born 1804. Organist of St. Mary's, Gateshead, and subsequently (1833) of Carlisle Cathedral. Composer of Vocal Music, &c.

JAMES STIMPSON 1841 1842
Born at Lincoln, 1820. Chorister in Durham Cathedral. Articled Pupil of Ingham, at Carlisle. Organist of St. Andrew's, Newcastle-on-Tyne, 1836; Organist of Carlisle Cathedral, 1841. Subsequently Organist of Birmingham Town Hall, and Organist and Chorus-master of Birmingham Festival. Trained the chorus for the production of Mendelssohn's "Elijah," in 1846. For many years Professor of Music at the Birmingham Blind Institution. Died at Birmingham, 1886. Composer of Songs, Pianoforte pieces, &c. Author of a "Manual of the Theory of Music." Editor of Church and Organ Music, &c.

HENRY EDMUND FORD, Mus.D., Cantuar., 1891 ... 1842 ——
Born near Croydon. Chorister in Rochester Cathedral and Assistant Organist there, under R. Banks. Organist of Carlisle Cathedral, 1842. Dr. Ford has been Organist of Carlisle Cathedral for the long period of fifty-seven years. On the attainment of his Jubilee as Organist of the Cathedral, 1892, he was presented with a testimonial at the County Hotel, Carlisle.

The specification of the present Cathedral organ, by Willis, was drawn up by Dr. Ford and his friend, the late Mr. W. T. Best, who was a native of Carlisle. Created Mus.D. by the Archbishop of Canterbury, 1891.

CHESTER.

JOHN BYRCHELEY 1541 1550

THOMAS BARNEYS 1550 1563

He was previously a Conduct, or singing man, in the Choir.

—— WHITE (or WHYTE) 1563 1569

The following appears as an item of expenditure relating to the Chester Plays, from the Harleian MSS., as quoted in "Chester in the times of Plantagenets and Tudors," by the Rev. Canon Morris, D.D.:—

"1568. To Mr. Whyte for singinge . . iiis."

ROBERT STEVENSON, Mus.D., Oxon., 1596 ... 1569 1602

Supplicated for a degree at Oxford in 1583, stating that he had been thirty-three years a student. Was granted the degree of Mus.B. in 1587 and of Mus.D. in 1596.

THOMAS BATESON, Mus.B. (?Dub.) 1602 1609

A distinguished Madrigal writer. Subsequently Organist of Trinity (now Christ Church) Cathedral, Dublin, where he is supposed to have taken the degree of Mus.B., probably the first Musical Degree granted by that University. The year of his death is unknown. Some of his Church Music was published by the Musical Antiquarian Society in their "Anthems by Composers of the Madrigalian Era."

JOHN ALLEN, Mus.B., Oxon., 1612 ... ... 1609 1613

Previously a Chorister and a Conduct.
He was required to compose a "Song," in seven parts, for his degree.

MICHAEL DONE 1613 1614

THOMAS JONES, Mus.B. (?) 1614 1637

A document referring to the lease of a farm and tenements (&c.), quoted in the "Cheshire Sheaf," February 11, 1891, commences thus:—

"This Indenture made the 7 Feb. 1625 [6] between William Trafford, of Bridge Trafford, co. Chester, gent., on the one part, and *Thomas Johnes*, of the city of Chester, *Bachelor of Music*, and Anne Johnes, now wife of the same Thomas Johnes on the other part (&c., &c.)."

The *locale* of his Degree cannot be ascertained.

RICHARD NEWBOLD 1637 1643

RANDALL (or RANDOLPH) JEWITT, Mus.B., Dub. 1643 (?)1644

Formerly a Chorister at Chester. (See under Winchester.)

PETER STRINGER 1661 1673

Successively Chorister and Conduct; afterwards simultaneously Minor Canon, Precentor, Organist, and Treasurer. Died 1673.
The words of some of his Anthems are included in Clifford's Collection.

He appears to have been Organist of Manchester Collegiate Church (now the Cathedral) for a short time in 1666.

The following curious extract from a letter of Dr. Henry Bridgman Dean of Chester and Bishop of Sodor and Man (he was a Pluralist), illustrates the esteem in which Peter Stringer was held:—

"Mr. Subdeane Bispham and
"Mr. Chanter Stringer.

"There is an hon'ble Maid lately deceased at Mr. John Anderson's, being the Hope and Anchor in our Northgate St., within the City of Chester, viz.: The Lady Jane Montgomery, sister to the Right Hon'ble Hughe, Earle of Mount Alexander in the Kingdome of Ireland; who, being a great lover of the ceremonyes of our Church while shee lived, desired to bee buried in our Church when shee dyed. And since shee had the quire so much in her heart living, I adjudged it fitt to bury her in the heart of our quire now shee is dead, her Executors paying to the Cathedrall all customarye dues and justifyable fees which belong unto us. Now, by reason of the late distraction in this Kingdome and my frequent absences from this Church, my memory not well serving mee in every particular thereof, and the R't. Reverend John, Lord Bishop of Chester, having a great kindness for her family, as well as a great love unto Justice, desiring that shee may not bee imposed upon by any kind of exaction: You two being the most *antient stagers* now resident in this Church, I doe require you, upon virtue of your oathes formerly taken, y't you declare unto mee in writing what the former fees and customes have been in the like case; that as I may not impose upon such hon'ble persons, so neither præjudice our Successors in this Church"; etc., etc.

"June ye 9th, 1673."

The two "antient stagers" duly replied, giving the required particulars, and not forgetting to add that "If the corps bee sung into the church and to the grave, the least that the Quiremen have usually had was forty shillings."*

JOHN STRINGER 1673 1686
(Son of the foregoing.) A Minor Canon.

WILLIAM KAY (KEY, or KEYS) 1686 1699
A Minor Canon. (See also under St. Asaph.)

JOHN DEMONTICALL 1699 1704

EDMUND WHITE 1704 1715

WILLIAM DAVIES 1715 1726
Afterwards a Conduct.

BENJAMIN WORRALL 1726 1727
Previously a Conduct.
He was probably a son (or some other relative) of the Rev. John Worrall, M.A., a Vicar Choral and Minor Canon of St. Patrick's Cathedral, Dublin, and afterwards successively Vicar Choral, Dean's Vicar, and Master of the Choristers of Christ Church Cathedral, Dublin.

* For this and much other interesting information concerning the Organists of Chester Cathedral, I am indebted to Dr. Joseph C. Bridge, M.A., the present Organist.

EDMUND BAKER 1727 1764

A Conduct.

Pupil of Dr. Blow, and musical instructor of Dr. Burney.

Baker is mentioned in the following anecdote, related by Burney in his "Commemoration of Handel" (1785):—"When Handel went through Chester, in his way to Ireland, this year 1741, I was at the Public-School in that city, and very well remember seeing him smoke a pipe, over a dish of coffee, at the Exchange-Coffee-house; for being extremely curious to see so extraordinary a man, I watched him narrowly as long as he remained in Chester; which, on account of the wind being unfavourable for his embarking at Parkgate, was several days. During this time, he applied to Mr. Baker, the organist, my first music-master, to know whether there were any choirmen in the cathedral who could sing *at sight;* as he wished to prove some books that had been hastily transcribed, by trying the choruses which he intended to perform in Ireland. Mr. Baker mentioned some of the most likely singers then in Chester, and, among the rest, a printer of the name of Janson, who had a good base voice, and was one of the best musicians in the choir. At this time Harry Alcock, a good player, was the first violin at Chester, which was then a very musical place; for besides public performances, Mr. Prebendary Prescott had a weekly concert, at which he was able to muster eighteen or twenty performers, gentlemen, and professors. A time was fixed for this private rehearsal at the *Golden Falcon*, where Handel was quartered; but, alas! on trial of the chorus in the Messiah, '*And with His stripes we are healed,*' poor Janson, after repeated attempts, failed so egregiously, that Handel let loose his great bear upon him; and after swearing in four or five languages, cried out in broken English: 'You shcauntrel! tit not you dell me dat you could sing at soite?' 'Yes, sir,' says the printer, 'and so I can; but not at *first sight.*'"

EDWARD ORME 1764 1776

A Conduct.

Originator of the Chester Musical Festivals. A prominent Freemason. Deputy Herald of the city. He also served as Sheriff. Died March 25, 1777, aged 61. Buried in the Cathedral.

JOHN BAILEY 1776 1803

A Conduct.

Died November 26, 1823, aged 73. Buried in the Cathedral.

EDWARD BAILEY 1803 1823

A Conduct.

Probably a brother of the preceding. Died November 4, 1830, aged 72. Buried in the Cathedral. Edward Orme and the Baileys were connected by family relationship. (See also under St. Asaph.)

GEORGE BLACK 1823 1824

THOMAS HAYLETT 1824 1840

Died October 6, 1843, aged 49. Buried in St. John's Cemetery, Chester.

The following amusing anecdote concerning Thomas Haylett is related by his present successor at Chester Cathedral, Dr. J. C. Bridge:—

"One day Haylett, according to custom, had been teaching in Warrington, whence he duly returned in the evening to Chester. Upon opening the door of the coach he discovered the huge figure of a man stretched across two seats. As the occupant seemed disinclined to move his portly figure,

Haylett reminded him that the coach was constructed to hold more than *one* passenger. The traveller then removed his feet, but uttered not a word. Haylett thereupon remarked that it was 'a fine night.' Silence greeted even this meteorological utterance. Similar observations were treated in like manner, with the result that Haylett held *his* peace, but only till Chester—the destination of the pair—was reached. Addressing his fellow-traveller for the last time, Haylett said to him, 'I think it right to inform you, sir, that you are a d——d disagreeable fellow.' This anathema caused the silent one to remove his muffler and thus unmask his features. The process revealed to Haylett's astonished gaze the face of Canon Slade, one of the Cathedral dignitaries, who was on his way to take up residence. The Canon, however, treated the matter very good-humouredly and often reminded Haylett of the joke."

FREDERICK GUNTON 1841 1877

Born at Norwich, 1813. Pupil of Alfred Pettet (Organist of St. Peter Mancroft, Norwich). Organist of Southwell Minster, 1835. Organist of Chester Cathedral, 1841. Director of the King's School Concerts, &c. Resigned the Cathedral appointment, 1877, at which time he was presented with a testimonial in the form of a handsome piece of plate. Died at Chester, 1888. Buried in Upton Churchyard.

Dr. Anson, upon being appointed Dean of Chester, brought Gunton, his Organist, with him from Southwell. Gunton effected great improvements in the musical services at Chester Cathedral, and the present organ, by Whiteley, was erected under his superintendence. It is said that Mendelssohn, having on one occasion heard Gunton play upon the Cathedral organ, remarked to someone present that his (Gunton's) touch was "like velvet."

JOSEPH COX BRIDGE, M.A., 1878: Mus.D., Oxon., 1885 F.R.C.O. ... ... 1877 ——

Born at Rochester, 1853. Chorister in Rochester Cathedral, and afterwards Assistant Organist there, and Pupil of John Hopkins. Pupil also of his brother, Sir Frederick Bridge, and Assistant Organist to him at Manchester Cathedral. Organist of Exeter College, Oxford, 1871, where he graduated in Arts and Music. Assistant Organist of Chester Cathedral, 1876; Organist, ditto, 1877. Was mainly instrumental in re-establishing the Chester Triennial Musical Festivals in 1879, of which he is now Conductor. Composer of an Oratorio, "Daniel"; a Cantata, "Rudel"; a Symphony for Orchestra, Church Music, Part-songs, &c.

Dr. Joseph Bridge has on more than one occasion acted as Conductor in the place of Sir Charles Hallé at Concerts in Bristol and Manchester.

The choir of Chester Cathedral has always been noted both for its discipline and musical efficiency, and its singing evoked the highest commendation from the American musicians who visited England in 1895.

CHICHESTER.

The earliest record of an Organist is in the time of Henry VIII., when WILLIAM CAMPYON "received 6s. 8d. for playing on the Organs in the Choir, and 3s. 4d. for playing on the Organs in the Lady Chapel."—(Walcott's "Early Statutes of the Cathedral Church of Chichester.)

THOMAS WEELKES, Mus.B., Oxon., 1602 ... (?)1578 1623

Formerly Organist of Winchester College. Better known at the present time by his Madrigals than by his Church Music. There is an Anthem by him, "O Lord, grant the king a long life," in Barnard's Collection; two were also published by the Musical Antiquarian Society, and others are extant in MS.

"The Organist shall remain in the Choir until the last psalm be sung and then go up to the organs, and there having done his duty, return into the Choir again to bear his part all along, under the amercement of iij. toties quoties. This is thought a meet matter in all double choirs, much more is it necessary in all half-choirs, as ours is."—("Statutes of the Dean and Chapter, 1616.")

BARTHOLOMEW WEBB ... ... 1668 (?)1674

JOHN READING 1674 1720

There were two other well-known musicians of the same name. One was Organist of Winchester Cathedral and College; the other was Organist successively of Dulwich College; St. John at Hackney; St. Mary, Woolnoth; St. Dunstan in the West; and St. Mary, Woolchurchhaw, London.

THOMAS KELWAY ... ... {Probationer 1720, Sworn 1733} 1733 1747

Born at Chichester. Chorister in the Cathedral, and probably a pupil of Reading, whom he succeeded as Organist. Died at Chichester, May 21, 1749. Buried in the South Aisle of the Cathedral.

Kelway's gravestone having been lost sight of for many years, was found and replaced, and the inscription re-cut, about 1846. This circumstance gave rise to the following pleasing sonnet by Mr. Charles Crocker, a former well-known Verger of Chichester Cathedral:—

"Kelway! thy memory, fresh as vernal day,
In many a heart's most secret holiest cell,
Where love of sacred song delights to dwell,
Lives—and shall live while music holds her sway
Within these hallowed walls, where day by day,
Year after year, he plied the wondrous art
Which bids the spirit from its prison start,
And soar awhile to happier realms away.
His strains full oft—still fall upon the ear
Of those who tread yon aisle, while, at their feet,
His name and record of his hope appear.
Peace to his ashes—be his slumbers sweet,
Till that glad morn when he shall wake to hear
The angel choir in nightless Heaven's bright sphere."

("The Organists and Composers of St. Paul's Cathedral." By J. S. Bumpus. Footnote, p. 246.)

Seven Services and nine Anthems in his own handwriting are in the Cathedral Library. His Evening Services in B minor, A minor, and G minor are still in frequent use. His brother, Joseph Kelway, was one of the most celebrated organists of his time.

THOMAS CAPELL ... ... {Probationer 1744 / Sworn 1747} (?)1794

RICHARD HALL (Deputy) ... ... 1771 ——

THOMAS TREMAINE (Deputy) ... ... 1771 ——

WILLIAM WALOND 1794 1801

Probably a son of William Walond, Mus.B., of Oxford. Deputy-Organist, 1775. Organist, 1794. Resigned his post at the Cathedral and lived for some time in the city in extreme poverty, his only means of subsistence being a small annuity raised upon the sale of some houses. Died February 9, 1836. Portions of his compositions are to be found in the Cathedral Choir books.

JAMES TARGETT ... ... Probationer 1801 1803

Born near Kidderminster, October, 1778. Chorister in Chichester Cathedral, and afterwards Organist there. Died May 15, 1803, aged 24.

John Marsh, a distinguished amateur of Chichester, edited "Three Anthems and a Hymn in four parts, composed by the late James Targett."

There are also three Chants by him in Marsh's "Cathedral Chants."

THOMAS BENNETT ... ... {Probationer 1803 / Sworn 1817} 1848

Born at Fonthill, 1779. Chorister in Salisbury Cathedral. Organist of St. John's Chapel, Chichester, and afterwards of the Cathedral. Died March 21, 1848. Buried in the Cathedral Yard. Published "Sacred Melodies," "Cathedral Selections," and "An Introduction to the Art of Singing."

HENRY R. BENNETT ... ... {Probationer 1848 / Sworn 1849} 1860

Son of the preceding, and elder brother of Alfred Bennett, Organist of New College, Oxford. Chorister in Magdalen College, Oxford. Pupil of his father. Succeeded him at Chichester. Resigned the post at Chichester and became Organist of St. Andrew's, Wells Street, London, exchanging appointments with Dr. Philip Armes.

PHILIP ARMES, M.A., Dunelm; Mus.D., Oxon. et Dunelm.; F.R.C.O. 1861 1862

(See under Durham.)

EDWARD HENRY THORNE, F.R.C.O. 1863 1870

Born at Cranbourne, Dorset, 1834. Pupil of Sir George Elvey. Organist of the Parish Church, Henley-on-Thames, 1853; Chichester Cathedral, 1863; St. Patrick's, Hove, 1870; St. Peter's, Cranley Gardens, London, 1873; St. Michael's, Cornhill, 1875; and now at St. Anne's, Soho, London. Composer of Church Music, Organ pieces, &c. His Anthem "I was glad" was written for the re-opening Service at Chichester Cathedral in 1867, after the falling in of the spire.

FRANCIS EDWARD GLADSTONE, Mus.D., Cantab.; F.R.C.O. 1870 1873
(See under Norwich.)

JAMES KENDRICK PYNE, F.R.C.O. 1873 1874
(See under Manchester.)

CHARLES HENRY HYLTON STEWART 1874 1875
Choral Scholar of St. Catherine's College, Cambridge, 1873. Afterwards took Holy Orders and became Curate of Pebmarsh, Essex, 1875; Precentor of Chester Cathedral, 1877; Vicar of New Brighton (Cheshire), 1889.

DANIEL JOSEPH WOOD, Mus.B., Oxon., Mus.D., Cantuar.; F.R.C.O. 1875 1876
(See under Exeter.)

THEODORE EDWARD AYLWARD 1876 1886
Great grandnephew of Dr. Theodore Aylward. Born at Salisbury, 1844. Pupil of Dr. S. S. Wesley. Organist successively of St. Matthew's, Cheltenham; St. Columba's College, Rathfarnham, 1866; St. Martin's, Salisbury; Llandaff Cathedral, 1870; Chichester Cathedral, 1876; St. Andrew's Church and the Public Halls, Cardiff, 1886. Composer. Editor of the Sarum Hymnal (1870).

FREDERICK JOHN READ, Mus.D., Oxon., 1891; F.R.C.O. ... ... 1887 ——
Born at Faversham. Pupil of Drs. Sloman, Corfe, and Sir Frederick Bridge. Organist of Christ Church, Reading, 1877. Founder of the Reading Orpheus Society, and Conductor of the same since 1882. Professor of Harmony, Royal College of Music, 1886. Examiner for the Associated Board of the Royal Academy of Music and the Royal College of Music, 1892. Composer of Church Music, Cantatas, Madrigals, Part-songs, &c.

CORK.

I am indebted to Dr. Richard Caulfield's interesting book, "Annals of St. Fin Barre's Cathedral, Cork,"* for much of my information regarding the Organists of Cork Cathedral.

"1633. The Dean and Chapter unanimously decree that the sum of Ten Pounds shall be paid for the completion of a musical instrument, called in English *Organs*, as is the custom to have in Cathedral Churches.—4th November."

WILLIAM LOVE ... ... —— ——
He is mentioned as Organist in 1677.
Probably the duties of Organist had, up to that time, been performed by one or other of the Vicars Choral in turn.
In 1684 "The Bishop orders the Vicars Choral, Organist, and Choir, to

* Kindly lent to me by Dr. J. C. Marks, the present Cathedral Organist.

attend the Cathedral daily, and perform the service 'in the best melodies they can, according to Cathedral use.'"*

"1688. The Organist monished to reside 'inter pomœria Ecclesiæ,' or at least in the suburbs of Cork." The same admonition had previously been given in 1686.

THOMAS HOLLISTER (Assistant) ... ... 1695 ——

Salary, £10 per annum.

WILLIAM TOOLE 1703 1711

Afterwards Organist of Armagh Cathedral, which post he resigned in 1722.

EDWARD BROADWAY 1712 1720

Lay Vicar, 1704. "Master of the Song," 1707. Organist, 1712. Resigned the post of Organist, 1720, and was recommended to the Bishop "for some provision for him as Organist for the time he served."

On the 7th November, 1723, "Mr. Broadway, and his successors, Lay Vicars, are ordered to sing a Solo Anthem every Sunday in the afternoon, and provide a variety of them, and that he instruct two boys to join him in singing said Anthems (&c.)." According to the records he appears to have failed to provide these boys, and an application was made to the Bishop to withhold a portion of his salary. In 1725-6 Broadway petitioned the Bishop for the sum of £30 withheld from him.

WILLIAM SMYTH ... ... 1720 (?)1721

Salary, £20 per annum. At the time of his appointment application was made to the Bishop for funds to purchase some additional stops for the Cathedral organ. Various sums of money were paid from time to time to Smyth, for tuning and cleaning the instrument. In 1781 it was reported to the Chapter that he had left a legacy of £200 for the poor of the parish.

HENRY DE LA MAINE 1782 1796

A French refugee who settled in Ireland at the time of the Revolution. Died 1796. Two Chants by him are in Joule's Collection, and some Psalm Tunes in Weyman's "Melodia Sacra."

On October 28th, 1791, he presented a memorial to the Dean and Chapter, alleging that he had a right to a fifth part of the emoluments of the Vicars Choral.

JAMES ROCHE 1797 1811

Organist and Master of the boys. Died 1811. He was, like Smyth, paid for keeping the organ in repair and tune.

JAMES BREALSFORD STEPHENS 1811 1860

Organist and Master of the boys. Died March 3, 1860.

JAMES CHRISTOPHER MARKS, Mus.Doc., Oxon., 1868 1860 ——

Born at Armagh, 1835. Chorister of Armagh Cathedral. Pupil of R. Turle. Assistant Organist at Armagh Cathedral, 1852, until his appointment to Cork. Conductor of Cork Harmonic Society, 1860-1, and of Cork Musical

* In the following year, however, the Vicars were admonished "for neglect in not attending the daily service in the Choir of the Cathedral according to the statutes of the same, and for the fuller publication thereof," it was ordered "that the monition be fixed over their stalls in the Church (&c.).—13th May." The "notorious neglect of the Vicars Choral" in their attendance at the Cathedral was the subject of a representation to the Bishop in 1720.

Festival in 1862. Now Conductor of Cork (New) Harmonic Society. Composer of an Oratorio "Gideon," (his degree exercise), Church Music, &c.

Shortly after Dr. Marks's appointment Full Choral Service was re-established in the Cathedral. This had been discontinued since Bishop Wetenhall's time, at the end of the seventeenth century. The present Cathedral was also completed in 1870, and, in commemoration of its consecration, Dr. Marks was publicly invested, by the Dean, with a gold medal.

DUBLIN.

THE CATHEDRAL OF THE HOLY TRINITY,

COMMONLY TERMED

CHRIST CHURCH.

AN early agreement with an Organist in the Reformation period—after the suppression of the Priory of the Holy Trinity Dublin.

Dated 16 March, 37 Hen. VIII. (1546).

Thomas Lokwod, dean, and the Chapter of the Holy Trinity, &c., in consideration of his instructing the Chorister-children, grant to ROBERT HAYWARD of Dublin, Singing man for life, a yearly stipend of £6 13s. 4d., twelve pecks of wheat, and eight pecks of malt, payable at the feasts of the Nativity, Easter, Nativity of St. John Baptist, and Michaelmas; a livery coat, a cart-load of wood at Christmas, and the Chamber* by the east of the Churchyard; and the Vicars Choral grant him four pecks of malt in equal portions, at said feasts, his daily finding, table and board, sitting and taking same with them.

Grantee, who is empowered to distrain grantors' lands in Dublin County and City for his stipend, undertakes to play the organ, to keep Our Lady's Mass and Anthem daily, Jesus' Mass every Friday, according the custom of St. Patrick's, and Matins when the organs play on the eight principal feasts and the feasts of "Majus duplex" (grantors finding a blower); to procure, at the expense of the Church, suitable songs; to behave humbly and well to grantors, and soon as he shall have the above Chamber, to instruct the Choristers in Pricksong and Descant to "four minims," and to play Our Lady's Mass, all instruments being found for them during the time of their child's voice, and to present them to the Chauntor to be admitted; to remain in the service of the Church during his life and not to absent himself without license.

Signed by—THOMAS LOKWOD, Dean.
RICHARD BELL, Chauntor.
WALTER WHYT, Chancellor.
JOHN MOS, Treasurer.
JOHN CORRAGHE, JOHN KERDYTT, CHRIST. RATHE } Prebendaries.

WM. LYNSHE.
WM. OWEN.
ROBT. LYDE.
JOHN DILLON, Vicar.
JOHN DOURY.

Dated 16 March, 1546.

(From the Calendar of Christ Church Documents [1892], deposited in the Public Record Office, Ireland).

* The Scriptorium of the Monastic Buildings.

JOHN FERMOR ... ... 1595 ——

THOMAS BATESON, Mus.B. (? Dub.) ... ... 1609 ——
(See under Chester.)

RANDALL (or RANDOLPH) JEWITT, Mus.B., Dub. 1631 1639
(See under Winchester.)

BENJAMIN ROGERS, Mus.B., Cantab., Mus.D., Oxon. 1639 1641
(See under Magdalen College, Oxford.)

JOHN HAWKSHAW (Senr.) 1661 1688

According to the Cathedral records, leases were granted to him in 1645 and 1647, but he is not mentioned as either Vicar Choral or Organist until after the Restoration, when in 1661 he appears to have been elected to the former post, which he held until his death in 1688. His appointment as Vicar Choral of St. Patrick's Cathedral is dated 1660, when he was also made Organist there "during the absence of Mr. Randall Jewet." Jewitt had returned to England on the breaking up of the Cathedral Establishment at the Rebellion (see his appointment at Chester Cathedral). He was evidently expected to resume his duties in Dublin after the Restoration, and, as he failed to do so, Hawkshaw was permanently appointed in his place.

His son (John Hawkshaw, Junr.) is supposed to have succeeded him as Organist of St. Patrick's Cathedral. One John Hawkshaw, Organist of Armagh Cathedral, is supposed by some authorities to have been this said son; but a comparison of the dates against this name at both Cathedrals leaves the matter doubtful.

THOMAS GODFREY 1688 1689

Also Organist of St. Patrick's Cathedral, 1686.

THOMAS MORGAN 1690 1691

Appointed January 2, 1690, his salary commencing from Christmas before. On March 25, 1691, the Proctor was ordered to "transmit five pounds into England to Thos. Morgan for his reliefe and encouragement to use his best to endeavour to attain the . . . * of an Organist.

PETER ISAAC(KE) 1692 1694

A native of England. Appointed a Vicar Choral of St. Patrick's, Dublin, 1673; but deprived of that office for neglect of duty, 1688, when he returned to England, and became Organist of Salisbury Cathedral. In 1691 he was invited by the Dean and Chapter of Christ Church Cathedral, Dublin, to

* This word is illegible in the Chapter books. Probably it is "position."

"come over" and serve as Vicar Choral and Organist of that Cathedral, which post he accepted, and was admitted, 1692, "on account of his extraordinary skill in music." Died 1694.

THOMAS FINELL ... ... 1694 (?)1698

Also Organist of St. Patrick's Cathedral, 1689-1691; and again in 1692. Vicar Choral of St. Patrick's Cathedral, 1677, and of Christ Church Cathedral, 1693. It is said that he was admitted *on probation* as Organist of Christ Church Cathedral on October 10, 1694. Died about 1709.

DANIEL ROSINGRAVE 1698 1727

Chorister in the Chapel Royal. Pupil of Henry Purcell and Dr. Blow. Organist of Gloucester Cathedral, 1679; Winchester Cathedral, 1682; Salisbury Cathedral, 1692; Organist and Vicar Choral of St. Patrick's Cathedral, and Organist and Stipendiary of Christ Church Cathedral, Dublin, 1698. Died in Dublin, 1727.

RALPH ROSINGRAVE 1727 1747

(See under St. Patrick's Cathedral.)

GEORGE WALSH 1747 1765

Appointed a Vicar Choral of St. Patrick's Cathedral, 1760; Organist, ditto, 1761. Died 1765. Composer of a Morning Service in D, which is still in use at Christ Church, and copies of which are said to exist in some of the English Cathedrals. Sir Robert Stewart thought so highly of it that he added a Communion Service in the same key and style. A fine score copy of "Walsh in D" is in the possession of Mr. J. S. Bumpus.

RICHARD WOODWARD, Mus.D., Dublin, 1771 ... 1765 1777

Son of Richard Woodward, a Vicar Choral of St. Patrick's Cathedral. Born in Dublin, 1744. Vicar Choral of St. Patrick's Cathedral, 1772. Organist of Christ Church Cathedral, 1765. Master of the Choristers at Christ Church and St. Patrick's Cathedrals. Died November 22, 1777. Buried in Christ Church Cathedral. On his monument is inscribed his Prize Canon "Let the words of my mouth."* Composer of Church Music, Songs, &c. His Church Music, which included a Service in B flat and seven Anthems, was published in London in a folio volume, and dedicated to Archbishop Smyth.

SAMUEL MURPHY, Mus.D., Dub. 1777 1780

(See under St. Patrick's Cathedral.)

LANGRISHE DOYLE, Mus.D., Dub., (?)1788 ... 1780 (?)1813

Chorister in Christ Church. Stipendiary, 1775. Organist of Armagh Cathedral, 1776. Master of the Choristers of both Christ Church and St. Patrick's Cathedrals in 1780, and Organist and Stipendiary of Christ Church Cathedral. Elected a Half Vicar of St. Patrick's Cathedral, 1781, and a Full Vicar, 1784. Also Organist of Trinity College Chapel, 1781.

By an Order of November 25, 1805, Warren and Doyle were made joint Organists and a Patent was made out accordingly. Doyle probably retired in 1813, as the books state that he was "licensed to be absent" in that year

WILLIAM WARREN, Mus.D., Dub. {Joint Org., 1805 / Sole Org., 1814} 1841

(See under St. Patrick's Cathedral.)

* Awarded the gold medal of the Glee and Catch Club in 1764.

FRANCIS JAMES ROBINSON, Mus.D., Dub. ... 1816 ——
Assistant Organist. (See under St. Patrick's Cathedral.)

JOHN ROBINSON 1841 1844
(See under St. Patrick's Cathedral.)

SIR ROBERT PRESCOTT STEWART, Mus.D., Dub., 1851; Hon. F.R.C.O. 1844 1894
Born in Dublin, December 16, 1825. Chorister in Christ Church Cathedral. Organist of Christ Church Cathedral and Trinity College Chapel, 1844. Organist of St. Patrick's Cathedral, 1852. Resigned the post of Organist, St. Patrick's Cathedral, 1861, in order to obtain a Vicar Choralship there, but the latter office was divided, and he only succeeded to one half. He still, however, played the Sunday afternoon services, by arrangement with his successor, Mr. Murphy, who on these occasions sang for Sir Robert in the choir. Half Vicar Choral of St. Patrick's Cathedral, 1861. Professor of Music in Dublin University, 1862. Knighted 1872. Died in Dublin, Easter Eve, March 24, 1894. Composer of Odes, Cantatas, Church Music, Organ pieces, Songs, Glees, &c. Editor of and Lecturer on music.

Inscription on the Brass placed to his memory in Christ Church Cathedral, Christmas, 1896:—

"To the Glory of God,
and in Memory of
ROBERT PRESCOTT STEWART, Knt.,
Doctor of Music.
Trained as a Chorister in the Cathedral School,
he was appointed Organist at the age of eighteen,
and continued in that post during fifty years.
His name stands foremost among the many who
for seven centuries
devoted their musical talents to the Service of God
within this Ancient Sanctuary.
Upright in life and modest in spirit,
he gained the warm affection of a large circle of
friends, and universal honour and respect.
A brilliant Organist and Composer, he impressed
his genius on the Use and Mode of Services
in this Cathedral Church,
and
enriched its Library with many noble compositions.
Born 1825.
He entered into his Rest on Easter Eve, 1894.

[Here are engraved the opening bars of the Te Deum from Stewart's Service for Double Choir, in E flat.]

A statue, erected to his memory on Leinster Lawn, Dublin, was unveiled by the Lord Lieutenant of Ireland (Earl Cadogan) on March 8, 1898.

JOHN HORAN ... ... 1894 ——
Born at Drogheda, February 26, 1831. Pupil of his father. Chorister in Christ Church Cathedral and frequently deputised as Organist there. Apprenticed to Telford and Telford, organ builders, Dublin. Organist successively of Booterstown Church; St. John's, Sandymount; and St. Andrew's, Dublin. Afterwards Solo Bass of Limerick Cathedral. Organist of Adare Parish Church, 1856; Organist of Tuam Cathedral, 1857; Organist of Derry Cathedral, 1862; Assistant Organist and Choirmaster of Christ Church Cathedral, 1873; succeeding to the full office on the death of Sir Robert Stewart. Composer of Services, Anthems, &c.

DUBLIN.

ST. PATRICK'S CATHEDRAL.

WILLIAM HERBIT ... ... 1509 ——

According to the Chapter books his annual stipend was £3 6s. 8d.

WILLIAM BROWNE ... ... 1555 ——

Appointed on the restoration of the Cathedral during the reign of Philip and Mary.

ANTHONY WILLIS (or WILKES) ... ... 1606 ——

Appointed a Vicar Choral of St. Patrick's Cathedral, 1639.

RANDALL (or RANDOLPH) JEWITT, Mus.B., Dub. 1631 (?) 1643

See under Winchester.)

JOHN HAWKSHAW (Senr.) 1661 1678

(See under Christ Church Cathedral.)

(?) JOHN HAWKSHAW (Junr.) 1678 1685

Son of the foregoing. He is said to have succeeded his father at St. Patrick's Cathedral, and to have been suspended for neglect of duty in 1685. In this case, however, the *John Hawkshaw* mentioned under *Armagh* would scarcely be the same person.

THOMAS GODFREY ... ... 1686 ——

(See under Christ Church Cathedral.)

THOMAS FINELL 1689 1691

(See under Christ Church Cathedral.)

WILLIAM ISAAC 1691 1692

Evidently a relative of Peter Isaac, Organist of Christ Church Cathedral.

THOMAS FINELL ... ... 1692 ——

(?) Re-appointed.

—— ROBERTS ... ... 1694 ——

ROBERT HODGE ... ... —— 1698

Probably the Robert Hodge who left Wells Cathedral, 1690. He was elected a Vicar Choral of St. Patrick's Cathedral, 1693, and a Vicar Choral of Christ Church Cathedral, 1695. The date of his appointment as Organist of St. Patrick's cannot be ascertained, but the Chapter minutes under the date June 9, 1698, state that "Robert Hodge resigns the post of Organist, and Daniel Rosingrave is appointed." Hodge afterwards became Master of the Choristers at Christ Church Cathedral, and died 1709.

DANIEL ROSINGRAVE 1698 1727

(See under Christ Church Cathedral.)

RALPH ROSINGRAVE 1727 1747

Son of the preceding. Appointed a Vicar Choral of St. Patrick's Cathedral, 1719; Assistant Organist there, 1726. Organist of Christ Church and St. Patrick's Cathedrals, 1727. Died 1747. Two Services, in C and F, and several of his Anthems are in the Dublin Cathedral books. An old organ book in the possession of Mr. J. S. Bumpus contains a Service in F by R. Rosingrave, with a setting of the Benedicite. Ralph Rosingrave was probably the "young Rosingrave" mentioned as being appointed Organist of Trinity College Chapel in 1705.

RICHARD BROADWAY ... ... 1748 ——

Probably son of Edward Broadway, Organist of Cork Cathedral. He was also a Vicar Choral of St. Patrick's Cathedral.

GEORGE WALSH 1761 1765

(See under Christ Church Cathedral.)

HENRY WALSH 1765 1769

Probably son of the preceding.

MICHAEL SANDYS, M.A., Dub. 1769 1773

Son of the Rev. Michael Sandys, B.A., Dublin. Appointed a Vicar Choral of St. Patrick's, 1772; Minor Canon and Dean's Vicar, ditto, 1778.

SAMUEL MURPHY, Mus.D., Dub. 1773 1780

Appointed a Half Vicar of St. Patrick's Cathedral, 1759; Organist ditto, 1773; Organist of Christ Church Cathedral, 1777; Organist of Trinity College Chapel, 1775; also Stipendiary of Christ Church Cathedral and Master of the Choristers in both Christ Church and St. Patrick's Cathedrals. Died 1780.

PHILIP COGAN, Mus.D., Dub. 1780 1806

Born at Cork about 1750. Chorister, and afterwards Lay Clerk of Cork Cathedral. Organist of St. Patrick's Cathedral, 1780. Died about 1834. Composer of Sonatas, &c.

JOHN MATHEWS 1806 1827

WILLIAM WARREN, Mus.D., Dub. 1827 1828

Joint Organist with Dr. Doyle at Christ Church Cathedral, 1805; sole Organist, ditto, 1814; Organist of St. Patrick's Cathedral, 1827; Organist also of Trinity College Chapel. Died in Dublin, 1841.

FRANCIS JAMES ROBINSON, Mus.D., Dub., *honoris causâ*, 1852 ... ... 1828 1829

Born in Dublin, 1799. Chorister in Christ Church Cathedral. Assistant Organist of Christ Church Cathedral, 1816; Organist of St. Patrick's Cathedral, 1828. Vicar Choral of Christ Church Cathedral, 1833; Vicar Choral of St. Patrick's Cathedral, 1843. Died October 21, 1872. Composer of Church Music, Songs, &c. Editor of a collection of Irish Melodies. The greatest Tenor singer that the Dublin Cathedrals have ever possessed.

JOHN ROBINSON 1829 1843

Brother of the preceding. Born 1812 (?). Chorister in Christ Church Cathedral. Organist of St. Patrick's Cathedral, 1829; Trinity College Chapel, 1834; Christ Church Cathedral, 1841. Died 1844.

RICHARD CHERRY 1843 1844

WILLIAM HENRY WHITE 1844 1852
Organist of the Chapel of Dublin Castle, 1836 to 1845.

SIR ROBERT PRESCOTT STEWART, Mus.D., Dub.; Hon. F.R.C.O. 1852 1861
(See under Christ Church Cathedral.)

WILLIAM MURPHY, Mus.B., Dub. 1861 1878

CHARLES GEORGE MARCHANT, Mus.B., Dub. ... 1879 —
Born in Dublin, 1857. Chorister in St. Patrick's Cathedral. Organist of Holy Trinity Church, Rathmines; Christ Church, Bray, 1876; St. Matthias', Dublin (for one week only), from whence he was appointed Organist and Choirmaster of St. Patrick's Cathedral. Organist to Dublin University, and Conductor of the University Choral Society. Professor of the Organ at the Royal Irish Academy of Music, &c. Composer of a Service in A and other Church Music, &c.

DURHAM.

JOHN BRIMLEY (or BRIMLEI) ... ... — 1576
Said to have been Organist when the monks were still in possession of the Monastery. "He was at his post in the Cathedral during the abortive rising in the North in 1569. Oliver Ashe, Curate of St. Giles's, Durham, deposed that whilst a priest named Holmes was saying Mass, when the sacring bell rang, he looked toward the priest but could not discern the elevation; whereupon he looked up to Mr. Brimlei, then in the loft over the quire door, and smiled at him. Examined himself, John Brimlei, Master of the Choristers in the Cathedral Church of Durham, aged sixty-seven, admitted that he was twice at High Mass, but he sang not himself at them, but played the organs, and did divers times help to sing Salvaes at Mattins and Evensong, and played on the organs, and went in procession, as others did, after the Cross. He owned also that he put forward the Service, and instructed the choristers in such things as they did in the Quire pertaining to service at that time. He expressed his contrition, seems to have conformed, and to have been confirmed in possession of his post, for he was at it when death overtook him in 1576. From which it appears that Master John Brimlei had not in him the stuff of which martyrs are made."—(Communicated by Mr. William Brown, of Durham, to Mr. Joseph Bennett.—See *Musical Times*, June, 1895.) Buried in the Galilee Chapel of the Cathedral. Some music by him is in the Durham MSS. books.

EPITAPH TO BRIMLEY IN THE "GALILEE."

John Brimlei's body here doth ly,
Who praysed God with hand and voice.
By musicke's heavenlie harmonie,
Dull myndes he maid in God rejoice.
His soul into the heavenes is lyft,
To prayse Him still that gave the gyft.
Obiit Ao. Dni. 1576, Octo. 13.

WILLIAM BROWNE (? Senr.) 1576 1587

ROBERT MASTERMAN 1588 1594

WILLIAM SMYTH 1594 1599

Some Anthems and Responses by him are to be found in the Durham books.

WILLIAM BROWNE (? Junr.) ... ... 1599 (?)1609

EDWARD SMYTH 1609 1611

Son of William Smyth. Died 1611. Composer also of Anthems and Responses in the Cathedral books.

—— DODSON was Organist for a year and a half.

RICHARD HUTCHINSON ... ... 1614 (?)1644

Died 1646.

There are three Anthems by him in the Cathedral books and in the Ely and Peterhouse (Cambridge) Collections.

According to the Cathedral Baptismal Registers, John Hutchinson, son of Richard Hutchinson, *Organist*, was baptized July 2, 1615.

JOHN FOSTER 1661 1677

"April 21, 1677. Joh'es Foster, Organista, naturæ concessit vicesimo die mensis Aprilis, et die sequente sep^ts^ est."—(Burial Registers.)

ALEXANDER SHAW 1677 1681

Composer of Services in G and E minor, and two Anthems in the Cathedral books.

Extract from an Organ book at Durham: "Prick'd by Alexr. Shaw, Orgt.—Mr. Alex^r^ Shaw was paid to pricking thus far, Oct. 30, 1678 (and again), 1679, by me, Thos. Smith, Treasurer."

WILLIAM GREGGS 1681 1710

Son of J. Greggs (Gentleman), of York. Succeeded Foster as Organist, 1677. Appointed Master of the Song School, 1690. Died 1710. Buried in the Church of St. Mary-the-less, Durham, where an Epitaph on him is to be found on the South Wall. His Anthem, "My heart is inditing," is in the Cathedral books.

JAMES HESLETINE 1710 1763

Pupil of Dr. Blow. Was Organist of St. Katherine's Church at the Tower, London, which post he retained on his appointment to Durham Cathedral, performing the London office by deputy. Died 1763. Buried in the Cathedral. Composer of many Anthems, &c. The greater part of these were destroyed by him in revenge for some slight by the Dean and Chapter of Durham. An Anthem, "Praise the Lord," is extant in the Cathedral books.

THOMAS EBDON 1763 1811

Son of Thomas Ebdon, "Cordwainer." Born at Durham, 1738. Chorister in Durham Cathedral. Died at Durham, September 23, 1811. Buried in St. Oswald's Churchyard. His name is still to be seen carved upon a wooden screen in the Cathedral. This screen separates the North Aisle from the Presbytery, and is one of those erected by Bishop Cosin after the Restoration. In the same place is carved the name of Ralph Banks, who was also a Chorister in Durham Cathedral, becoming a pupil of Ebdon and afterwards Organist of Rochester Cathedral.

Ebdon published two volumes of Church Music, six Glees, Songs, Sonatas for the Harpsichord, &c. The Evening portion of his Service in C attained a considerable amount of popularity some years ago, and is still a favourite with admirers of Church music of that time. The Communion Service is completed by a *Gloria in Excelsis*, very unusual for the period.

(See under Rochester.)

CHARLES ERLIN JACKSON CLARKE 1811 1813

Born at Worcester, December, 1795. Chorister in Worcester Cathedral. Appointed Organist of Durham Cathedral at the early age of sixteen. Resigned that post, 1813, and became Organist of Worcester Cathedral and Conductor of the Worcester Festivals. Died of paralysis at Worcester, April 28, 1844.

Hackett's "National Psalmist" (1842) contains a Double Chant in F by him. The words of his Anthem, "Gather yourselves together," are given in Marshall's "Words of Anthems" (1840.)

WILLIAM HENSHAW, Mus.D., Dunelm ... 1813 1862

Born 1791, Organist of Durham Cathedral, 1813. Died at Clapham, September 30, 1877. Buried in Nunhead Cemetery.

Composer of Chants, &c.

PHILIP ARMES, M.A., Dunelm; Mus.D., Oxon., 1864, et Dunelm., 1874; F.R.C.O. ... ... 1862 ——

Born at Norwich, August 15, 1836. Chorister in Norwich Cathedral, and afterwards in Rochester Cathedral. Assistant Organist of Rochester Cathedral, under Dr. J. L. Hopkins. Organist of Holy Trinity Church, Gravesend, 1854; St. Andrew's, Wells Street, London, 1857; Chichester Cathedral, 1861; and Durham Cathedral, 1862. Appointed Resident Examiner in Music to Durham University, 1890, and now Professor of Music to the same. Composer of Oratorios, Cantatas, Church Music, Organ pieces, Madrigals, &c.

EDINBURGH.

ST. MARY'S CATHEDRAL.

SEE ESTABLISHED IN 1879.

THOMAS HENRY COLLINSON, Mus.B., Oxon., 1877 1878 ——

Born at Alnwick, April 24, 1858. Pupil of Dr. Armes, and Assistant Organist at Durham Cathedral. Organist of St. Oswald's, Durham, 1876; St Mary's Cathedral, Edinburgh, 1878 (prior to its consecration). Lecturer in Church Music to the Episcopal Theological College, 1880. Conductor of Edinburgh Choral Union, 1883. Composer of Anthems, &c.

ELY.

THOMAS BARCROFTE ... ... —— ——

He is said to have been Organist in 1535, but the Cathedral records furnish no proof. An early copy of his Service in G (composed in 1532) is in the Cathedral Library.

CHRISTOPHER TYE, Mus.D., Cantab., 1545 et Oxon., 1548 ... ... 1541 1562

"Magister Choristarum" and Organist. At one time musical instructor to the children of Henry VIII. Took Orders, and held successively the Rectories of Little Wilbraham, Newton, and Doddington-cum-March. Afterwards became Organist of the Chapel Royal of Queen Elizabeth. A prominent Organist and Composer of the Reformation period. Commenced rhythmical paraphrase of the Acts of the Apostles, and set it to music. It was unsuccessful, and he never completed the task. Early copies of his Evening Service in G minor and of four Anthems are in the Cathedral Library.

According to Anthony Wood: "Dr. Tye was a peevish and humorsome man, especially in his later days, and sometimes playing on the organ in the Chapel of Queen Elizabeth, which contained much music but little to delight the ear, she would send the verger to tell him that he played out of tune, whereupon he sent word that *her ears* were out of tune."

ROBERT WHITE, B.A., Mus.B., Cantab., 1561 ... 1562 1567

Very little is known of his biography, but Morley mentions him in his "Introduction" as one of the famous English musicians of his time. He was probably the Robert White who became Organist of Westminster Abbey in 1570. An early copy of his Anthem "O praise God" is in the Cathedral Library, and there are some Latin Services and Anthems by him in MS. in the Library of Christ Church, Oxford.

JOHN FARRANT 1567 1572

He is supposed to have been a son of Richard Farrant. He subsequently became Organist successively of Hereford Cathedral; Christ Church, Newgate Street, London; and Salisbury Cathedral. Hawkins assigns the post at Christ Church, Newgate Street, to another John Farrant, but it is quite possible that all the above appointments were held in turn by the same person. The Service—Farrant in D minor—which has been attributed to *Richard* Farrant, is the composition of *John* Farrant.*

WILLIAM FOX 1572 1579

An old Chapter account of 1572, quoted by Willis ("Survey"), records that his yearly stipend was £13 6s. 8d. Composer of an Anthem, "Teach me Thy way," an early copy of which is in the Cathedral Library. It was published in "The Parish Choir" (1847).

GEORGE BARCROFTE, B.A. 1579 1609

Probably a son of Thomas Barcrofte. Styled "Vicar" in the Cathedral books, and he may have been a Minor Canon. Early copies of two Anthems in the Cathedral Library are probably by him, and not by *Thomas* Barcrofte.

* This fact can be proved by reference to the Ely, Peterhouse (Cambridge), and other MSS., and to various old Part books still extant.

JOHN AMNER, Mus.B., Oxon., 1613; et Cantab., 1640 1610 1641

Organist and Master of the Choristers. A "Vicar" like Barcrofte. Died 1641. Much of his neat handwriting, chiefly of Organ parts, is still extant in the Cathedral books. His compositions include three Services (one of them known as "Cæsar's," from the fact that it was written for his friend Henry Cæsar, D.D., Dean of Ely, in 1614) and fifteen Anthems.

ROBERT CLAXTON 1641 1662

In the Cathedral books called "Lay Clerke." In another list, one of "other instructors in music, and on the viols occasionally." The organ was silenced in 1644, and Claxton's occupation as *Organist* must then have ceased. He is said, however, to have been "displaced," 1662. Died 1668.

JOHN FERRABOSCO, Mus.D., Cantab., 1671 ... 1662 1682

Probably grandson of Alphonso Ferrabosco, an Italian musician resident in England during Elizabeth's reign. His degree was granted by royal letters patent of James II. Died 1682. The Ely books contain fourteen Services and eleven Anthems by him.

On his death, in 1682, "THOMAS BULLIS, Junr., officiated 6 mo. in ye vacancy." Bullis is mentioned as "Lay Clerke," and is included in the list of "other instructors," like Claxton. The Cathedral books contain three Services and six Anthems by Thomas Bullis, Junr. A Service and five Anthems are attributed to Thomas Bullis, who was probably his father.

JAMES HAWKINS (Senr.), Mus.B., Cantab., 1719 ... 1682 1729

Formerly a Chorister in St. John's College, Cambridge. The Cathedral is indebted to this indefatigable musician for its valuable collection of MS. scores and part-books, carefully preserved to this day. He also left behind him a large number of original compositions, those at Ely amounting to as many as seventeen Services and seventy-five Anthems!

He lies buried in the South Transept of the Cathedral. The following is the inscription on his tomb—

"Under this marble
(Among many of his relations)
Lieth the body of James Hawkins, B.M.,
46 Years Organist of this Church;
Eminent in his Profession,
Regular in the discharge of his Duty,
Chearful and friendly in his Deportment.
He died the 18th of October 1729,
In the 67th year of his Age."

THOMAS KEMPTON 1729 1762

Born 1694. Died June 16, 1762. Buried in St. Mary's Churchyard, Ely. Some of his descendants have sung in the Cathedral Choir up to the present time. Composer of the well-known Service, Kempton in B flat, the autograph score of which, together with those of four other Services and three Anthems, is included in the Cathedral MSS.

JOHN ELBONN 1762 1768

No particulars are known concerning Elbonn, except that he died June 7, 1768, and lies buried near the Western end of the Lady Chapel of the Cathedral.

DAVID WOOD 1768 1774

The Anthem, "Lord of all power and might" is attributed by Page, in his "Harmonia Sacra," Vol. II., to a "David Wood, *Gentleman of the Chapel Royal, and Vicar-Choral of St. Paul's Cathedral.*" Possibly Wood resigned the appointment at Ely and went to London.

JAMES ROGERS 1774 1777

Very little is known of him except that he resigned. Most probably, however, he was the James *Rodgers* who became Organist of Peterborough Cathedral, 1777. He composed an Evening Service in A, in continuation of Boyce (Verse Service).

RICHARD LANGDON, Mus.B., Oxon., 1761 ... ... 1777 1778

Grandson of the Rev. Tobias Langdon, a Priest Vicar of Exeter Cathedral. Organist and Sub-Chanter of Exeter Cathedral, 1753; Organist of Ely Cathedral, 1777; Organist of Bristol Cathedral, 1778; Organist of Armagh Cathedral, 1782. Died at Exeter, September 8, 1803. Buried in St. Paul's Church, Exeter. Composer of "Chanting Services,"* Anthems, Glees, &c. Chiefly known at the present day by the Double Chant in F, usually attributed to him, and published anonymously in his "Divine Harmony."

HIGHMORE SKEATS (Senr.) 1778 1803

(See under Canterbury.)

HIGHMORE SKEATS (Junr.) 1804 1830

(See under St. George's Chapel, Windsor.)

ROBERT JANES 1831 1866

Born, 1806. "Sol-fa Scholar" (*i.e.*, Chorister) of Dulwich College. Pupil of Dr. Z. Buck at Norwich. Appointed Organist of Ely Cathedral at the age of eighteen. Died at Ely, 1866. Composer of the well-known "Ely Confession" and other Church Music. Editor of a Psalter, which, in a revised form, is still in use at Ely.

Janes had a very large teaching connection in Norfolk and Suffolk, and in later years was wont to relate how he rode long distances on horseback to fulfil his engagements; also how he had arranged a pair of lamps, attached to his saddle like pistol holsters, to light his lonely road at night through the Fen country. It is said that his income at this time could not have been expressed in less than four numerals. (See "Fifty Years of Church Music," by the Rev. W. E. Dickson, M.A.).

EDMUND THOMAS CHIPP, Mus.D., Cantab., 1861... 1867 1886

Son of T. P. Chipp, the drum player. Born Christmas-day, 1823. Chorister in the Chapel Royal. Violinist in Her Majesty's Private Band and other Orchestras. Organist successively of Albany Chapel, Regent's Park; Percy Chapel, Tottenham Court Road; St. Olave's, Southwark; St. Mary-at-Hill; Royal Panopticon, Leicester Square; Holy Trinity, Paddington; St. George's Church and Ulster Hall, Belfast; Kinnaird Hall, Dundee, 1866; St. Paul's, Edinburgh, 1866; and Ely Cathedral, 1867. Died at Nice, December 17, 1886. Buried in Highgate Cemetery. Composer of Church Music, Organ Music, &c.

BASIL HARWOOD, M.A., Mus.D., Oxon.... ... 1887 1892

(See under Oxford.)

THOMAS TERTIUS NOBLE 1892 1898

(See under York.)

HUGH PERCY ALLEN, M.A., Mus.D., Oxon., F.R.C.O. ... ... 1898 ——

(See under St. Asaph.)

* He appears to have borrowed the idea for these from his predecessors at Ely—Ferrabosco, Hawkins, and Kempton, whose compositions in the books at Ely include Services of this kind.

EXETER.

MATTHEW GODWIN, Mus.B., Oxon., 1585 ... ... —— 1586

Previously Organist of Canterbury Cathedral. Died January 12, 1586. Buried under the North Tower of Exeter Cathedral, with the following Inscription:—

"Matthei Godwin adolescentis pii mitis ingeniosii
musicæ bacchalaurii dignissimi scientissimi
Ecclesiarum Cathed.: Cantuar: et Exon.; Archimusici.
Æternæ memoriæ posuit G: M: Fr: vixit annos XVII:
menses V: Hinc ad cœlos migravit XII Januarii, 1586."

(*Translation by Mr. J. S. Bumpus.*)

"G. M. Fr. placed this to the eternal memory of Matthew Godwin, a pious, gentle, and clever youth, Bachelor in Music and most skilful chief-musician of the Cathedrals of Canterbury and Exeter. He lived seventeen years and five months, and departed hence to heaven, 12 January, 1586."

ARTHUR COCK (or COCKE), Mus.B., Oxon., 1593 ... —— ——

Supplicated for his degree in 1593, and was mentioned in this connection as *Organist of Exeter Cathedral.* Afterwards became Organist of the Chapel Royal. Some of his compositions are to be found in the Music School, Oxford.

EDWARD GIBBONS, Mus.B., Cantab. et Oxon. ... 1609 1644

According to the Chapter books he was elected a Priest Vicar, August 8, 1609, but there is no particular mention of him as Organist. Most likely, however, he took his turn in playing the organ.

(See under Bristol.)

It has frequently been stated that HENRY LOOSEMORE, Mus.B., Cantab. (See under Cambridge—King's College), became Organist of Exeter Cathedral after the Restoration; but it can be proved by entries in the records of King's College, Cambridge, that he continued as Organist of the latter uninterruptedly from 1627 until his death in 1670.

In the Chapter records of Exeter, moreover, there is no mention whatever of any Loosemore but John, the organ builder (probably a brother of Henry), concerning whom there are several entries during the period 1660-1665, in connection with the organ which he was then building for the Cathedral. One such entry, dated 1663, is to the effect that his charges were to be paid by the Dean and Chapter in riding to Salisbury, "to see the organ there, the better to inform himself to make the new organ of this Cathedral." Loosemore's organ was completed in 1665, and was long considered to be one of the finest in the country. It was highly praised by the Hon. Roger North on his visit to Exeter with his brother, the Lord Keeper Guildford. Macaulay's History of England also mentions it in connection with the visit to the Cathedral of William, Prince of Orange. After undergoing several alterations and additions from time to time, the instrument was entirely rebuilt in 1891 by Willis.

Epitaph on John Loosemore, in the Cathedral—

"Hic jacet spe Resurrectionis
Johannes Loosmore (*sic*).

quondam Decano et Capitulo hujus Ecclesiæ Curator fidelissimus, et inter Artifices sui Generis facile Princeps. Sit organum hoc augustum prope situm perpetuum istius Artis et Ingenii Monumentum. Obiit 18 Aprilis an: 1681—æta: suæ 68."

Translation (kindly supplied by Mr. J. S. Bumpus).

"Here lies, in hope of the Resurrection, John Loos(e)more, formerly the most faithful Curator to the Dean and Chapter of this Church, and by far the chief among the workmen of his kind: may this noble organ, placed near, be a perpetual monument of his art and genius.

"He died 18 April, 1681, in the 68th year of his age."

THEODORE COLEBY (or COLBY) 1665 1674

Previously Organist of Magdalen College, Oxford.

"A.D. 1667, Sept. 20. Admitted and sworn in the Colledge Hall, by the Custos, as Lay Vicar of the said Colledge, Theodore Colby" (Registers of the College of Vicars, Exeter). "The last signature to his stipend is dated Midsummer, 1674, and is made by a cross only, which renders it probable that he was then in an infirm state of health, possibly on the verge of death" (Bloxam, "Magdalen Registers"). Wood (Fasti) describes Coleby as "a German."

HENRY HALL (Senr.) ... ... 1674 (?)1688

Son of Captain Henry Hall, of Windsor. Born about 1655. Chorister in the Chapel Royal. Pupil of Dr. Blow. Organist of Exeter Cathedral, 1674; Organist (and Vicar Choral) of Hereford Cathedral, 1688. Took Holy Orders, 1698. Died 1707. Buried in the Cloister of Vicars' College, Hereford. Some of his Church Music is to be found in the Tudway Collection. He also acquired some celebrity as a poet.* His son (Henry Hall, Junr.) succeeded him as Organist of Hereford Cathedral.

{ PETER PASMORE. }
{ JOHN WHITE. }

They are mentioned together as Organists in 1686. The name of the latter, however, appears alone in 1693.

RICHARD HENMAN 1694 1741

Dismissed on June 27, 1741, "for his long absence and disorderly life."

An Anthem, "Have mercy," by Henman, in the Ely Collection, is probably his composition.

JOHN SILVESTER .. .. 1741 (?)1753

RICHARD LANGDON 1753 1777

(See under Ely).

WILLIAM JACKSON 1777 1803

Son of a grocer in Exeter. Born May 29, 1730. Pupil of Silvester and afterwards of John Travers in London. Returned to Exeter and established himself as a teacher. Appointed Organist to the Cathedral, 1777. Died July 5, 1803. Buried in the Vestry of St. Stephen's Church, Exeter. Composer of Operas, Odes, Songs, Sonatas, and a quantity of Church Music, including the popular Service in F. Writer on musical and other subjects; also skilled as a painter. Thomas Gainsborough, the great artist, was one of his intimate friends.

* See the concluding lines of his Ode to Purcell on page 115.

Inscription on the white marble monument to Wm. Jackson, in the Vestry of St. Stephen's Church, Exeter:—

"In the Science of Music an eminent Professor, whose genius united elegant expression with pure and original melody and delicacy of harmonic combination. In painting, in literature, in every liberal study that enlightens the intellect, or expands the heart, his attainments were rare and distinguished: a writer, novel and acute in observation, a correct and discriminating critic: endeared to his select associates by a conversatior and demeanour of impressive and fascinating simplicity. Born in this city xxix May, 1730. Died v July, 1803."

JAMES PADDON 1804 1835

Born at Exeter about 1768. Chorister in the Cathedral. Pupil of William Jackson. Organist of the Cathedral, 1804. Died 1835. Buried in the South Aisle of the Cathedral Nave. Composer of Church Music. Editor of Jackson's Cathedral Music.

SAMUEL SEBASTIAN WESLEY, Mus.D., Oxon. 1835 1842

(See under Gloucester.)

ALFRED ANGEL 1842 1876

Born 1816. Chorister in Wells Cathedral and afterwards Assistant-Organist there. Succeeded Dr. Wesley at Exeter Cathedral, 1842. Died at Exeter, May 24, 1876. Buried in the Old Cemetery. Composer of Church Music, Part-songs, &c. His Anthem, "Blow ye the trumpet in Zion," gained the Gresham Prize in 1842.

DANIEL JOSEPH WOOD, Mus.B., Oxon., 1874; Mus.D., Cantuar., 1896 F.R.C.O. ... ... 1876 ——

Born at Brompton near Chatham, August 25, 1849. Chorister in Rochester Cathedral, and afterwards Assistant Organist there. Organist of Holy Trinity, New Brompton (Kent), 1864; Parish Church, Cranbrook, 1866; Parish Church, Lee, 1868; Parish Church, Boston (Lincs.), 1869; Chichester Cathedral, 1875; and Exeter Cathedral, 1876. Conductor of the Western Counties Musical Association, 1877. Composer of Church Music, Organ pieces, &c.

GLOUCESTER.

ROBERT LICHFIELD ... ... —— (?)1582

Inscription on a stone in the South Transept of the Cathedral: "Here lyeth under this marbel stone, Robert Lichfield, Organist and Maister of the Choresters of this Cathedral Church 20 years. He dyed the 6 of January, 1582."

ELIAS SMITH ... ... —— (?)1620

PHILIP HOSIER 1620 1638

BERKELEY WRENCH 1638 1640

JOHN OKER (or OKEOVER), Mus.B., Oxon. ... 1640 (?)1644
(See under Wells.)

ROBERT WEBB 1662 1665

THOMAS LOWE 1665 1666
Probably a relative of Edward Lowe, of Oxford Cathedral.

DANIEL HENSTRIDGE 1666 1673
One Daniel Henstridge is also mentioned as Organist of Rochester Cathedral and afterwards of Canterbury Cathedral; but he is more likely to be the son of this Daniel Henstridge of Gloucester.

CHARLES WREN 1673 1679
"10 April, 1679. First monition for beating and wounding one of the singingmen."—(Cathedral Records.)
Afterwards Organist of Rochester Cathedral.

DANIEL ROSINGRAVE 1679 1681
(See under Dublin—Christ Church Cathedral.)

STEPHEN JEFFRIES (or JEFFERIES) 1682 1710
Born 1662. Chorister in Salisbury Cathedral and afterwards Assistant Organist there. Appointed Organist of Gloucester Cathedral at the age of twenty. Composer of one of the melodies played by the Gloucester Cathedral chimes.* Died 1712.
Buried in the Cathedral Cloisters.
31st Janry, 1684. Jefferies' first monition "for manifold neglect and unreasonable absence from the Church without leave desired or obtained."
8th Feby, 1688. Jefferies' second monition for playing over upon the organ a common ballad, "insomuch that the young gentlewomen invited one another to dance."†
5th Decr, 1699. Jefferies' first admonition for frequent absences, especially on

* A set of Variations on this melody has been written for the pianoforte by the lately-retired Organist of Gloucester Cathedral, Mr. C. Lee Williams, Mus.B., and published by Messrs. Novello.

† "8th Feby, 1688. Mr. Subdean pronounced against Mr. Stephen Jefferies, Organist of this Church, his second monition to depart this Church, for that he, the said Stephen Jefferies, did upon Thursday last in the morning (being Thanksgiving day), immediately after the sermon ended and the blessing given, play over upon the organ a common ballad in the hearing of 1500 or 2000 people, to the great scandal of religion, prophanation of the Church, and grevious offence of all good Christians. And further, because though Dr. Gregory (the Senior Prebendary of this Church) did immediately express his great detestation of the same to Mr. Deighton, the Chaunter of this Church, and Mr. John Tyler, the senior singingman of the Choir, informing them of the unspeakable scandal that universally was taken at it, and that they immediately acquainted the said Stephen Jefferies therewith, yet he, the said Stephen Jefferies, in direct despite to religion and affront to the said Dr. Gregory, did after evening prayer, as soon as the last Amen was ended, in the presence and hearing of all the congregation, fall upon the same strain, and on the organ played over the same common ballad again, insomuch that the young gentlewomen invited one another to dance, the strangers cryed it were better that the organs were pulled down than they should be so used, and all sorts declared that the Dean and Chapter could never remove the scandal if they did not immediately turn away so insolent and profane a person out of the Church."

Sunday mornings; but more particularly for not educating the Choristers in the grounds of music.

According to Hawkins ("History of Music," p. 770), there was a story concerning Jeffries amongst the Choirmen of Gloucester, who used to relate that: "To cure him of a habit of staying late at the tavern, his wife drest up a fellow in a winding-sheet, with directions to meet him with a lanthorn and candle in the cloisters through which he was to pass on his way home; but that, on attempting to terrify him, Jeffries expressed his wonder only by saying 'I thought all you spirits had been abed before this time.'" Hawkins also gives the following story as a proof of Jeffries' eccentric character: "A singer from a distant church, with a good voice, had been requested and undertook to sing a solo anthem in Gloucester Cathedral, and for that purpose took his station at the elbow of the organist in the organ loft. Jeffries, who found him trip in the performance, instead of palliating his mistake and setting him right, immediately rose from his seat, and leaning over the gallery, called out aloud to the choir and the whole congregation—'He can't sing it!'"

WILLIAM HINE 1710 1730

Born at Brightwell, 1687. Chorister in Magdalen College, Oxford. Pupil of Jeremiah Clark.* Succeeded Stephen Jeffries as Organist of Gloucester Cathedral. It is said that, in consideration of his musical skill and gentlemanly qualities, his salary was augmented by £20 a year. Died August 28, 1730. Buried in the Cathedral Cloisters. Some Anthems and an Organ Voluntary by him were published after his death, under the title of "Harmonia Sacra Glocestriensis," edited by his widow. He was joint composer, with Hall, Junr., of the Morning Service known as Hall and Hine in E flat.†

A tablet to his memory on the Cloister wall bears the following inscription:—

"M. S. Gulielmi Hine,
hujusce Ecclesiæ Cathedralis
Organistæ et Choristarum Magistri.
Qui morum candore et eximiâ in
arte cœlesti peritiâ omnium amorem
et admirationem, venerandi autem
Decani et Capituli gratium (voluntario
Stipendii incremento testatum) meritissimo
affecutus est. Morte præmatura ereptus
Obiit Aug. 28vo, Anno Christi 1730, ætatis 43."

BARNABAS GUNN 1730 1740

Previously Organist of St. Philip's, Birmingham. Died 1743. His extempore playing is said to have been remarkable. A Te Deum and Jubilate by him are extant in MS. He published "Two Cantatas and Six Songs" (to which Handel was one of the subscribers), and some Sonatas for the Harpsichord.

MARTIN SMITH 1740 1782

Father of John Stafford Smith, Master of the Children and Organist of the Chapel Royal.

* "From whom," says Dr. Arnold ("Succinct Account" of Hine—*Cath. Mus.*), "he imbibed his master's excellence, and became distinguished for his elegant manner of playing the Church Service."

† Dr. William Hayes wrote a Communion and Evening Service in continuation of this, the correct title of the whole Service being Hall, Hine and Hayes.

WILLIAM MUTLOW... ... ... 1782 1832

Born 1761. Chorister in the Cathedral. Succeeded Martin Smith as Organist, 1782. First conducted the Festival of the Three Choirs, 1790, and continued as conductor of the Gloucester performances until his death in 1832. Buried in the Cloisters. His Verse Anthem—"Unto Thee, O Lord"—was included in one of Novello's early Catalogues. A Chant by him is to be found in Dr. Beckwith's Collection.

As a boy, Mutlow was very fat, and it is related of him that he once fell from the Triforium into the Choir, bouncing like an india-rubber ball, and was not in the least hurt.

The following description in Henry Phillips's "Musical and Personal Recollections during Half-a-Century" is said to apply to Mutlow: "A gentleman of eccentric habits and appearance, very short and fat, an epicure of no ordinary stamp, the length of whose arm was as near as possible the measure of his baton." The anecdotes which Phillips relates concerning this "conductor" of a "celebrated triennial festival" should, like many others to be found in his book, be taken *cum grano salis.* After describing a scarcely credible practical joke which he alleges that Malibran, Braham, and Loder played upon Mutlow at a morning performance of the Festival, by arranging with the band that not a note should be sounded upon his giving the signal to start a certain piece, he (Phillips) goes on to say: "When this little conductor gave a lesson on the pianoforte it was always in a room next to the kitchen: in the middle of the lesson he would say, 'There, go on; I can hear ye, I'm only going to baste the air' (hare); so he walked into the kitchen, did what he proposed, came back, and finished the lesson. The Queen's English was a matter sadly disregarded by this gentleman: . . . when going out he would call to the servant, 'Hann, where's my at?' He was, however, a kind, good-tempered soul, took all that happened in the best part, and when the Festival had terminated said—'Some very droll things have occurred this week; but never mind, come and dine with me, and we'll enjoy the haunch of venison, and drink success to the next Festival in some of the finest port in England.'"

JOHN AMOTT 1832 1865

Born at Monmouth, 1798. Pupil of W. Mutlow. Appointed Organist of the Abbey Church, Shrewsbury, 1820. Succeeded Mutlow at Gloucester. Died February 3, 1865. Buried in Gloucester Cemetery. Composer of Services and Anthems. Compiler of "A selection of Chants, Kyrie Eleison, &c., arranged in Score." A Sanctus and Kyrie in G, by him, were printed in Bunnett's "Sacred Harmony" (1865). One of the compilers of "Annals of the Three Choirs."

SAMUEL SEBASTIAN WESLEY, Mus.D., Oxon., 1839 1865 1876

Son of Samuel Wesley and grandson of the Rev. Charles Wesley, the hymn writer. Born in London, August 14, 1810. Chorister in the Chapel Royal. Organist of St. James's Chapel, Hampstead Road, 1826; St. Giles's, Camberwell, January 12, 1829; St. John's, Waterloo Road, 1829; Parish Church, Hampton-on-Thames, 1830; Hereford Cathedral, 1832; Exeter Cathedral, 1835; Leeds Parish Church, 1842; Winchester Cathedral, 1849; and Gloucester Cathedral, 1865. Died at Gloucester, April 19, 1876. Buried in the Old Cemetery, Exeter. There is a tablet to his memory in the North Aisle of the Nave at Exeter Cathedral, and a stained glass window in the South Chantry of the Lady Chapel at Gloucester Cathedral. Distinguished Church Composer and Organist. Composer of Church Music, Odes, Madrigals, Organ pieces, Pianoforte pieces, Songs, &c. Author of pamphlets on Cathedral music. Editor of a "Selection of Psalms and Hymns" and "The European Psalmist" (1872). There is an interesting Organ book at Hereford Cathedral containing the organ part of Wesley's Anthem "The Wilderness," in the composer's own handwriting. The same book also contains his "Blessed be the God and Father," and "O God, Whose nature and property."

Dr. Wesley was a prominent advocate of reform in musical matters at our Cathedrals, and wrote and lectured with considerable insight and ability on the subject. But his efforts to obtain from the Cathedral authorities a larger amount of interest, and to place the musical service on a higher and more satisfactory footing, were only partly successful during his lifetime; and being a man of unusually sensitive temperament, it is more than probable that the many troubles and disappointments which he experienced in his Cathedral duties, helped in a great measure to shorten his days.

There can be no doubt that these troubles largely accounted for the migratory character of his career as a Cathedral Organist.

The following extracts from a pamphlet by him, entitled "A few words on Cathedral Music and the Musical System of the Church, with a plan of Reform" (London: Rivingtons, 1849), will serve to illustrate one or two of his views:—

"Painful and dangerous is the position of a young musician who, after acquiring great knowledge of his art in the Metropolis, joins a country Cathedral. At first he can scarcely believe that the mass of error and inferiority in which he has to participate is habitual and irremediable. He thinks he will reform matters, gently, and without giving offence; but he soon discovers that it is his approbation and not his advice that is needed. The choir is 'the best in England' (such being the belief at most Cathedrals), and, if he give trouble in his attempts at improvement, he would be, by some Chapters, at once voted a person with whom they 'cannot go on smoothly,' and 'a bore.'

. . . .

"He must learn to tolerate error, to sacrifice principle, and yet to indicate, by his outward demeanour, the most perfect satisfaction in his office, in which, if he fail, he will assuredly be worried and made miserable. If he resign his situation a hundred less scrupulous candidates soon appear, not one of whom feels it a shame to accept office on the terms, and his motives being either misunderstood, or misrepresented wilfully, or both, no practical good results from the step."

Referring to the careless performances and to the inferior quality of the music often performed, he says:

"The illusive and fascinating effect of musical sound in a Cathedral unfortunately serves to blunt criticism, and casts a veil over defects otherwise unbearable. No coat of varnish can do for a picture what the exquisitely reverberating qualities of a Cathedral do for music. And then, the organ! what a multitude of sins does *that* cover!"

His argument with those who would have nothing but Plain-song in the musical service is thoroughly characteristic and convincing:

"Some would reject all music but the unisonous Chants of a period of absolute barbarism—which they term 'Gregorian.' All is 'Gregorian' that is in the black, diamond, note! These men would look a Michael Angelo in the face and tell him Stonehenge was the perfection of architecture."

Here is another characteristic passage referring to the want of support many composers of eminence have experienced, and their pecuniary embarrassments resulting therefrom:

"Why should we not have monuments to perpetuate the fame of those who *neglect* their duty, as well as of those who perform it?"

As a part of his "Plan of Reform" he suggests that the minimum number of lay singers at one Cathedral should be fixed at twelve, with the addition of a few competent volunteer members. He considers it absolutely necessary that there should be a Musical College for the efficient training of Cathedral Organists and Singers, every Cathedral being required to contribute to its support.

The Cathedral Organist "should in every instance be a professor of the highest ability—a master in the most elevated departments of composition—and efficient in the conducting and superintendence of a choral body."

One of the concluding sentences of the pamphlet runs thus:

"Amongst the dignitaries of the Church are several distinguished persons who are fully alive to the high interests of music, and who do not forget that whatever is offered to God should be as faultless as man can make it. Music should not be compelled to bring her worst gift to the altar! Is it too much to ask of them some public effort in support of Cathedral Music? From whom could it so well come?"

On the recommendation of Mr. Gladstone, Wesley was offered the honour of knighthood, with the alternative of a Civil List pension of £100 per annum, for his distinguished services to Church Music. He chose the latter, remarking that "it was a nice little nest egg." This pension was continued to his widow. The last time Dr. Wesley played the organ in Gloucester Cathedral was on the afternoon of Christmas Day, 1875. Before the Service was over he asked his assistant, Mr. C. E. Clarke, for an old full score of "The Messiah," which he kept in the organ loft, and from it he played, as the concluding voluntary, the "Hallelujah" chorus, an unusual thing for him to do, as he generally extemporized or played one of Bach's Fugues from memory. He never touched the Cathedral organ again, and in April of the following year the gifted brain and clever fingers were at rest. His last words were, "Let me see the sky," a fitting request from a man of such high ideals and noble inspirations.

CHARLES HARFORD LLOYD, M.A., Oxon., 1875
Mus.D., Oxon., 1892; F.R.C.O. 1876 1882

Born at Thornbury, Gloucester, October 16, 1849. Graduated in Arts and Music at Magdalen Hall, Oxford. Succeeded Dr. Wesley at Gloucester. Conductor of the Gloucester Festivals, 1877 and 1880. Resigned the post at Gloucester on his appointment as Organist of Christ Church Cathedral, Oxford, 1882. First President of Oxford University Musical Club. Succeeded Sir Joseph Barnby as Organist and Precentor of Eton College, 1892. Composer of Church Music, Cantatas, Organ pieces, Madrigals, Part-songs, Songs, &c.

CHARLES LEE WILLIAMS, Mus.B., Oxon., 1876;
F.R.C.O. 1882 1897

Born at Alton Barnes, Wiltshire, May 1, 1852. Chorister in New College, Oxford. Pupil of Dr. G. B. Arnold, and Assistant Organist of Winchester Cathedral. Organist of Upton Church, Torquay, 1870. Music Master of St. Columba's College, Rathfarnham, 1872. Organist of Llandaff Cathedral, 1876; Gloucester Cathedral, 1882. Conductor of the Gloucester Festivals, 1883-1895. Resigned at Gloucester owing to ill-health, 1897. Now an Examiner for the Associated Board of the Royal Academy of Music and Royal College of Music. Composer of Cantatas, Church Music, Part-songs, Organ pieces, The Gloucester Chimes arranged for the Pianoforte, Songs, &c. Joint compiler, with H. Godwin Chance, M.A., of the latest edition of "Annals of the Three Choirs."

ALFRED HERBERT BREWER, Mus.B., Dub., 1897;
F.R.C.O., 1897 ... ... 1897 ——

Born at Gloucester, June 21, 1865. Chorister in the Cathedral, and afterwards pupil of Dr. Harford Lloyd. First Organ Scholar of the Royal

College of Music. Organist of St. Catherine's Church, Gloucester, April, 1881; St. Mary-le-Crypt, November, 1881. Organ Scholar of Exeter College, Oxford, 1883. Organist of St. Michael's, Coventry, 1886. Organist and Music Master of Tonbridge School, 1892. Succeeded C. Lee Williams as Organist of Gloucester Cathedral and Conductor of the Gloucester Festivals, 1897. Composer of a setting of Psalm xcviii., Church Music, Part-songs, Organ pieces, an Operetta, &c.

HEREFORD.

THOMAS MASON ... ... —— ——

Organist in 1581.

JOHN HODGE ... ... —— ——

JOHN BULL, Mus.D., Cantab. (circa 1591) et Oxon., 1592 ... 1582 (?)1591

Born *c.* 1563. Chorister in the Chapel Royal, under Blitheman. Organist of Hereford Cathedral, 1582. Organist of the Chapel Royal, 1591. First Gresham Professor of Music, 1596,* but compelled to resign his Professorship on his marriage in 1607. "Went abroad without license" (Chapel Royal Cheque Book), 1613, and became Organist of the Chapel Royal at Brussels. Subsequently Organist of the Cathedral of Notre Dame, Antwerp. Died March 13, 1628. Buried in Notre Dame, Antwerp. Distinguished Organist and Composer of Church Music, Madrigals, Pieces for the Virginals, &c. To John Bull has been attributed the authorship of the music of our National Anthem, "God save the Queen," but the authority for this seems doubtful.

In 1601 Bull went abroad for the benefit of his health, having obtained permission to appoint Thomas Bird (son of William Bird, Organist of Lincoln Cathedral and afterwards of the Chapel Royal) as his deputy Gresham lecturer. While travelling through France *incognito* a famous musician showed him a song in forty parts, challenging anybody to add another part to it. Bull asked to be left alone with the score, which request being granted, he added *forty more parts* to it. On seeing these additions the famous musician burst into an ecstasy, declaring that the writer must be either the Devil or *John Bull!*

THOMAS WARROCK (or WARWICK) ... ... —— ——

Organist in 1586.

Descendant of an old Cumberland family, and father of Thomas *Warwick*, Organist of Westminster Abbey and the Chapel Royal, whose name appears among the benefactors to Hereford Library, belonging to the Vicars Choral.

THOMAS MASON (Re-appointed) ... . 1589 (?)1592

"To be Organist for one whole year."

---

* He was unable to deliver his lectures in Latin, according to the custom of his colleagues. An ordinance was therefore made in 1597, permitting him to read them in English. This permission has been extended to all subsequent Gresham Professors of Music.

JOHN FARRANT* 1592 1593

See under Ely.)

It is said that Farrant resigned the appointment at Hereford after being admonished for alleged insolence.

JOHN FIDOW ("Laicus") 1593 1594

Dismissed by the Vicars, February 22, 1594.

The Peterhouse, Cambridge, Collection contains an Anthem, "Hear me, O Lord," by John Fido (*sic*). In an old MS. Bass part-book, in the possession of Mr. J. S. Bumpus, the same Anthem is attributed to "Mr. Fidow of *Exetor*" (*sic*). It is evidently, therefore, the composition of either the Organist of Hereford Cathedral or a relative.

—— GIBBS 1595 1597

WILLIAM JUGLOTT ... ... 1597 ——

(Or Inglott? See under Norwich.)

HUGH DAVIES (or DAVIS), Mus.B., Oxon., 1623*... 1630 (?)1644

Vicar Choral, and afterwards Custos (or Warden) of the Vicars Choral.

Wood (Fasti., Oxon.) mentions that he was famous for his Church Compositions.

An Act in the College books relating to him orders "that he be spared from the Choir so that he be ready in ye Organ loft to play before ye reading of ye first Lesson."

JOHN BADHAM* ... ... 1661 (?)1688

Vicar Choral.

"1678. On April 27 John Badham took to his assistance Mr. Rbt. Griffiths one of ye Vicars Choral."

HENRY HALL (Senr.)* 1688 1707

(See under Exeter.)

HENRY HALL (Junr.) 1707 1713

Son of the foregoing. Succeeded his father in the appointment. Died January 22, 1713.

None of his compositions are extant, but it appears that as a poet he was even more gifted than his father.

EDMUND TOMSON (or THOMPSON) ... ... 1713 (?)1721

HENRY SWARBRICK (or SCHWARBROOK) 1721 1754

Supposed to have been a relative of Thomas Schwarbrook, the organ builder. Died 1754.

A Morning Service by him in MS. is at Hereford. In a curious old oblong MS. volume of Single Chants written on parchment, in the possession of Mr. J. S. Bumpus, there is a Chant by "Mr. Henry Swarbrick, Organist of Hereford, in E lami."

* These Organists were members of the College of Vicars Choral, and consequently in Holy Orders.

RICHARD CLACK* ... ... 1754 (?) 1779

Vicar Choral. Died 1779. Buried in the Cathedral. According to "Annals of the Three Choirs" he was Conductor of the Hereford Festivals of 1759 and 1765.

The performance of Handel's "Messiah," conducted by him in the Cathedral, at the Festival of 1759, was probably the first instance of the rendering, in a Cathedral, of a complete Oratorio at these Festivals.

WILLIAM PERRY ... ... 1779 (?) 1789

The Cathedral records give this name and date; but "Annals of the Three Choirs" states that the music at the Hereford Festival of 1780 "was conducted by Mr. Coyle, Organist of Hereford Cathedral. He *succeeded* Richard Clack."

MILES COYLE ... ... 1789 (?) 1805

Previously Organist of Ludlow Parish Church. Conductor of the Hereford Festivals, 1780-1804.

CHARLES JAMES DARE 1805 1818

Conductor of the Hereford Festivals, 1807-1816. Resigned 1818. Died 1820. Composer of a Service in G, which always used to be sung at Hereford on Audit Days.

AARON UPJOHN HAYTER 1818 1820

Born at Gillingham, December 16, 1799. Chorister in Salisbury Cathedral, and afterwards pupil of and assistant to A. T. Corfe. Succeeded C. J. Dare as Organist of Hereford. Conductor of the Hereford Festival of 1819. Resigned the post at Hereford and became Organist of the Collegiate Church, Brecon. Went to America, 1835. Organist of Grace Church, New York. Organist of Trinity Church, Boston, 1837. Organist (and Musical Adviser) to the Handel and Haydn Society, 1838. Died in Boston, 1873. There is a MS. Evening Service, in E flat, by him, at Hereford, and an Anthem, "Withdraw not Thou," is included in the Rev. W. Cooke's Words of Anthems, printed for the use of Hereford Cathedral (1825).

His name is mentioned in "Musical and Personal Recollections during Half-a-Century," by Henry Phillips; and the valuable services which he rendered to the Handel and Haydn Society, in Boston, are recorded in the published "History" of that Society, compiled by Charles C. Perkins, and issued in Boston, 1886.

JOHN CLARKE-WHITFELD, Mus.B., Oxon., 1793
Mus.D., Dub., 1795; Cantab., 1799; et Oxon., 1810... 1820 1832

Originally John Clarke, but on the death of his maternal uncle, H. Fotherley Whitfeld, 1814, he adopted his name. Born at Gloucester, December 13, 1770. Pupil of Dr. P. Hayes, at Oxford. Organist of the Parish Church, Ludlow, 1789; Master of the Choristers of Christ Church and St. Patrick's Cathedrals, Dublin, 1793; Organist of Armagh Cathedral, 1794; Trinity and St. John's Colleges, Cambridge, 1799; Hereford Cathedral, 1820; University Professor of Music, Cambridge, 1821. Retired from the post at Hereford, 1832. Died at Holmer, near Hereford, February 22, 1836. Buried in the East Walk of the Bishop's Cloister, Hereford Cathedral. Composer of an Oratorio, "The Crucifixion and Resurrection," Church Music, Glees, Songs, &c.

* See footnote, p. 41.

SAMUEL SEBASTIAN WESLEY, Mus.D., Oxon. ... 1832 1835
(See under Gloucester.)

JOHN HUNT 1835 1843
Born at Marnhull, Dorset, December 30, 1806. Chorister in Salisbury Cathedral, and afterwards pupil of A. T. Corfe. Lay Vicar of Lichfield Cathedral, 1827, and Organist of the Church attached to St. John's Almshouses in that city. Succeeded Dr. S. S. Wesley at Hereford, 1835. Conductor of the Hereford Musical Festivals. Died November 17, 1843, from the results of a fall over a dinner wagon, laden with plates and glasses, which had carelessly been left in a dark part of the Cloisters after an Audit dinner. His adopted nephew, a Chorister in the Cathedral, died three days afterwards from the effects of the shock of his uncle's death, and both bodies were buried in the same grave. There is a window to his memory and that of his nephew in the North Aisle of the Choir of the Cathedral.
A volume of his Glees and Songs, with a memoir prefixed, was published by subscription in 1843.

GEORGE TOWNSHEND SMITH 1843 1877
Son of Edward Smith, a Lay Clerk of St. George's Chapel, Windsor. Born at Windsor, November 14, 1813. Chorister in St. George's Chapel, Windsor, under Skeats. Pupil of Dr. S. S. Wesley. Organist of the Old Parish Church, Eastbourne; St. Margaret's, Lynn. Succeeded J. Hunt, at Hereford, 1843. Conductor and Hon. Secretary of the Hereford Festivals. Died suddenly, August 3, 1877. There is a stained glass window to his memory in the Cathedral. Composer of Church Music. A Jubilate by him was written expressly for and performed at the Hereford Festival of 1855; and an Anthem, "O, how amiable," was composed for and produced at the re-opening Service at Hereford Cathedral, after its restoration, in 1863.*

LANGDON COLBORNE, Mus.B., Cantab., 1864; Mus.D., Cantuar., 1883 ... ... 1877 1889
Born at Hackney, September 15, 1835. Pupil of George Cooper. Organist of St. Michael's College, Tenbury, 1860; Beverley Minster, 1874; Wigan Parish Church, 1875; Dorking Parish Church, 1877, succeeding J. Townshend Smith at Hereford the same year. Conductor of the Hereford Festivals. Died September 16, 1889. There is a stained glass window to his memory in the Cathedral. Composer of an Oratorio, "Samuel," Church Music, Part-songs, Songs, &c.

GEORGE ROBERTSON SINCLAIR ... ... 1889 ——
Born at Croydon, October 28, 1863. Student at the Royal Irish Academy of Music. Chorister in, and afterwards Assistant Organist at, St. Michael's College, Tenbury. Pupil of Dr. C. Harford Lloyd, and Assistant Organist of Gloucester Cathedral. Organist of St. Mary-le-Crypt, Gloucester, 1879; Truro Cathedral (at the age of seventeen), 1881; Hereford Cathedral, 1889. Conductor of the Hereford Festivals, Hereford Choral Society, Hereford Orchestral Society, &c. Composer of Church Music, &c.
The new organ in Truro Cathedral, by Willis, was built under Mr. Sinclair's direction; and since his appointment to Hereford the sum of £2,300 has been raised through his energy, and the Cathedral organ rebuilt (also by Willis) from his specification.

* For the same occasion there were also written Ouseley's eight-part Service in C and his Anthem "Blessed be Thou"; also Goss's "Stand up and bless." During the work of restoration (1842-1850) the Choral Services were entirely abandoned in the Cathedral, and were held in All Saints' Church. On Easter Day, 1850, the Services were resumed in the Nave, and on June 30, 1863, the Cathedral was re-opened in its entirety.

LICHFIELD.

According to Bishop Hacket's Statutes, "the Organist is reckoned as one of the Lay Vicars, whose salary as an Organist is to be £4 for himself, and 6s. 8d. for an Organ blower." These Statutes are still in force at the present day, in regard to the Organist, his salary being £4 per annum, largely augmented by that of a Vicar Choral and by other perquisites.

MICHAEL ESTE, Mus.B., Cantab., 1606 ... ...(?)1618 (?)1638
(His name is variously given as ESTE, EST, EASTE, and EAST).

Supposed to be son of the famous printer and music publisher, Thomas Este. Appointed Vicar Choral and Master of the Choristers of Lichfield Cathedral about 1618. Probably also took duty as Organist. Composer of Church Music, Madrigals, "Duos and Fancies for Viols," &c. Contributor to ' The Triumphs of Oriana." A work by him, entitled "The Sixt Set of Bookes, wherein are Anthemes for Versus, and Chorus of 5 and 6 parts; apt for Violls and Voices," is dedicated to Dr. John Williams, Bishop of Lincoln. This worthy prelate, who was a perfect stranger to Este, had settled upon him an annuity for life, in return for the pleasure he had experienced in hearing some of the composer's Motets. A number of Este's Anthems, with accompaniment for viols, were published by the Musical Antiquarian Society in 1845, under the editorship of Dr. E. F. Rimbault.

HENRY HINDE ... ... —— 1641

In a book entitled "The Life of Elias Ashmole, Esq.," occurs the following entry in his diary:—

"Mr. Henry Hinde, Organist of the Cathedral [Lichfield], who died the 6th of August, 1641, taught me the virginets and organ."

There is an Anthem by him, "Sing Praises," in Barnard's Collection.

—— LAMB (Senr.) ... ... —— 1688

Probably appointed at the Restoration. He was Organist in 1683. This information occurs on the fly-leaf of the Primus Contra-Tenor part of Barnard, at Lichfield.

—— LAMB (Junr.) ... ... (?)1688 ——

He was Organist in 1690 and in 1694.
(According to the fly-leaf above mentioned.)

A MS. Book at Lichfield contains an Anthem, "Lord, who shall dwell," by Mr. William Lamb, Junr.

From a note in another of the Barnard Part-Books, it would appear that Lamb, Junr., unlawfully claimed the authorship of a Service by a composer named Berchinshaw.

GEORGE LAMB ... ... —— 1749

Buried 1749, according to the Cathedral registers.

In the Muniment Room of the Cathedral there is a deposition of Thomas Cothall, organ builder, as to peculations of George Lamb, Vicar Choral and Organist. Mention is therein made of "a little organ in the Lady Choir." There is also a letter from George Lamb to the Dean and

Chapter as to charges against him, in which he makes astounding and infamous charges against the Vicars. This letter also treats of the organ and its repairs.

JOHN ALCOCK, Mus.D., Oxon., 1761 ... ... 1750 1760

Born in London, 1715. Chorister in St. Paul's Cathedral. Pupil of the blind Organist, John Stanley. Organist of St. Andrew's, Plymouth, 1737; St. Lawrence's, Reading, 1741; Lichfield Cathedral, 1750; Sutton Coldfield Parish Church, 1761-1786; St. Editha's, Tamworth, 1766-1790; also Private Organist to the Earl of Donegal. He suffered in health through attending to his duties in the damp, neglected Cathedral, and resigned the appointment of Organist; but continued to be a Vicar Choral until his death in 1806. Buried in the Cathedral. Composer of Church Music, Songs, and Instrumental pieces. Author of a novel, "The Life of Miss Fanny Brown."

Alcock had in contemplation the issue of a collection of Church Music by various composers. But upon hearing of Dr. Greene's intention, not only to make a similar compilation, but to supply the principal choirs with copies of the same at his own expense, he generously handed over to Greene all the materials which he had then collected for his own work, probably feeling that his own chances of success were small under the circumstances.*

In the Preface to a volume of his own Anthems, published in 1771, occurs the following foot-note, which may be taken as an illustration of the somewhat peculiar and over-sensitive nature of its writer, rather than of any *real* injustice to him on the part of the Cathedral authorities:—

"'Tis incredible what a number of baſe Artifices have been practiced by ſome People belonging to this Cathedral, in Order to prejudice me, in my Profeſſion, and diſtreſs my Family, for no cauſe whatever: Nay, even my Son,† as ſoon as ever he began to play for me, was turned out from being a choriſter, tho' he had been in the choir but *two Years*, and his Voice, (which was a very uſeful one,) not the leaſt fallen; when many of the Lads are continued in their Places, for *ten*, *twelve*, or *fourteen* Years, *and long after their Voices are broke:* Alſo, tho' he always officiated for me, yet I forfeited the ſame Money, when I went out of Town, as if the *Duty* had been totally neglected; Albeit the Salary *then* was *only* four Pounds *per annum*, besides the Vicar's Place; and there was much more *Duty* when I was Organiſt, *than now*, being obliged always to play a Voluntary after Morning, and Evening Prayers, even in the ſevereſt cold Weather, when, very often, there was only one Vicar, who read the Service, and an Old Woman at Church, beſides the Choriſters; which not only brought, but fix'd the Rheumatiſm ſo ſtrongly upon me, that I am seldom free from Pain, and ſometimes confin'd to my Bed, for eight or ten Days together, tho' I never had the leaſt Complaint of that Kind, till then; and no Body can live more regular than I have always done, as every one of my Acquaintance, can teſtify: I likewiſe play'd the Organ all *Paſſion-Week*, (except *Good-Friday*,) both which Cuſtoms, have *ever ſince*, *been diſcontinued*. All the Time I was Organiſt, which was upwards of Ten Years, there was not a Book in the Organ-loft fit for Uſe, but what I bought, or wrote myſelf, (for which I never was paid one Halfpenny,) and yet there

* Mr. J. S. Bumpus has in his possession a copy of Alcock's "Divine Harmony; or a Collection of Fifty-five Double and Single Chants for Four Voices, as they are sung at the Cathedral of Lichfield" (1752), perhaps the only copy now in existence, at the end of which is sewn up, between some blank pages, an interesting prospective "Advertisement," by Alcock, of his intended compilation of Services and Anthems.

† This must have been John Alcock, Mus.B., Oxon., who became Organist of St. Mary Magdalen, Newark-on-Trent in 1758, and of the Parish Church, Walsall, in 1773, and died 1791.

have been as many Books purchafed, within thefe few Years, as have coft, at leaft, Thirty Guineas."

. . . . . "Oh, 'tis excellent
To have a Giant's strength; but it is tyrannous
To use it like a Giant."—*Shakespeare.*

WILLIAM BROWN 1766 1807

A native of Worcester. Died March 3, 1807, aged 70. Buried (on March 11, 1807) in the North Transept of the Cathedral.

SAMUEL SPOFFORTH 1807 1864

Younger brother of Reginald Spofforth, the Glee writer. Born 1780. Pupil of his uncle, Thomas Spofforth, of Southwell. Organist of Peterborough Cathedral, 1799; of Lichfield Cathedral, 1807. Died 1864. Buried in the Cathedral Close, Lichfield. His Double Chant in G was once a favourite.

THOMAS BEDSMORE 1864 1881

Born at Lichfield, 1833. Chorister in the Cathedral. Pupil of S. Spofforth, and Assistant Organist at the Cathedral. Organist, 1864. Held several other appointments in and around Lichfield, in addition to that at the Cathedral. Died 1881. Buried in the Cathedral Close. Composer of Church Music, Songs, Pianoforte pieces, &c.

There is a handsome memorial brass to him on the wall of the North Choir Aisle.

JOHN BROWNING LOTT, MUS.B., OXON., 1876; F.R.C.O. ... ... 1881 ——

Born at Faversham, 1849. Chorister in Canterbury Cathedral. Pupil of T. E. Jones and Dr. Longhurst, and Organist successively of St. Dunstan's and St. Paul's Churches, Canterbury. Assistant Organist of Canterbury Cathedral, 1873. Organist of the Parish Church, Margate, 1875. Organist of Lichfield Cathedral, 1881. Conductor of the Lichfield Musical Society. Composer of Church Music, Part-songs, &c. Joint Editor, with Mr. (now Dr.) C. Charlton Palmer, of a series of Arrangements for the Organ.

LINCOLN.

Much interesting information concerning the early history of the musical staff of Lincoln Cathedral is to be found in the Rev. Canon A. R. Maddison's excellent book, entitled "A short account of the Vicars Choral, Poor Clerks, Organists, and Choristers of Lincoln Cathedral" (London, 1878). To its pages, and to a series of valuable papers by Canon Maddison in continuation of the same subject, read, at various periods, before the Lincoln Archæological Society, I am greatly indebted for much of the following information concerning the Lincoln Organists.

JOHN INGLETON ... ... 1439 ——

JOHN DAVY ... ... 1489 ——

Appointed Master of the Choristers in singing.

Leonard Pepir ... ... 1506 ——

Appointed "ad lusus organorum in alto choro."

John Gilbert ... ... 1524 ——

Appointed Organist for Life. Previously elected Master of the Choristers in Singing, 1518.

Thomas Appilby ... ... 1538 ——

Singing Master, or Teacher of the Choristers, and Organist.

James Crowe ... ... 1539 ——

Singing Master and Organist.

William Byrd (or Bird) 1563 1572

One of the most eminent musicians of the sixteenth century.

Chorister in the Chapel Royal. Pupil of Tallis. Organist of Lincoln Cathedral, 1563-1572. Gentleman of the Chapel Royal, and afterwards Organist there, 1585. It is said that, upon his appointment as Gentleman of the Chapel Royal, the Dean and Chapter of Lincoln allowed him to continue his office at the latter place by means of his deputy, Thomas Butler, who afterwards, upon Byrd's recommendation, succeeded him as Organist. Died 1623. Composer of Church Music, Madrigals, pieces for the Virginals, &c.

Byrd took out a Patent, with Tallis, for the sole right of publishing music in England.

By an Act of Chapter passed on September 29, 1570, the Organist was directed to set the tune before the commencement of the Te Deum and the "Canticle of Zachary" at Morning Prayer, and before the Magnificat and Nunc dimittis at Evening Prayer, and to accompany the Anthem.*

Thomas Butler 1572 1595

Previously Deputy-Organist (for William Byrd). Appointed Organist and Master of the Choristers on Byrd's recommendation. Salary, £10 per annum. Admonished for negligence, 1595, and shortly afterwards resigned, when William Boys was appointed temporarily.

John Hilton is mentioned as Organist (in 1593 and 1594), but he was probably only deputy to Butler. Afterwards appointed Organist of Trinity College, Cambridge. He was a counter-tenor, and in 1593 the Chapter gave him 30s. for his services in arranging for the acting of two Comedies by the choristers.

Thomas Kingston 1599 1616

On the 30th of March, 1611, he was arraigned before the Chapter "for beating the boys and calling Mr. Dye, the Master of the Choristers, an ass! He confessed all the misdemeanours charged against him, and submitted to the censure of the Chapter. Whereupon they gave him an admonition, and gave him order to amend upon pain of being turned out and deprived." In 1612, however, he "is ordered never hereafter to meddle with teaching the Quiristers." In 1615 again admonished: "He

* According to the Rev. Canon Maddison, these injunctions are carried out almost to the letter on Friday mornings at the present day; the Organist simply gives a chord at the commencement of the Te Deum and Canticle.

ys verye often drunke and by means therof he hathe by unorderlye playing on the organs putt the quire out of time and disordered them." Replaced in 1616 by John Wanless(e).

JOHN WANLESS(E) ... ... 1616 ——

Admitted Organist by the Chancellor after Evening Prayers. Salary, £20 per annum.

In 1625 the Gate House Chambers in Vicars' Court were assigned to him at a rent of 10s. per annum.

—— MUDD ... ... 1662 (?)1663

Great complaints were made to Dean Honywood of his drunkenness, as will be seen from the following extracts from letters, written by the Precentor to the Dean:—

"14 March, $166\frac{2}{3}$.

"Mr. Mudd hath been so debauched these assizes, and hath so abused Mr. Derby that he will hardly bee persuaded to stay to finish his worke unlesse Mudd bee removed.* And I have stuck in the same *Mudd* too;† for he hath abused mee above hope of Pardon. I wish you would be pleased to send us downe an able and more civill organist."

"16 March, $166\frac{2}{3}$.

"Yesterday Mr. Mudd shewed the effects of his last weeke's tipling, for when Mr. Joynes was in the midst of his sermon Mudd fell a-singing aloud, insomuch as Mr. Joynes was compelled to stopp; all the auditorie gazed and wondered what was the matter, and at length some neere him, stopping his mouth, silenced him, and then Mr. Joynes proceeded: but this continued for the space of neere halfe a quarter of an houre. So that now wee dare trust him no more with our organ, but request you (if you can) to helpe us to another; and with what speed may be."

ANDREW HECHT (or HIGHT) ... ... (?)1663 1693

a Dutchman, was therefore appointed in the place of Mudd. Buried in the Cathedral, March 31, 1693. Two of his Anthems in MS., "God is our hope" and "Out of the deep," are included in the Cathedral Library.

A writ appears to have been taken out against him in 1670 by John Jameson, Clericus Rivestriæ (Vestry Clerk), for striking him in the Church; but the suit was afterwards withdrawn.

THOMAS HECHT ... ... —— ——

Son of the foregoing. Admitted Organist in 1693, at a salary of £30 per annum, but did not take duty, being afterwards (1695) appointed Organist of Magdalen College, Oxford (see Magdalen College, Oxford), and

THOMAS ALLINSON (or ALLANSON) 1693 1704

was admitted in his place, salary £40 per annum, on condition that he taught a Chorister to play the organ from time to time—"Cautionem autem ut unum Choristarum ad Organum pulsandum de tempore in tempus doceat ei imposuerunt." Died 1704. Buried in the Cathedral. Composer of several Anthems in MS. in the Cathedral Library.

---

* Derby was an organ builder, and at the time was evidently repairing the organ, or building a new one.

† By this little joke the Precentor meant to imply, not that he had indulged in the same dissipated habits as his Organist, but that he had been subjected to the same annoyance from him as had Mr. Derby.

GEORGE HOLMES 1704 1721

Probably son of Thomas Holmes (a Lay Vicar of Winchester Cathedral), and grandson of John Holmes (Organist of Winchester Cathedral, and afterwards of Salisbury Cathedral).

Previously Organist to the Bishop of Durham. Succeeded Allinson at Lincoln Cathedral. Died 1721. Buried in the Cathedral Cloisters. Composer of several Anthems, two of which, "Arise, shine, O daughter of Zion" (composed on the Union with Scotland, 1706), and "I will love Thee, O Lord," are included in the Tudway and Ely Collections, and an Ode for St. Cecilia's Day. His setting of the Burial Sentences is still sung in Lincoln Cathedral at funerals. A Toccata for Single or Double Organ, in a book of organ music, once in his possession, and now in the British Museum, is probably his own composition.

CHARLES MURGATROYD§ (or MURGETROYD) ... 1721 1741

Appointed, "cum approbatione Chori,"* Organist and Junior Vicar,† having previously been Organist of York Minster.

On June 26, 1731, it was ordered that "the Organist should play a short Voluntary before the Second Lesson."‡

On March 24, 1733, Murgatroyd was suspended from his post for negligence, and SAMUEL WISE was ordered to play "for the present in his stead." Died September 4, 1741.

WILLIAM MIDDLEBROOK 1741 1756

"Son of Robert Middlebrook of the city of Lincoln." Burghersh Chanter in the Cathedral, 1717, and a Chorister, 1719. Died 1756.

LLOYD RAYNOR§ 1756 1784

Previously a Chorister in the Cathedral, 1746, and Master of the Song School, Newark-on-Trent.

On September 10, 1771, he was "arraigned and reproved for playing one Anthem while Mr. Binns was singing another"; and, "for insolence," was suspended from his office till he apologized. Dismissed from the post September 17, 1784; but afterwards "submitted," and was allowed a pension of £10 a year, which, however, was discontinued after the first year.

JOHN HASTED§ 1784 1794

Resigned the office, 1794.

REGINALD SPOFFORTH, the glee writer, is said to have been Organist, and to have resigned in 1789 (see his "Life"), but this is obviously wrong.

GEORGE SKELTON 1794 1850

Son of George Skelton, a blacksmith of Lincoln. Admitted a Burghersh Chanter in the Cathedral, 1782; Chorister, 1785. Succeeded Hasted as Organist, 1794. Resigned 1850.

His son, G. J. Skelton (with whom he resided after his retirement), was Organist of Holy Trinity Church, Hull, and composer of the well known Chant Service—Skelton in D.

---

* The Choir were evidently allowed a voice in the matter of selection of their Organist.

† The title of Junior Vicar is now superseded by that of "Lay Clerk."

‡ This curious and unnecessary interpolation was only abolished during the organistship of the late Mr. J. M. W. Young.

§ Chants by all of these three Organists are contained in Warren's "Chanter's Hand Guide," 1850.

JOHN MATTHEW WILSON YOUNG 1850 1895

Organist and Master of the Choristers.*

Born at Durham, December 17, 1822. Chorister in Durham Cathedral, and afterwards pupil of Henshaw and Assistant Organist there. For some time Professor of Music at the Training School, York. Succeeded Skelton as Organist of Lincoln Cathedral. Resigned 1895. Died at West Norwood, March 4, 1897. Buried in the Cemetery, East Gate, Lincoln. Composer of a Sacred Cantata, "The Return of Israel to Palestine," Church Music, &c. Compiler of the Lincoln Psalter.

Under Mr. Young's *régime* the musical services at Lincoln Cathedral greatly improved. The organ was considerably enlarged, and pedals were for the first time used.

GEORGE JOHN BENNETT, Mus.D., Cantab., 1893; F.R.C.O. ... . 1895 ——

Born at Andover, May 5, 1863. Chorister in Winchester College. Student of the Royal Academy of Music under Macfarren, Steggall, and others. Afterwards studied abroad (through the kindness of Messrs. Novello) under Kiel and Rheinberger. On his return to England he was appointed a Professor of Harmony at the Royal Academy of Music. Organist of St. John's, Wilton Road, 1890; Lincoln Cathedral, 1895. Fellow and Member of the Council of the Royal College of Organists. Conductor of the orchestra at the London Organ School, and for some time Conductor of the Church Orchestral Society. Composer of Church Music, Orchestral Music, Organ pieces, Songs, Chamber Music, Pianoforte pieces, &c.

Under Dr. Bennett's direction a new and unusually complete four-manual organ has been erected by Mr. Henry Willis, from a specification drawn up by the late Mr. J. M. W. Young, with large additions. It was opened on Thursday, November 17 (St. Hugh's Day), 1898, with a Special Service, followed by two Recitals by Sir Walter Parratt.

LIVERPOOL.

SEE ESTABLISHED IN 1880.

FREDERICK HAMPTON BURSTALL, F.R.C.O. ... 1880 ——

Born at Liverpool, January 29, 1851. Pupil of Dr. Röhner at Liverpool. Organist of Childwall Parish Church, 1870; Wallasey Church, 1876. Elected Organist of Liverpool Cathedral by the Chapter on the formation of the See. Organised a large special choir for Oratorio Services, 1883. Composer of Church Music, Songs, Pianoforte pieces, &c.

---

* It appears that the two offices must have been separate from the time of Butler's resignation, 1595, until 1850; that of Master of the Choristers being sub-divided for a short time, after the Restoration, between two of the Lay Clerks, the one teaching vocal and the other instrumental music.

LLANDAFF.

Very scanty records exist of the earlier Organists of Llandaff Cathedral. For some considerable period both the fabric and the establishment had been in a declining state, and in 1691 the Choir was suppressed and the organ destroyed. As a substitute, the National Schoolmaster was appointed to lead the singing, for which he received £4 per annum. At Bishop Ollivant's enthronement, on March 13, 1850, these crippled musical arrangements appear to have been still in force, for we read that "On the opening of the door to the bishop's summons . . . . the National Schoolmaster, heading the procession, gave out a Psalm, which was sung by about a dozen of his scholars, a bass viol being the only instrument then in the possession of the Cathedral. In this way the bishop was conducted to his throne," &c. (Bishop's Charge, 1869). Under the rule of this worthy prelate Choral Service was re-established in 1861.*

—— RESE (Rees) was Organist in 1608.

In that year £7 was granted to him "as his wage to be paid unto him quarterly by even quantities." A marginal note in the records states that "The Chapter did disagree and not consent to this Act."

GEORGE CARR ... ... 1629 ——

At a stipend of £8.

—— NIXON was Organist in 1672.

"Ordered that Mr. Nixon shall have £4 quarterly."

[Choral Service discontinued from 1691 until 1861.]

JOHN BERNARD WILKES 1861 1865

Student of the Royal Academy of Music, 1842-1846. Organist successively of Monkland Church, near Leominster; St. David's, Merthyr Tydvil; and Llandaff Cathedral. Composer of the tune "Lyte" to "Far from my heavenly home," in "Hymns Ancient and Modern."

JAMES HAMILTON SIREE CLARKE, MUS.B., OXON., 1867 ... ... 1865 1866

Born at Birmingham, January 25, 1840. Organist of Parsonstown Parish Church, 1862; Zion Church, Rathgar, Dublin, 1863; Carnmony Church, 1864; Queen's College, Oxford, 1866; Kensington Parish Church, 1871; St. Peter's, South Kensington, 1872. Appointed Conductor of the Victorian National Orchestra, Australia, 1889-1891. During the past

* From a letter addressed by Archbishop Wake to Browne Willis, on November 2, 1721, it seems that the re-establishment of Choral Service at Llandaff had been contemplated in the last century.

twenty years has been Director of the music at several of the London Theatres. Composer of Church Music, Cantatas, Operettas, Incidental Music to various Plays, two Symphonies, and other music for Orchestra, Chamber Music, Organ pieces, Pianoforte pieces, Part-songs, Songs, &c. Author of "A Manual of Orchestration."

FRANCIS EDWARD GLADSTONE, Mus.D., Cantab.; F.R.C.O. 1866 1870

(See under Norwich).

THEODORE E. AYLWARD 1870 1876

(See under Chichester).

CHARLES LEE WILLIAMS, Mus.B., Oxon., F.R.C.O. 1876 1882

(See under Gloucester).

HUGH BROOKSBANK, Mus.B., Oxon., 1874; F.R.C.O. 1882 1894

Born at Peterborough, September 13, 1854. Chorister in St. George's Chapel, Windsor. Pupil of Dr. Keeton at Peterborough. Organ Scholar at Exeter College, Oxford. Organist of St. Alban's, Birmingham, 1881; Llandaff Cathedral, 1882. Died at Cardiff, April 28, 1894. Composer of Church Music, Songs, &c.

GEORGE GALLOWAY BEALE, Mus.B., Dunelm, 1891; F.R C.O. ... ... 1894 ——

Born in London, 1868. Educated at Marlborough College, and for some time a Chorister there. Pupil of Sir Frederick Bridge. Organist, successively, of St. John's School, Leatherhead, and St. John's Church, Paddington. Succeeded Hugh Brooksbank as Organist of Llandaff Cathedral.

LONDON.

ST. PAUL'S CATHEDRAL.

JOHN REDFORD 1491 1547

Organist and Almoner, the latter appointment including the duties of Master of the Boys. His Anthem, "Rejoice in the Lord alway," is still sung at St. Paul's and elsewhere. An edition in 8vo size, by Dr. (now Sir George) Martin, was issued some few years ago by Messrs. Novello & Co. Redford also composed some pieces for the organ.

Tusser, in his "Five Hundred Points of Husbandry," gives the following eulogy of him:—

. . . .

"By friendship's lot to Paul's I got,
So found I grace a certain ſpace
Still to remaine
With Redford there, the like no where,
For cunning ſuch and vertue much
By whom ſome part of muſic's art
So did I gaine."

THOMAS GILES (or GYLES) ... ... (?)1547 ——

Father of Dr. Nathaniel Giles (Organist of St. George's Chapel, Windsor).

THOMAS MORLEY, Mus.B., Oxon., 1588 ... (?)1591 1592

Born about 1557. Chorister in St. Paul's. Pupil of Bird. Resigned the post of Organist of St. Paul's on his appointment as a Gentleman of the Chapel Royal in 1592, which he held until 1602. Died in 1604. Composer of Church Music (including a Service for the Burial of the Dead), Madrigals, Canzonets, Lessons for the Virginals. Author of "A Plaine and Easie Introduction to Practicall Musicke, set down in the forme of a dialogue. Divided into three partes. The first teacheth to sing with all things necessary for the knowledge of prickt song. The second treateth of descante and to sing two parts in one upon a plain song or ground, with other things necessary for a descanter. The third and last part entreateth of composition of three, foure, five, or more parts, with many profitable rules to that effect, with new songs of 2, 3, 4, and 5 parts (London, 1597)." This work was dedicated to "the most excellent musician Maister William Birde." In 1598 Morley was granted a patent for the exclusive right of printing music.

JOHN TOMKINS, Mus.B., Cantab., 1607 ... ... 1622 (?)1638

Brother of Thomas Tomkins (see Gloucester). Previously Organist of King's College, Cambridge (1606). Gentleman of the Chapel Royal. Died 1638. Buried in St. Paul's Cathedral. Some Anthems by him are to be found in Barnard's Collection.

An inscription to him in the North Aisle of the Old Cathedral, where he was buried, reads as follows:—

"Johannes Tomkins, Musicæ
Baccalaureus, organista sui
temporis celeberrimus, post-quam
Capellæ regali, per annos
duodecim, huic autem Ecclesiæ
per novem decem sedulo inser-
viisset, ad cœlestem chorum
migravit Septembris 27, Anno
Domini 1638. Ætatis suæ 52.
Cujus desiderium mœrens uxor
hoc testatur marmore."

(See also under Cambridge—King's College.)

ADRIAN BATTEN ... ... (?)1624 1637

Tomkins and Batten appear to have been *Joint* Organists during the greater part of their period of office.

Chorister in Winchester Cathedral, and pupil of John Holmes. Lay Vicar of Westminster Abbey, 1614. Organist and Vicar Choral of St. Paul's Cathedral, 1624. Died 1637. Voluminous composer of Church Music, much of it being in MS. Batten's music appears to have been among the earliest that was measured out by means of bar lines.

ALBERTUS BRYAN (BRIAN or BRYNE) 1638 1666

Pupil of John Tomkins. Appointed Organist of St. Paul's Cathedral in 1638, at the early age of seventeen. Deprived of his post during the

Civil Wars and re-appointed at the Restoration. After the Great Fire (in 1666) he became Organist of Westminster Abbey, and was eventually buried in the Cloisters there. Composer of Services, Anthems, and Organ pieces.

PETITION OF ALBERTUS BRYAN TO CHARLES II. FOR HIS ADMISSION AS ORGANIST OF THE CHAPEL ROYAL:—

"To the King's Most Excellent Majesty.

The humble petition of Albertus Bryne,

Sheweth,

That your Majesty's late Royal father, of blessed memory, was pleased in his lifetime to make Choice of your petitioner to be Organist of the Cathedral Church of St. Paul's, London, in which said place he was by your said late Royal father confirmed when your petitioner was about the age of seventeen years.

And since then he hath so industriously practised that Science that he hath very much augmented his skill and knowledge therein.

And therefore most humbly presents himself to serve your Majesty as Organist in your Majestie's Chapel at Whitehall, if your Majesty would be graciously pleased to admit of him accordingly.

And he shall ever pray.

1660."

(Musical Petition to Charles II., from the State Paper Office: never before published. *Musical Standard*, April 11, 1868).

Bryan's petition appears to have been of no avail, for his name does not occur in the Cheque Book of the Chapel Royal as Organist. His son, Albertus Bryan, Junr., was Organist of Dulwich College, 1671-1674.

The Cathedral was destroyed in the Great Fire, 1666.

JEREMIAH CLARK 1695 1707

The first Organist of the present Cathedral. Chorister in the Chapel Royal. Organist of Winchester College, 1692. Almoner and Master of the Choristers of St. Paul's,* 1693; Organist of St. Paul's, 1695; Vicar Choral of St. Paul's, 1705, having previously (1699) been admitted on probation. Gentleman of the Chapel Royal, 1700; one of the Organists of the same, 1704. Committed suicide, in consequence of an unsuccessful love affair, by shooting himself, December 1, 1707, at his house in St. Paul's Churchyard. Buried in St. Gregory's Vault in the New Crypt of St. Paul's, December 3, 1707. Composer of Church Music, Lessons for the Harpsichord, Incidental Music to various plays, &c.

His sister married Charles King, Mus.B., Almoner and Master of the Choristers, 1707-1748, alluded to by Dr. Greene as the "serviceable" composer.

RICHARD BRIND 1707 1718

Chorister in St. Paul's, and eventually Organist. Died 1718. Composer of two thanksgiving Anthems. The words of five of his Anthems are in a Collection by Dr. Croft, entitled "Divine Harmony."

MAURICE GREENE, Mus.D., Cantab., 1730 ... 1718 1755

Born in London, 1696. Son of the Rev. Thomas Greene, Rector of St. Olave's, Jewry. Chorister in St. Paul's, and pupil of Brind. Organist of St. Dunstan in the West, 1716; St. Andrew's, Holborn, 1717. Organist of St. Paul's, 1718, and afterwards Vicar Choral of the same. Organist and

* It is said that Dr. Blow resigned this post in favour of Clark.

Composer to the Chapel Royal, 1727. Professor of Music in the University of Cambridge, 1730. Master of the King's Band, 1735. Associated with Michael Festing in the foundation of the Royal Society of Musicians. For some time a friend of Handel, the latter frequently playing on the organ in St. Paul's, which instrument, it is said, greatly pleased him. Greene is supposed to have acted as *blower* on some of these occasions.* Died December 1, 1755. Buried in St. Olave's, Old Jewry, London, of which his father was formerly Rector. On the demolition of St. Olave's, Greene's remains were removed to St. Paul's and placed in the grave of Boyce, May 18, 1888. Composer of Oratorios, Cantatas, an Opera, Odes, Songs, Catches, Organ and Harpsichord Music, a Service in C, and "Forty Select Anthems," 2 vols. (1743). Commenced a collection of Church Music by various composers, which he gave to Dr. Boyce for completion just before his death.

Greene seems to have been a man of attractive and courteous manners, and a great favourite in society, notwithstanding the fact that he was physically deformed. Upon the death of an uncle—Sergeant Greene—he became possessed of a large estate in Essex, called Bois Hall, where it is said that he spent the greater part of his later years.

JOHN JONES ... (Appointed Christmas Day) 1755 1796

Also *Vicar Choral* of St. Paul's. Organist of the Temple Church, 1749; Charterhouse, 1753. He held the three appointments—Temple, Charterhouse, and St. Paul's—until his death, February 17, 1796. Buried in the Charterhouse Chapel Cloisters. Composer of "60 Chants, Single and Double, respectfully dedicated to the Dean and Chapter of St. Paul's," Lessons for the Harpsichord, Songs, &c. There are two MS. Services by him in the St. Paul's books. His well-known Double Chant in D was admired by Haydn, who heard it at a Festival of the Charity Children in St. Paul's, 1791, and noted it, in an improved form, in his Diary.

"Jones . . . appears not to have been worthy of the situation, for he was not capable of doing the duty for a length of time after the appointment: and as he could not play from score, he employed himself in arranging the Anthems in two lines. The same book is now in use at the Cathedral."†—(From "A description of the Organ at St. Paul's Cathedral," in *The English Musical Gazette*, January 1, 1819.)

THOMAS ATTWOOD 1796 1838

Born in London, November 23, 1765. Chorister in the Chapel Royal and pupil of Nares and Ayrton, and afterwards studied at Naples and Vienna (in the latter city under Mozart). Some time after his return to England was appointed Assistant Organist to Reinhold at St. George the Martyr, Queen's Square, Holborn, and one of the Chamber Musicians, and Page, to the Prince of Wales. Succeeded Jones at St. Paul's, 1796, and was appointed Composer to the Chapel Royal the same year, in succession to Dr. Dupuis. Organist of the King's Private Chapel, Brighton, 1821, and Organist of the Chapel Royal, 1836. Died at 17, Cheyne Walk, Chelsea, March 24, 1838, and is buried in the Crypt at St. Paul's. Composer of Church Music, Musical Dramas, Glees, Songs, &c.

Attwood used to say with reference to the Dignitaries of St. Paul's and his appointment there: "It is all very well that they agree to pay me for playing, for if they did not, I should be happy to pay *them* for letting me play."

Mendelssohn, when in England, frequently accompanied his friend Attwood

* We read that on one occasion "their Royal Highnesses the Princess Anne and Princess Caroline came to St. Paul's Cathedral and heard the famous Mr. Handel (their musick-master) perform upon the organ"; . . . *Applebee's Weekly Journal*, August 29, 1724.

† This was in 1819.

to St. Paul's, and played on the Organ. It is said that on one occasion, when he was playing at the end of the afternoon service, the vergers experienced such difficulty in dispersing the congregation, that they caused the bellows to be stopped in the midst of his performance, much to his disgust and that of his hearers.

SIR JOHN GOSS, Knt., Mus.D., Cantab., 1876 ... 1838 1872

Born at Fareham, December 27, 1800. Chorister in the Chapel Royal. Pupil of Attwood. Was an unsuccessful candidate for the Organistship of Old Chelsea Church, 1819. Organist of Stockwell Chapel, 1821; St. Luke's, Chelsea, 1824; St. Paul's Cathedral, 1838. Appointed Composer to the Chapel Royal, 1856. Knighted 1872, retiring from St. Paul's the same year. Died at Clarewood Terrace, Brixton Rise, May 10, 1880. Buried in Kensal Green Cemetery, May 15. Composer of Church Music, Glees, Madrigals, Overtures for Orchestra, Songs, &c. Compiler of Organ Arrangements, Chant and Hymn Books. Author of a Treatise on Harmony and a Catechism of the Rudiments of Music.

Inscription on the Monument to Sir John Goss in the Crypt of St. Paul's Cathedral:—

"In remembrance of Sir John Goss, Knt., Mus.D., Cantab.; Composer to H.M. Chapels Royal, and for 34 years Organist and Vicar Choral of this Cathedral. Born 27th December, 1800. Died 10th May, 1880. His genius and skill are shewn in the various compositions with which he has enriched the music of the Church. His virtues and kindness of heart endeared him to his pupils and friends, who have erected this monument in token of their admiration and esteem."

GEORGE COOPER (Junr.) was Sub-Organist from 1843 to 1876. He succeeded his father in this office.

(See under Chapel Royal.)

SIR JOHN STAINER, Knt., M.A., 1866, and Mus.D., Oxon., 1865; D.C.L., and Mus.D., Dunelm., 1895; F.R.C.O. 1872 1888

Born in London, June 6, 1840. Chorister in St. Paul's. Pupil of W. Bayley, Dr. Steggall, and George Cooper. Organist of St. Benet and St. Peter, Paul's Wharf, 1855; St. Michael's College, Tenbury, 1857; Magdalen College, Oxford, 1859. Organist to the University of Oxford, 1860. Organist of St. Paul's Cathedral, 1872. Organist to the (Royal) Albert Hall Choral Society, 1873-1888. Musical Juror at the Paris Exhibition, 1878. Chevalier of the Legion of Honour of France, 1878. Principal of National Training School for Music, 1881-82. Appointed H.M. Inspector of Music in Schools, 1882. Resigned his post at St. Paul's in consequence of failing eyesight, 1888. Knighted 1888. Honorary Fellow of Magdalen College. Professor of Music in the University of Oxford, 1889. Resigned the latter post May, 1899. President of the Musical Association, 1899. Composer of an Oratorio, "Gideon," Cantatas, Services, Anthems, and other Church Music, Organ Music, Songs, Part-songs, &c. Author of "The Music of the Bible" and of works on Harmony, Composition, the Organ, Vocalization, &c. Joint author, with Dr. W. A. Barrett, of a "Dictionary of Musical Terms." Editor and Arranger. Lecturer on various Musical Subjects.

SIR GEORGE CLEMENT MARTIN, Knt., Mus.B., Oxon., 1868; Mus.D., Cantuar., 1883; F.R.C.O. 1888 ——

Born at Lambourne, Berkshire, September 11, 1844. Pupil of J. Pearson and Sir John Stainer. Organist of Lambourne Parish Church. Organist to

Duke of Buccleuch at Dalkeith, 1871, and St. Peter's Episcopal Church, Edinburgh, holding the two appointments simultaneously. Master of the Choristers at St. Paul's Cathedral, 1874. Sub-Organist of St. Paul's, 1876. Organist, 1888. Created Mus.D. by the Archbishop of Canterbury, 1883. Knighted in 1897, when he directed the musical arrangements at the great Thanksgiving Service, held June 22, on the West steps of St. Paul's Cathedral, in celebration of the sixtieth year of Her Majesty's reign. Composer of Services, Anthems, Hymns, Carols, Part-songs, Songs, &c. Editor and Arranger of Church and Organ Music. Author of "The Art of Training Choir Boys."

WILLIAM HODGE was Sub-Organist from 1888 until his death, in 1895, when he was succeeded by CHARLES MACPHERSON.

For a more detailed account of the Organists of St. Paul's the reader is referred to that interesting and valuable contribution to the history of Church Music by Mr. John S. Bumpus, entitled: "The Organists and Composers of St. Paul's Cathedral." To this able work I am, by the kind generosity of its author, largely indebted for much of the foregoing information.

LONDON.

SOUTHWARK (ST. SAVIOUR'S CATHEDRAL).

SEE ESTABLISHED IN 1897.

ALFRED MADELEY RICHARDSON, M.A., Oxon., 1890; Mus.D., Oxon., 1896; F.R.C.O. ... ... 1897 ——

Born at Southend, 1868. Pupil of W. Haynes at Malvern, and afterwards of Sir Walter Parratt, Sir Hubert Parry, and others. Organ Scholar at Keble College, Oxford, 1885; Organist of Hindlip Church, Worcester, 1889; Holy Trinity, Sloane Street; St. Jude's, Gray's Inn Road; Holy Trinity, Scarborough, 1892; resigning the latter appointment upon being offered that at Southwark Cathedral. Composer of Church Music, Part-songs, &c.

MANCHESTER.

The Collegiate Church of St. Mary the Virgin, Manchester, was made a Cathedral in 1847.

As a Collegiate Church it held three separate Charters. The first was granted by King Henry V. on May 22nd, 1421, with the following foundation: A Warden, Four Fellows, Four Singing Priests, and Six Choristers. This was dissolved by Edward VI., and was afterwards re-established by Queen Mary. In 1578 Queen Elizabeth granted a new Charter, with a foundation of—A Warden, Four Fellows, Two Chaplains (Singing Priests), Four Lay Singers, Four Children. The third Charter was that of King Charles I., granted on September 30th, 1635, and provided for—A Warden, Four Fellows, Two Chaplains, Two Clerks, Four Singers (Lay or Clerical), Four Boys, a Sub-Warden, Treasurer, Collector, Registrar, Master of the Choristers, Instructor, and Organist.

The following is a complete succession of Organists from the date of the last-named Charter down to the present time, all the earlier registers of the Church having perished, it is said, in the great Fire of London.*

JOHN LEIGH 1635 1637

WILLIAM CARTER ... ... 1637 (?)1644

WILLIAM CARTER (re-appointed) 1662 1666

PETER STRINGER ... ... 1666 (?)1666
Probably Organist for only a short time.
(See under Chester.)

WILLIAM TURNER 1666 1670

WILLIAM KEYS 1670 1679
(See under St. Asaph.)

RICHARD BOOTH ... ... 1679 (?)1682

—— (?)SMITH ... ... (?)1682 1696

EDWARD TETLOW 1696 1702

JAMES HOLLAND 1702 1704
Dismissed in 1704.

* I am indebted to Mr. James Kendrick Pyne, the present Cathedral Organist, for much of my information concerning the Organists of Manchester.

EDWARD EDGE 1704 1714

EDWARD BETTS 1714 1767

Compiler of "An Introduction to the Skill of Musick, Anthems, Hymns, and Psalm Tunes, in several parts." London, 1724.

The Cheetham College Grace is said to have been composed by Betts.

JOHN WAINWRIGHT... ... ... 1767 1768

Previously Deputy-Organist.

Born at Stockport, 1723. Baptized April 14, 1723. Buried at Stockport, January 28, 1768. Composer of Anthems, Hymns, Chants, &c. His well-known tune to "Christians, awake, salute the happy morn," was first published in his "Collection of Psalm Tunes, Anthems, Hymns, and Chants, for One, Two, Three, and Four voices," in 1766.

ROBERT WAINWRIGHT, Mus.D., Oxon., 1774 ... 1768 1775

Son of the preceding. Born 1748. Organist of the Collegiate Church, Manchester, 1768; St. Peter's, Liverpool, 1775. Died July 15, 1782. Buried in St. Peter's, Liverpool. Composer of an Oratorio, "The Fall of Egypt," a Te Deum, Psalm Tunes, &c.

In 1766 Robert Wainwright competed for the post of Organist at Halifax Parish Church. Dr. Miller, in his "History of Doncaster," relates the following story in connection with that occasion:—

"A new organ by Snetzler had been erected in the Parish Church, and was opened with an Oratorio by Mr. Joah Bates. There were seven candidates for the situation of Organist: among them were Robert Wainwright and F. W. Herschel, then leader of the concerts at Halifax, and an intimate friend of Dr. Miller. Concerning the others we have no information. On the day of trial, August 30, they attended at the church, and the order in which they were to play was decided by lot. The second was drawn by Wainwright and the third by Herschel. Wainwright's execution was so rapid that old Snetzler ran about exclaiming, 'Te tevil, te tevil, he run over te keys like von cat; he vill not give my piphes room for to shpeak.' During this performance Miller said to Herschel, 'What chance have you to follow this man?' He replied, 'I don't know, but I am sure fingers will not do.' In due time he ascended the gallery and drew from the organ such a full volume of slow solemn harmony as Miller could by no means account for. After a short extempore effusion of this character, he finished with the Old 100th tune, which he played better than his opponent had done. 'Aye, aye,' cried Snetzler, 'tish is very goot, very goot inteet; I will luff tish man, for he gives my piphes room for to shpeak.' Herschel being afterwards asked by Miller by what means he had produced so uncommon an effect, answered, 'I told you fingers would not do,' and, taking two pieces of lead from his waistcoat pocket, he said, 'One of these I placed on the lowest key of the organ and the other on the octave above; thus, by accommodating the harmony, I gained the power of four hands instead of two.' Herschel was thereupon appointed, but soon after entered upon other pursuits, and the Musician has been long forgotten in the Astronomer."—(See Parr's "Church of England Psalmody.")

RICHARD WAINWRIGHT 1775 1782

Brother of the preceding. Born 1758. Organist of the Collegiate Church and St. Anne's, Manchester. Succeeded his brother at St. Peter's, Liverpool, 1782. Organist for some time at St. James's, Toxteth Park. Reappointed Organist of St. Peter's, 1813. Died August 20, 1825. Composer of Church Music, Glees, &c.

GRIFFITH JAMES CHEESE... ... ... 1783 1804

Born May 2, 1751. Organist at Leominster in 1771. On resigning the appointment at Manchester he became a teacher of music in London. Died November 10, 1804. He was blind. Composer of Songs, &c. Author of a treatise on playing the Organ and Pianoforte, containing useful information to teachers and people born blind.

WILLIAM SUDLOW 1804 1848

Son of a music dealer in Hanging Ditch, Manchester. Born 1772. Died 1848. Composer of Anthems, Songs, &c. He was also a Violoncellist.

JOSEPH JOHN HARRIS ... { Joint Organist 1831 (with W. SUDLOW) Sole Organist 1848 } 1869

Born in London, 1799. Chorister in the Chapel Royal. Organist of St. Olave's, Southwark, 1823; Blackburn Parish Church, 1828; Manchester Cathedral, 1848 (having previously been Choirmaster, and Joint Organist with Sudlow). Died February 10, 1869. Buried in Harpurhey Cemetery. Composer of Anthems, Glees, a selection of Psalm Tunes, "The Cathedral Daily Service," consisting of the Versicles, Litany, &c., with music, &c. For the occasion of the laying of the foundation stone of the new tower of the Cathedral, in 1864, Harris composed an Anthem, "The Lord is my strength."

JOHN FREDERICK BRIDGE, Mus.D., Oxon.; F.R.C.O. 1869 1875

NOW SIR FREDERICK BRIDGE. (See under Westminster Abbey.)

JAMES KENDRICK PYNE, F.R.C.O. ... ... 1875 ——

Son of James Kendrick Pyne, for fifty-three years Organist of Bath Abbey Church. Born 1852. Appointed Organist of All Saints', Bath, at the age of eleven. Pupil of Dr. S. S. Wesley. Assistant Organist of Winchester Cathedral, and afterwards of Gloucester Cathedral. Organist, successively, of Christ Church, St. Mark's, and St. Mary-le-Crypt, Gloucester; St. James's, Cheltenham; Aylesbury Parish Church; Christ Church, Clifton; Chichester Cathedral; St. Mark's, Philadelphia, U.S.A. Returned to England and was appointed Organist to Manchester Cathedral, and afterwards Organist to Corporation of Manchester. Organist of the Royal Jubilee Exhibition, Manchester. Professor of the Organ at the Royal Manchester College of Music. Composer of Church Music, Songs, &c. Lecturer, &c.

NEWCASTLE.

(Formerly the Parish Church of St. Nicholas.)

SEE ESTABLISHED IN 1884.

William Jamson Ions 1857 1894

Born at Newcastle-on-Tyne, November 3, 1833. Chorister in St. Nicholas' Church. Pupil of his brother, Thomas Ions, the then Organist of St. Nicholas', and Assistant Organist to him in 1850. Studied in Germany, 1852-1854. Returning to England, he was appointed Organist at St. Nicholas' on the death of his brother. Organised several Choral Festivals (with orchestra) at St. Nicholas' and elsewhere. Designed the new organ in St. Nicholas', which was opened in 1891. Presented with a testimonial, 1893. Retired 1894 upon becoming afflicted with deafness. Composer of Church Music.

George Frederick Huntley, Mus.D., Cantab., 1894; F.R.C.O. 1894 1895

Born at Datchet, May 31, 1859. Pupil of Sir George Elvey and Dr. Keeton and Dr. Hancock. Organist of St. George's, Kensington, 1880; St. Andrew's, Westminster, 1890; Newcastle Cathedral, 1894; St. Peter's, Eaton Square, 1895. Revived the Orchestral Services at Newcastle Cathedral during his organistship there, and is now Conductor of the Church Orchestral Society. Composer of an Oratorio, "Dies Domini," Cantatas, Church Music, Operettas, &c.

John Edward Jeffries, F.R.C.O. ... ... 1895 ——

Born at Walsall, October 18, 1863. Chorister, and afterwards Assistant Organist at St. Paul's, Walsall, under his father. Student at the Royal College of Music, under Dr. (now Sir George) Martin, Dr. (now Sir F.) Bridge, Dr. Gladstone, and Mr. Franklin Taylor. Appointed Organist of Walsall Parish Church, 1881, where he frequently introduced Oratorio Services with orchestral accompaniment. Organist of Newcastle Cathedral, 1895. Conductor of Jarrow Philharmonic Society and Newcastle Amateur Vocal Society. Composer of an Oratorio and other Church Music, Songs, &c.

NORWICH.

"Adam the Organist" is mentioned as early as 1333.

Henry Baker was Organist in 1593.

William Cobbold 1598 1608

Born at Norwich, January 5, 15$\frac{59}{60}$. In 1599 he appears in the Cathedral records as William *Cobbald*, Organist, his salary being "as in previous years." In 1600-3 the name is spelt *Cobold;* in 1604-5, *Cobhold;* and in 1606-8, *Cobbold*. From 1608 he became a singing-man in the Cathedral, the post of Organist being transferred to William Inglott. Died at Beccles, November 7, 1639, and was buried in the Parish Church there. Composer of

Anthems, Madrigals, &c. Contributor to Este's "Book of Psalms," also to "Triumphs of Oriana." A Madrigal by him in the latter, entitled "With Wreaths of Rose and Laurel," is eulogised by Burney ("History of Music"). It has been edited by Dr. A. H. Mann and published in 8vo form (Novello).

Inscription to Cobbold, upon a stone at the East end of the South Aisle of the Parish Church, Beccles:—

"Here lyeth the body of William Cobbold,
sometimes Organist of Christ Church,
in Norwich, who died the 7th of November, 1639.
The body rest here
But the soule above
Sing heavenly anthems
Made of peace and love."

In his Will occurs the following bequest—"to the Canons, singing-men and queristers of the Cathedral of Christ Church within the quere, 20s." He also leaves money to the poor in the parishes of the Close, St. Andrew, St. John de Timberhill, and St. George's, Tombland.

WILLIAM INGLOTT 1608 1621

Born 1554. Died 1621. Buried in the Cathedral Nave. Composer of pieces for Virginals, &c. His monument, on the pillar near the Organ screen, was repaired at the expense of Dr. Croft, and bears the following inscription:—

"Here William Inglott, Organist, doth rest,
Whose art in Music this Cathedral blest;
For Descant most, for Voluntary all,
He passed on Organ, Song, and Virginall.
He left this life at age of sixty-seven,
And now 'mongst Angels all sings first in Heaven.
His Fame flies far, his Name shall never die,
See, Art and Age here crown his memorie.
Non digitis, Inglotti, tuis terrestia tangis;
Tangis nunc digitis Organa celsa poli.
Anno Dom. 1621."

"Buried the last day of December, 1621." "This erected on the 15th day of June, 1662."

"Ne forma hujusce monumenti injuriâ
Temporum penè deleti, dispereat, exculpi
Ornavit Gul. Croft, Reg. Capellæ in
Arte Musicâ Discipul. Præfectus."

Dr. Croft evidently held this musician in high estimation.

RICHARD GIBBS ... ... (?)1622 (?)1630

Composer of Anthems, &c. (See Clifford's Collection). There is an Anthem, "Have mercy upon me, O God," by Richard Gibbs, in a Collection of "Easy Anthems for Parish Church Choirs," edited by Sir W. H. Cope. From its style of writing it is probably the work of this same composer.

RICHARD AYLEWARD 1660 1669

Buried October 18, 1669, in the North Aisle of the Cathedral Nave. Dr. Mann, of Cambridge, has in his possession an oblong quarto volume, in the autograph of Dr. Philip Hayes, containing a Service in D, with Responses and Litany, and thirteen Anthems by Ayleward; also a folio Organ book, in Ayleward's autograph, containing two Evening Services, one complete Service in D, and twenty Anthems.

According to the Chapter accounts a THOMAS GIBBS (probably son of *Richard* Gibbs) was also Organist about this time—see entries against his name in the years 1664 and 1665. He died of the plague, and was buried on July 16, 1666.

THOMAS PLEASANTS 1670 1689

Died November 20, 1689. Buried November 23, in the North Transept of the Cathedral. Composer of Church and other music.

JAMES COOPER ... ... —— (?)1721

Died January 26, 1721. Buried January 29, in the Cathedral Nave (at the foot of Inglott's monument).

HUMPHRY COTTON 1721 1749

Son of Edward Cotton. Organist of St. Peter Mancroft, Norwich, 1717-1720. Elected a Freemason of the City of Norwich, August 25, 1722. Died September 19, 1749. Buried September 22, in the South Transept of the Cathedral.

THOMAS GARLAND 1749 1808

Probably born in the Cathedral Precincts. Baptized July 5, 1731. Organist of the Cathedral for fifty-nine years. Died March 1, 1808. Buried under the Organ Screen in the Cathedral. Composer of the Ordination Hymn "Come, Holy Ghost, our souls inspire," printed in Bunnett's "Sacred Harmony," 1865.

JOHN CHRISTMAS BECKWITH, Mus.D., Oxon., 1803 1808 1809

Born at Norwich, December 25, 1750. Articled pupil of Drs. William and Philip Hayes at Oxford. Organist of St. Peter Mancroft, Norwich, 1794. For some years Master of the Choristers at the Cathedral before his appointment as Organist. His powers as an extempore player (especially of fugues) are said to have been exceptional. He was also considered a good painter. Died of paralysis, June 3, 1809. Buried in St. Peter Mancroft Church. Composer of Anthems, Organ pieces, Glees, a Sonata for the Harpsichord, Songs, "The First Verse of every Psalm of David, with an Ancient or Modern Chant in score, adapted as much as possible to the sentiment of each Psalm" (1808), &c.

His name, Christmas, is, of course, accounted for by the fact that his birthday fell upon December 25. It is said that Bishop Horne, when President of Magdalen College, Oxford, "usually joined in the singing with a very loud voice, but always came in at the wrong places. Having once complained to a Deputy-Organist, *Mr. Beckwith*, that he played so loud that he could not hear himself sing: 'Can you not?' said the musician, 'I can hear you very plain indeed, sir.' The President smiled, and said no more."—(Reg. Magdalen College.—Bloxam.)

JOHN CHARLES BECKWITH 1809 1819

Son of the preceding. Born 1788. Died October 11, 1819. Buried in St. Peter Mancroft Church. Was considered an Organist of great ability.

ZECHARIAH BUCK, Mus.D., Cantuar., 1853 ... 1819 1877

Born at Norwich, September 9, 1798. Chorister in Norwich Cathedral, and afterwards articled pupil of J. Charles Beckwith. Was a very successful trainer of boys' voices, also teacher of many well-known organists of to-day. Resigned 1877. Died at Newport (Essex), August 5, 1879, and was buried in the Churchyard there. Composer of Anthems, Chants, &c., most of which were published in Dr. Bunnett's "Sacred Harmony" (1865).

Very amusing anecdotes have been related by Dr. Buck's pupils concerning the eccentric but apparently successful methods of voice production which he practised during their period of choristership at Norwich. At first nuts, marbles, and beans were amongst the various articles placed between the teeth to keep the mouth properly open whilst singing. After a little while, however, the boys began to find it difficult to avoid *cracking* the nuts, and the worthy Doctor, suspecting that this was less the result of accident than design, found it expedient to invent a substitute for them. A kind of mouthpiece was therefore introduced, made of boxwood, to fit in with the teeth, and in the exact shape of the mouth. Each boy was provided with one of these and a small looking-glass (the latter for the purpose of checking all contortions or unnatural expressions of the face), and both these articles were put into regular use at the morning practices, when the actual voice training was gone through. Certain exercises for the proper control of the tongue during singing were practised daily before anything else was attempted. The vocal *shake*, being an ornament much in use at that period, was assiduously cultivated, and a prize of half-a-crown was awarded from time to time to successful "shakers."

FRANCIS EDWARD GLADSTONE, Mus.D., Cantab., 1879 1877 1881

Born at Summertown, near Oxford, March 2, 1845. Pupil of Dr. S. S. Wesley at Winchester Cathedral. Organist of Holy Trinity, Weston-super-Mare, 1864; Llandaff Cathedral, 1866; Chichester Cathedral, 1870; St. Patrick's, Hove, 1873; St. Peter's, Brighton, 1875; St. Mark's, Lewisham, 1876; Norwich Cathedral, 1877. Resigned at Norwich and was appointed Organist of Christ Church, Lancaster Gate, London, W., 1881. Joined the Roman Catholic Church, and was Director of the Music at St. Mary of the Angels, Bayswater, until 1894. Professor of Harmony and Counterpoint at the Royal College of Music and Trinity College, London. Examiner, &c. Composer of Cantatas, Church Music, Organ pieces, Part-songs, Songs, &c.

FREDERICK COOK ATKINSON, Mus.B., Cantab., 1867 1881 1885

Born at Norwich, August 21, 1841. Pupil of Dr. Z. Buck and Assistant Organist of the Cathedral. Organist of Manningham Church, Bradford; Norwich Cathedral, 1881; St. Mary's Parish Church, Lewisham, 1886. Composer of Church Music, Part-songs, Songs, Pianoforte pieces, &c. Died at East Dereham.

FRANK BATES, Mus.D., Dub., 1884 ... ... 1886 ——

Born at March, 1856. For some time Assistant Organist of Leamington Parish Church. Organist of St. Beldred's Episcopal Church, North Berwick, 1874; St. John's, Edinburgh, 1882; Norwich Cathedral, 1886. In 1888 he organized a special choir and commenced a series of Musical Services for the people. Conductor of Norwich Diocesan Church Choral Association. Lecturer. Composer of an Oratorio, "Samuel," Church Music, &c.

OXFORD.

CHRIST CHURCH CATHEDRAL.

JOHN TAVERNER .. .. (?)1530 ——

Previously Organist of Boston, Lincolnshire. He is said to have narrowly escaped martyrdom for being concerned with heretics.—(See Hawkins's "History of Music," p. 354.)

BARTHOLOMEW LANT ... ... 1564 ——

Wood (Fasti., I, 175) mentions him as living in 1569.

MATTHEW WHITE, Mus.D., Oxon., 1629 ... (?)1611 (?)1613

He is supposed to have been Organist. He was previously a Bass Singer in Wells Cathedral, and afterwards became a Gentleman of the Chapel Royal. Much of his music is among the Aldrich MSS. at Christ Church.

WILLIAM STONARD, Mus.B., Oxon., 1608 ... ... —— (?)1630

Composed a Choral Hymn in eight parts for his degree. Composer also of Church Music, &c. Died 1630.

EDWARD LOWE ... ... (?)1630 1682

Born at Salisbury about 1610. Chorister in Salisbury Cathedral. Organist of Christ Church Cathedral, Oxford, (?)1630. Probably deprived of this post during the period of the Commonwealth, and re-appointed at the Restoration. Appointed Organist of the Chapel Royal, 1660. University Professor of Music at Oxford, 1661. Died July 11, 1682. Buried in the Divinity Chapel of Christ Church Cathedral. Composer of Church Music. Author of "Some short directions for the performance of Cathedral Service," published at Oxford, 1661. Three years later he published a "Review of his Short Directions," in which he adapted his original instructions to the Prayer Book of 1662.

WILLIAM HUSBANDS 1682 1690

Probably a son of Charles Husbands, a Gentleman of the Chapel Royal, who died 1678. Appointed Chaplain, 1690.

CHARLES HUSBANDS 1690 1691

(?) Son of the preceding.

RICHARD GOODSON (Senr.), Mus.B., Oxon., circa 1682 1691 1718

Born 1655. Also Organist of New College, 1682. Appointed University Professor of Music, 1682. Died January 13, 1718. Buried in South Aisle of Christ Church. A few of his MS. Compositions are included in the Library of Christ Church and the Music School.

RICHARD GOODSON (Junr.), Mus.B., Oxon., 1716 ... 1718 1741

Son of the preceding. Previously Organist at Newbury. Succeeded his father as Organist of the Cathedral and University Professor of Music, 1718. Died 1741. Buried in Christ Church. MS. Compositions at Christ Church and the Music School.

RICHARD CHURCH ... ...(?)1741 1776

Pupil of William Hine. Clerk of Magdalen College, 1732-1736. Organist of New College, 1732-1776. Matriculated at Christ Church, 1735. Resigned the Organistship at Christ Church, (?)March, 1776. Died July, 1776. Buried, July 23, in the Churchyard of St. Peter's-in-the-East, Oxford.

"A.D. 1732, Ap. 2. On Thursday last, Mr. Church was chosen Organist of New College. He is also Organist of St. *Peter's*-in-the-East, Oxford, in which parish he lives, and hath been Organist of the said St. Peter's ever since the organ was placed there from the theatre."—("Hearne's Diary.")

[PHILIP HAYES, Mus.D., Oxon.

(See under Magdalen College, Oxford.)

He is said (*Magdalen Register*, Bloxam) to have been Organist, 1763-1765, and to have been "ousted by a man named Norris"; but there is no evidence in the Cathedral records to show that he ever held the office. Moreover, it would appear from the following Chapter Order that Norris succeeded Church in the appointment: "17 April, 1776. Mr. Norris the Organist, having agreed that £30 a year shall be paid out of his salary to *Mr. Church the late Organist*, ordered that the Treasurer do pay the same to Mr. Church accordingly." Amongst the subscribers to Dr. Alcock's "Six and twenty select Anthems" is "*Mr. Church*, Organist of *Christ Church* and New College, Oxford."]

THOMAS NORRIS, Mus.B., Oxon., 1765 ... ... 1776 1790

Born at Mere, Wilts, 1741. Chorister in Salisbury Cathedral. Organist of St. John's College, Oxford, 1765. Lay Clerk of Christ Church, 1767; Lay Clerk of Magdalen College, 1771.* He possessed a fine tenor voice, and sang at several of the leading Musical Festivals. Died at Himley Hall, Staffordshire, September 3, 1790, it is said, through over-exertion at the Birmingham Festival. Buried at Himley. Composer of Anthems, Instrumental Symphonies, Glees, &c.

As a chorister "Master Norris" sang at the Worcester Festival of 1761. He afterwards became, as a tenor, one of the chief supports of the Festivals of the Three Choirs. Unfortunately, however, an early love disappointment caused him to give way to intemperate habits, and it is said that at the Musical Festival of 1789 in Westminster Abbey he was quite unable to hold the book from which he was singing.

The following is his inscription in Himley Churchyard:—

"In memory of Mr. Thomas Norris, Bachelor of Music, who came to Himley Hall for the benefit of his health, and breathed his last there on the 3rd of Sept., 1790, aged 50:

"Though human efforts were too weak to save,
The tear of friendship has bedewed his grave;
That tear, by nature to his memory shed,
Honours alike the living and the dead."

* "Unfortunately the Quire of Magdalen College had not often the opportunity of admiring his excellence. When admitted as a Clerk, he was mildly desired by the President, Dr. Horne, to attend at the chapel *occasionally*. This he understood so literally, as to make his appearance only once a quarter, on the days that the Clerks received their salary. On these rare occasions a servant in livery preceded him with his surplice and hood."—(*Magdalen Registers*, Bloxam.)

WILLIAM CROTCH, Mus.D., Oxon., 1799 .. 1790 (?)1807 (or 8)

Son of a carpenter. Born in Green Lane, Parish of St. George's, Colegate, Norwich, July 5, 1775. Showed unusual musical capabilities at a very early age. Pupil of Dr. Randall at Cambridge. Succeeded Norris at Christ Church, Oxford, 1790. Succeeded P. Hayes as Organist of St. John's College, St. Mary's Church, and University Professor of Music, 1797. Afterwards settled in London as a teacher and became the first Principal of the Royal Academy of Music, 1823. Resigned 1831. Died December 29, 1847. Buried at Bishop's Hull, near Taunton. Composer of Oratorios, "Palestine" and "Captivity of Judah" (two with the latter title), an Ode, &c. Author of "Elements of Musical Composition," Lecturer, &c. Was also skilled in Drawing.

Crotch possessed an unusual facility in the use of his hands, and was able to write as easily with his left as with his right. It is also said that, in order to save time, he would often write down the notes of two separate staves of music simultaneously.

WILLIAM CROSS ... ... (?)1807 (or 8) 1825

Born at Oxford, 1777. Organist of St. Martin's, Oxford; Organist of St. John's College, 1807; succeeded Dr. Crotch as Organist of the Cathedral and of the University Church, 1807 (or 8). Died June 20, 1825. Composer of Church Music. His familiar Chant in C minor was composed for the funeral of the Rev. Dr. White, Canon of Christ Church.

The Rev. W. H. Havergal remarked of Cross that he was "a good organist, but no musician," a criticism which is justified on reference to the (undated) Collection of Chants compiled by him during his organistship, and also to his edition of Dr. W. Hayes' "Psalms."

WILLIAM MARSHALL, Mus.D., Oxon., 1840 ... 1825 1846

Born at Oxford, 1806. Chorister in the Chapel Royal. Pupil of Braham, Neate, and Horsley. Organist of Christ Church Cathedral and St. John's College, Oxford, 1825; Organist of All Saints', Oxford, 1839; Organist of St. Mary's, Kidderminster, 1846. Died at Handsworth, August 17, 1875. Composer of Church Music, &c. Editor, with A. Bennett, of a Collection of Chants, and a book of Words of Anthems. Author of "The Art of reading Church Music."

During the vacancy, lasting some months, between the resignation of Marshall and the appointment of Corfe, SIR FREDERICK OUSELEY officiated as Organist gratuitously. He was then an undergraduate of Christ Church.

CHARLES WILLIAM CORFE, Mus.D., Oxon., 1852 ... 1846 1882

Son of A. T. Corfe, Organist of Salisbury. Born at Salisbury, July 13, 1814. Pupil of his father. Organist of Christ Church, 1846. Conductor of the University Motet and Madrigal Society, 1848. University Choragus, 1860. Died at Oxford, December 16, 1883. Composer of Church Music, Glees, &c.

A stained glass window, designed by Sir Edward Burne-Jones, was presented to the Cathedral by Dr. C. W. Corfe.

CHARLES HARFORD LLOYD, M.A., Mus.D., Oxon.; F.R.C.O. 1882 1892

(See under Gloucester.)

BASIL HARWOOD, M.A., Oxon., 1884; Mus.D., Oxon., 1896 ... ... 1892 ——

Son of Edward Harwood, J.P. Born at Woodhouse, Olveston, Gloucestershire, April 11, 1859. Educated at Charterhouse, and Trinity College,

Oxford. Pupil of J. L. Roeckel, Mrs. Roeckel, George Riseley, and Dr. C. W. Corfe. Also studied at the Leipzig Conservatorium. Organist of Trinity College, Oxford, 1878; Organist of St. Barnabas', Pimlico, 1883; Organist of Ely Cathedral, 1887, resigning the latter post on his appointment to Christ Church, Oxford. Conductor of Oxford Orchestral Association, 1892-8, and Oxford Bach Choir, 1896. President of the University Musical Club, 1881 and 1895. Precentor of Keble College, 1892. Composer of Church Music, Organ pieces, Pianoforte pieces, Songs, &c.

(For Magdalen and New Colleges, Oxford, see pages 118-124.)

PETERBOROUGH.

RICHARD STOREY ... ... 1541 —

He was Organist in the time of the Monastery, and continued to hold the office at the Reformation, at a salary of £10 per annum.

RICHARD TILLER ... ... — 1583

JOHN MUDD ... ... 1583 —

Organist and Epistoler. Probably grandfather or some early relative of the Mudd who was Organist of Lincoln Cathedral. In 1629 he was awarded £4 as "benevolence money." A Complete Service and four Anthems by him are included in the Ely MS. Collection.

DAVID STANDISH 1661 1676

His salary was £20 per annum. Died 1676. Buried in the Cathedral. His epitaph runs thus:—

"David Standish, Deo in Ecclesia Petriburgh. Annos 50. Serviens, & plusquam 80 Annorum tædio lassatus, attritas Mortalitatis exuvias deposuit." Dec. 6, 1676.—(Willis's "Survey.")

WILLIAM STANDISH 1677 1690

Salary, £20 per annum.

ROGER STANDISH 1690 1713

Salary, £20 per annum. In 1691 he was allowed £8 for pricking eight new books and filling up eight old ones. Died 1713. Buried in the Cathedral.

JAMES HAWKINS (Junr.) 1714 1759

Son of James Hawkins, Mus.B., Organist of Ely Cathedral.

His Anthem, "O praise the Lord," is to be found in the Ely and Tudway Collections.

GEORGE WRIGHT 1759 1774

Organist and Master of the Choristers.

CARTER SHARPE 1774 1777

Dismissed in 1777 for negligence in the duties of his office.

JAMES RODGERS 1777 1784

Presumably the James *Rogers* who was Organist of Ely Cathedral, 1774-1777.

(See under Ely.)

RICHARD LONGDON... ... ... 1784 1785

Resigned in 1785.

JOHN CALAH 1785 1798

Born 1758. Organist of St. Mary's Church and Master of the Song School, Newark-on-Trent, 1782. Organist of Peterborough Cathedral, 1785. Died 1798. Buried in the "New Building" of the Cathedral. Composer of Church Music, Songs, Sonatas for pianoforte, &c. A Double Chant by him was formerly very popular.

SAMUEL SPOFFORTH 1799 1807

(See under Lichfield.)

THOMAS KNIGHT 1808 1811

Born 1789. Died November 21, 1811.

EDMUND LARKIN 1812 1837

Appointed at a salary of £45 per annum, afterwards increased to £63, with an additional sum of £6 for tuning the Cathedral Organ and the Harpsichord in the Music Room.

Born 1785. Was also Organist of St. John's Church, Peterborough; afterwards Organist of Stamford Parish Church. Died at Stamford, December 9, 1839.

JOHN SPEECHLY 1837 1869

Born at Peterborough, 1811. Also held appointment of Organist of St. John's Church, Peterborough. Died August 7, 1869. He is buried in the South Choir Aisle of the Cathedral, where there is a tablet to his memory.

HAYDN KEETON, Mus.D., Oxon., 1877; F.R.C.O. 1870 ——

Born at Mosborough, Derbyshire, October 26, 1847. Chorister in St. George's Chapel, Windsor. Pupil of Sir George Elvey. Organist of Datchet Parish Church, 1867, and afterwards at Hawtrey's School at Slough, which he resigned on his appointment to Peterborough. Conductor of Peterborough Choral and Orchestral Societies. Conductor and Organist of Peterborough and Lincoln Festivals. Composer of Church Music, a Symphony for Orchestra, Pianoforte pieces, Songs, &c. Author of "Church and Cathedral Choristers' Singing Method."

RIPON.

SEE ESTABLISHED IN 1836.

PREVIOUSLY A COLLEGIATE CHURCH.

The first mention of "Organs" in the Fabric Rolls of Ripon Cathedral is in 1399, and the first payment to an Organist in 1447, when THOMAS LITSTER received the annual fee of 10s.

In 1478 LAURENCE LANCASTER was Organist, and received a like sum, but out of this only 3s. 6d. was for playing on the organs, and the remainder was for singing Mass in the Lady Chapel.

In 1546 occurs "a rent of 13/4 payd yerlie to the organ player, comynge forthe of the comon of the saide Church."—("Memorials of Ripon," edited for the Surtees Society, by J. T. Fowler.)

—— WANLASS ... ... —— ——

Probably a relative of Thomas Wanless, Organist of York.

—— WILSON ... ... 1670 (?)1677

"Singing man," appointed to play instead of Wanlass, who had become deaf.

WILLIAM SORRELL ... ... 1677 ——

—— SHAW ... ... —— (?)1682

JOHN HAWKINS ... ... 1682 (?)1690

THOMAS PRESTON (Senr.) 1690 1730

Born 1662. Died 1730. Buried in South Transept of the Cathedral. A Chant by him is to be found in one or two Collections.

THOMAS PRESTON (Junr.) 1731 1748

Son of the foregoing.

WILLIAM AYRTON ... ... 1748 (?)1779

Born 1726. Died February 2, 1799. The Cathedral records state that he was son of Edward Ayrton, Chirurgeon (who in 1760-1 was Mayor of Ripon), and that he was baptized in the Cathedral on November 18, 1726. Dr. Edmund Ayrton (see under Southwell) was his brother.

WILLIAM FRANCIS MORRALL AYRTON ... ... 1779 (?)1802

THOMAS AYRTON 1802 1822

Born 178½. Died October 24, 1822, having been Organist for twenty years.

JOHN HENRY BOND ... ... 1823 (?)1829

Previously Organist of Portsmouth Dockyard Chapel.

GEORGE BATES 1829 1873

Born at Halifax, July 6, 1802. Organist of Ripon Cathedral, 1829. Retired 1873. Died January 24, 1881. Buried in Holy Trinity Churchyard. Composer of a Volume of Sacred Music, Hymns, &c. There is a brass to Bates in the North Nave Aisle of the Cathedral on which is engraved his *Veni Creator*.

EDWIN JOHN CROW, Mus.D., Cantab., 1883; F.R.C.O. 1873 ——

Born at Sittingbourne, September 17, 1841. Chorister in Rochester Cathedral, and pupil of Dr. J. L. and Mr. John Hopkins. Afterwards studied under G. A. Löhr, at Leicester. Organist successively of Trinity, St. Andrew's, and St. John's Churches, Leicester. Organist of Ripon Cathedral, 1873, commencing duty January 1, 1874. Conductor of the Cathedral Festival Choir and of Ripon Orchestral Society. Music Master of Ripon Grammar School. Composer of a Harvest Cantata, Services, Anthems, Organ pieces, Pianoforte pieces, Songs, &c.

At the time of Dr. Crow's appointment to Ripon there was no Cathedral Service. The Canticles were merely chanted and the Priest's part was read. Dr. E. G. Monk described the Service as "so bad that it could not by any possibility be worse." This state of things has since been entirely altered. Full Choral Services have been established, and on Sunday afternoons Oratorios, Cantatas, &c., are frequently given, either complete or in part. Perhaps the most notable achievement of the Cathedral Choir in its later days was the singing of Brahms's German Requiem by twelve boys and six men!

ROCHESTER.

Through the kindness of Mr. Thomas Shindler, M.A., LL.B., Registrar of the Royal College of Organists, I have been enabled to quote much valuable information regarding the earlier Organists of Rochester Cathedral from his interesting and researchful book, "Registers of the Cathedral of Rochester."

The particulars concerning the first five Organists below-mentioned are taken literally from that work.

JAMES PLOMLEY was Organist in 1559.

"He is mentioned in a Patent of this date, as 'Organist and Teacher of the Children.' The Patent is to Peter Rowle, to feed, lodge, and clothe the choristers after the death of Plomley."

ROPER BLUNDELL was Organist in 1588.

"He was appointed by Patent of this date to the office of 'Master of the Coristers or Singinge Children and player upon the Organs in the said Cathedral.' He was described as 'one of the ministers or companye of the Quire,' and was granted the 'Chambers being at the east side of the long gallery called the Cannon Place lately in the tenure of John Bartlett or Kinge deceased.' John Bartlett or Kinge was Curate of Chatham and Vicar of Dartford."—(Denne's Repertorium.)

JOHN WILLIAMS (the elder) was Organist in 1599.

"He was appointed Petty Canon by Patent of this date, and also 'teacher of the Children.' He is described as 'one of the ministers or company of the Quire,' and had the house of Roper Blundell deceased. In 1609 a Patent was granted to 'John Williams the elder, one of the ministers or company of the Quyer, and John Robinson the younger, one of the clerks or company of the Quyer,' to be 'Master of the Choristers' for the life of the longest liver."

JOHN HEATH was Organist in 1614.

"In the Treasurer's book of this date he appears as Organist, but I cannot find this Patent. In the Survey of the Parsonage of Chatham (Parliamentary Surveys, 1649, Lambeth Library) is the following: In 1608, the Dean 'granted unto Phillipp Heath and John Heath sonne of the sayd Phillipp Heath the office of Clerke and Organiste dureing the tearme of their naturall lives and the longest liver of either of them, with the annuall ffee or stipend of Twelve pounds of lawfull English Money, issueing and payeable out of the foresaide parsonage of Chatham. . . . Phillipp Heath is deceased. John Heath aged about sixty years.' John Heath appears as Organist of the Cathedral so late as 1668."

Composer of Church Music (mentioned in Clifford's Collection of Words of Anthems.) There is an Evening Service by him in the Peterhouse (Cambridge) Collection.

CHARLES WREN was Organist in 1672.

"He appears as Organist in the Treasurer's book of this date In the 'Red' Book of 1661 it was 'Ordered that Mr. William Rothwell for the reversion of the Organist's place at Mr. John Heath's death should have a Patent.' William Wrothwell had a Patent for a Petty Canon's place in 1662; I do not find him mentioned as Organist."

Wren was afterwards Organist of Gloucester Cathedral.

(See also under Gloucester.)

DANIEL HENSTRIDGE 1674 1698

(See under Canterbury.)

ROBERT BOWERS 1699 1704

Died 1704. Buried in the Cathedral Yard.

JOHN SPAIN 1704 1721

The Baptismal Registers of the Cathedral include the names of four of his children. Died 1721. Buried in the Cathedral.

CHARLES PEACH 1721 1753

Died 1753. Buried in the Cathedral.

JOSEPH HOWE ... ... 1753 (?)1781

There are Baptismal entries of four of his children in the Cathedral Registers.

RICHARD HOWE ... ... 1781 (?)1790

Son of the preceding.

RALPH BANKS 1790 1841

Born at Durham, 1762. Chorister in Durham Cathedral, and afterwards Assistant Organist there, under Ebdon; also Organist of Houghton-le-Spring Parish Church. Organist of Rochester Cathedral, 1790. During a part of the period of his appointment at Rochester he was also Voluntary Organist at the Evening Services at St. John's, Chatham. Died September 20, 1841, aged 79. Buried in the Nave of the Cathedral.

He published a Selection of Hymn Tunes from Purcell, Croft, &c. A volume of his Cathedral Music was published posthumously by Messrs. Chappell. It includes an Anthem, "O Sing unto the Lord," composed for the re-opening of the organ at Rochester Cathedral, after additions to it by Hill, on November 22nd (St. Cecilia's Day), 1840.

At the time of Banks's appointment the prayers at Rochester Cathedral were *read*, not *chanted*, by the Minor Canons. Through Banks's exertions this abuse was rectified.—(See Dr. Jebb on the "Choral Service.") The following entry, made by Banks in an Organ Book belonging to the Cathedral, has been kindly supplied to me by the present Organist, Mr. John Hopkins, and throws an additional light upon the limited scope of the musical services there at this time: "When I came from Durham to this Cathedral in 1790, only one Lay Clerk attended during each week. The daily service was chanted. Two Services (Aldrich in G and Rogers in D) and seven Anthems had been in rotation on Sundays for twelve years !!!—R. B." This entry appears in one of four Organ Books in the handwriting of Banks, who grouped their contents as follows: 1, Full Services; 2, Full Anthems; 3, Verse Services; 4, Verse Anthems.

JOHN LARKIN HOPKINS, Mus.D., Cantab., 1857 ... 1841 1856

Cousin to Dr. E. J. Hopkins. Born at Westminster, 1820. Chorister in Westminster Abbey. Organist of Rochester Cathedral, 1841. Left Rochester on his appointment as Organist of Trinity College, Cambridge, 1856; Organist to Cambridge University, 1856. Died at Ventnor, April 25, 1873. Buried in Ventnor Cemetery. Composer of Church Music, Glees, Songs, &c.

JOHN HOPKINS, F.R.C.O.... ... ... 1856 ——

Cousin to the foregoing, and brother to Dr. E. J. Hopkins. Born at Westminster, April 30, 1822. Chorister in St. Paul's Cathedral. Organist of Mitcham Parish Church, 1838; St. Stephen's, Islington, 1839; Holy Trinity, Islington, 1843; St. Mark's, Jersey, 1845; St. Michael's, Chester Square, London, 1846; and the Parish Church, Epsom, which he resigned on his appointment to Rochester Cathedral in 1856. Composer of Church Music, Organ pieces, Pianoforte pieces, &c.

ST. ALBAN'S.

The old Abbey Church was made a Cathedral in 1877 (the first See established since the Reformation), but at present there is no Cathedral foundation.

ROBERT FAIRFAX, Mus.D., Cantab., 1501-2, et Oxon. 1511 ... ... —— ——

He should be mentioned as one of the Organists of St. Alban's before its suppression as an Abbey. It is said that the organ then in use, built in 1438, was the finest in England. Fairfax was appointed one of the Gentlemen of the King's Chapel abont 1509. He died at St. Alban's in $15\frac{29}{30}$, and was buried in the Abbey. He composed much sacred and secular music, and portions of his compositions are to be found in the music libraries at Oxford, Cambridge, the British Museum, and elsewhere.

The Organist at the establishment of the See in 1877 was—

JOHN STOCKS BOOTH 1858 1880

Born at Sheffield, 1828. Pupil of Gauntlett, Thalberg, Sterndale Bennett, and Molique. Organist, successively, of Queen Street Chapel, Sheffield, and Wortley Church and St. Philip's, Sheffield (double appointment). Removed to Watford (Herts.), and was shortly afterwards appointed Organist at St. Alban's Abbey. Died of cerebral paralysis, December 7, 1879. Buried in the Cathedral Yard.

At the time of his appointment the Abbey organ was a small instrument by Father Smith and the Services were of a very primitive character. The *Tate and Brady* version of the Psalms were the only hymns in use. These were announced by the organ blower, who emerged from his corner in a surplice yellow with age, and performed his task in broad Hertfordshire brogue. The character of the Services was, however, gradually improved, and a new organ (the present one) was erected from Mr. Booth's specification (with the valuable help of Dr. E. J. Hopkins) by Messrs. Hill & Son, at a cost of £1,300, and opened with a special Musical Festival. Mr. Booth directed the musical arrangements at the Service of the enthronement of the first Bishop (Dr. Claughton, previously Bishop of Rochester), on June 12, 1877.

GEORGE GAFFE, F.R.C.O.... ... ... 1880 ——

Born at Cawston, Norfolk, July 27, 1849. Chorister in Norwich Cathedral, and pupil of and assistant to Dr. Z. Buck. Organist of Oswestry Parish Church, 1874, and afterwards appointed to St. Alban's. Founder and Principal of the St. Alban's School of Music; Fellow and Member of the Council of the Royal College of Organists. Composer of an Evening Service, a set of Offertory Sentences, &c.

ST. ASAPH.

WILLIAM KEYS ... ...

Previously Organist of Manchester Collegiate Church (now the Cathedral). William *Kay*, afterwards Organist of Chester Cathedral, may have been the same person, or a son.

"MR." LECHE ... ...

Was Organist in 1681.

"MR." KAY (or KEYS) 1690 1692

Probably a son of the William Keys above-mentioned.

THOMAS HUGHES 1692 1695

J. GERARD 1695 1712

ALEXANDER GERARD 1712 1738

—— GERARD 1738 1783

The last three were evidently all related. See also Richard Jarred or *Gerard*, Organist of Bangor Cathedral, 1778-1782.

JOHN JONES 1783 1786

EDWARD BAILEY 1786 1791

Possibly the Edward Bailey who was afterwards Organist of Chester Cathedral.

CHARLES SPENCE 1791 1794

Probably a relative of Thomas Spence, who was for seventy-nine years a member of the Choir of Chester Cathedral, and lies buried in the North Transept there.

WILLIAM HAYDEN 1794 1833

Composer of some Chants in MS. at the Cathedral.

ROBERT AUGUSTUS ATKINS 1834 1889

Son of Robert Atkins, Lay Vicar of Chichester Cathedral. Born at Chichester, October 2, 1811. Chorister in Chichester Cathedral. Organist of St. Asaph Cathedral for fifty-five years. Died at St. Asaph, August 3, 1889. Composer of Church Music, including MS. Services in A and G.

LLEWELYN LLOYD 1889 1897

Chorister in St. Asaph Cathedral. Pupil of R. A. Atkins, and afterwards Assistant Organist. Organist, 1889. Resigned 1897.

HUGH PERCY ALLEN, M.A., Mus.D., Oxon., 1898; F.R.C.O. 1897 1898

Born at Reading, 1870. Pupil of Dr. F. J. Read. Organist (when only eleven years of age) of St. Saviour's, Reading. Organist of Tilehurst Church, 1884; Eversley Parish Church, 1886; Assistant Organist at Chichester Cathedral, 1887; Organist to the Merchant Taylors' Schools, Bognor, 1890; Christ's College, Cambridge, 1892; St. Asaph Cathedral, 1897; Ely Cathedral, 1898. Composer of Odes, Church Music, &c.

ARCHIBALD WAYET WILSON, MUS.D., OXON., 1897; F.R.C.O. ... ... 1898 ——

Born at Pinchbeck, Lincolnshire, 1869. Student at the Royal College of Music under Sir Walter Parratt, Sir F. Bridge, &c. Organist of St. Paul's, East Moulsey, 1888. Organ Scholar at Keble College, Oxford, 1890. Music Master, Temple Grove, 1894. Organist of St. John's, St. Leonard's, 1896; St. Asaph Cathedral, 1898. Composer of Church Music, a Choral Ballad, Part-songs, &c.

ST. DAVID'S.

WALTER WARRYN ... ...

Was Organist, 1490.

The Priest Vicars in turn discharged the duties of Organist from 1490 to 1563.

Archdeacon Yardley, in his MSS. entitled "Memoria Sacra," mentions that in Bishop Vaughan's time (1509-1522) "MR. JOHN NORMAN, a Skillful and Learned Musician, was Organist and Master of ye Choristers."*

THOMAS ELLIOT 1563 1577

Priest Vicars officiated in turn, 1577-1713.

The following incident concerning the Organist of St. David's, at the time of the attack upon the Cathedral by the Parliamentary troops during the Civil Wars, is worth quoting: "The rebels were consulting in the Choir about what other sacrilegious mischiefs they should perform; it was at length agreed to destroy the organ. The Organist, who had secreted himself within the organ loft, heard the same, and knowing that, if they perpetrated their intended mischief, he should lose his bread, he threw a large stone into the Choir; which falling on the head of one of Cromwell's aides-de-camp killed him. Dreading the consequence of his being discovered and taken by the rebels, he fled; they perceived, and pursued him, when he had the presence of mind to get into one of the bells which hung low, and there supported himself by the clapper, until they had given up the search."—("History and Antiquities of the Parish of St. David's," by Captain Geo. W. Manby, R.N.)

R. MORDANT 1713 1714

Lay Vicar Choral.

HENRY MORDANT 1714 1719

Son of the preceding. Lay Vicar Choral.

RICHARD TOMKINS 1719 1719

Lay Vicar Choral.

---

* Probably the *John Norman* mentioned in Hawkins's "History" as one of the famous musicians who flourished before the Reformation.

WILLIAM BISHOP 1719 1720
Lay Vicar Choral.

HENRY WILLIAMS 1720 1725

MATTHEW MADDOX 1725 1734
Lay Vicar Choral.

MATTHEW PHILPOTT 1734 1793
Lay Vicar Choral.

ARTHUR RICHARDSON 1793 1826
Lay Vicar Choral. Formerly Assistant Organist at Armagh Cathedral. He appears, from entries in the St. David's books, to have also been *tuner* of the organ. Died 1826(?)

JOHN BARRETT 1827 1851
Lay Vicar Choral. Died 1851.

WILLIAM PEREGRINE PROPERT, LL.D. and M.A., Cantab.; Mus.B., Oxon., 1850, et Cantab. (?) ... 1851 1883
Since 1883 a Lay Vicar Choral of the Cathedral. Composer of Church Music.

During the restoration of the Cathedral, 1864-1883, the organ was not in use.

FREDERICK S. GARTON 1883 1894
Pupil of Dr. Done, and Assistant Organist of Worcester Cathedral. Organist of Dudley Parish Church; St. David's Cathedral, 1883. Organist of St. Martin's, Haverfordwest, 1894.

D. JOHN D. CODNER 1894 1896
Born 1851. Organist of St. Bride's, Fleet Street, E.C. Organist of St. David's Cathedral, 1894. Retired through ill-health, 1896. Composer of Church Music.

HERBERT C. MORRIS, F.R.C.O. ... ... 1896 ——
Born at Coventry, June 18, 1873. Pupil of Frank Spinney, at Leamington; A. H. Brewer, at Coventry; and Sir Walter Parratt and others, at the Royal College of Music. Organist successively at the Parish Church, Kenilworth, various Churches in London, and Boscombe Pavilion. Assistant Organist of Manchester Cathedral; Organist of St. Andrew's, Bath, 1896; Organist of St. David's Cathedral, 1896. Composer of Anthems, Services, &c.

SALISBURY.

JOHN FARRANT 1598 1602

(See under Ely.)

JOHN HOLMES 1602 1610

Previously Organist of Winchester Cathedral. Adrian Batten (Organist of St. Paul's) and Edward Lowe (Organist of Christ Church, Oxford) were among his pupils. Composer of Church Music, Madrigals, &c. Contributor to "The Triumphs of Oriana."

ELLIS GIBBONS ... ... —— ——

Brother of Orlando and Edward Gibbons. Born at Cambridge. Composer. Contributor to "The Triumphs of Oriana."

EDWARD TUCKER ... ... —— (?)1631

Composer of Church Music. The Anthem "This is the day," generally attributed to the *Rev. Wm.* Tucker (Minor Canon of Westminster, 1660), is more probably the composition of *Edward* Tucker, from the fact that it appears in an old MS. Bass part-book, in the possession of Mr. J. S. Bumpus, bearing evidences of belonging to a pre-Restoration period. It is there attributed to "Mr. Tucker."

GILES TOMKINS 1631 1668

According to the records at Salisbury his appointment there was made "Salvo Jure Ed. Tucker, Organiste."

Brother of Thomas and John Tomkins. Organist of King's College, Cambridge, 1624-1626; Salisbury Cathedral, 1631. Re-appointed to the latter post at the Restoration. Died 1668.

(See also under Cambridge—King's College.)

MICHAEL WISE 1668 1687

Born at Salisbury, 1638. Chorister in the Chapel Royal, and afterwards a Gentleman of the same, 1675. Organist of Salisbury Cathedral, 1668. Appointed Almoner and Master of the Choristers at St. Paul's Cathedral, 1687. He was a man of very quick temper, and was killed in a quarrel with the midnight watch at Salisbury, August, 1687. Was buried in the Cathedral, near the West door, but the stone is missing. Composer of Church Music.

"He is said to have been in great favour with Charles II., and being appointed to attend him in progress, claimed, as King's Organist for the time, the privilege of playing to his Majesty on the organ, at whatever church he went."—(Burney's "History of Music.") On one occasion, however, he incurred the King's displeasure by interrupting a sermon by a voluntary of his own. Notwithstanding his hasty temper, he seems to have exhibited a character of some pleasantry, for we are told that when in Charles II.'s reign he was asked to set his hand to a petition of which he did not approve (it was for the sitting of the Parliament), he wittily answered, "No, gentlemen, that is not my business; but I'll set a tune to it an you please."

The particulars of his death are these: "He had quarrelled with his wife on some trivial matter, and rushed out of his house. The watchman met him while he was boiling with rage, and commanding him to stand and give an account of himself, he struck the guardian of the peace to the ground, who in return aimed a blow at his assailant with his bill, which broke his skull, of the consequence whereof he died."

PETER ISAAC(KE) 1688 1692
(See under Dublin—Christ Church Cathedral.)

DANIEL ROSINGRAVE* 1692 1698
(See under Dublin—Christ Church Cathedral.)

ANTHONY WALKELEY ... ... (?) 1698 1717
Born 1672. Chorister in Wells Cathedral, and afterwards Vicar Choral there. Organist of Salisbury Cathedral, (?) 1698. Died at Salisbury, 1717. Buried in the Cathedral Nave. A Morning Service by him in E flat is included in Tudway's Collection, and some of his Anthems are extant in MS. His Morning Service in A was for a long time a favourite at Salisbury.

EDWARD THOMPSON 1718 1746
Was previously a Chorister in Magdalen College, Oxford, and probably an articled pupil to his cousin, Thomas Hecht, the Organist there.

JOHN STEPHENS, Mus.D., Cantab., 1763 ... ... 1746 (?) 1780
Previously a Chorister in Gloucester Cathedral. He conducted the Gloucester Festival of 1766. Died at Salisbury, December 15, 1780. Buried in the Cathedral, North Aisle of Nave. A volume of his Church Music was issued in 1805, edited by Highmore Skeats, Senr. He composed one of the four melodies still to be heard on the Gloucester Cathedral chimes.

ROBERT PARRY 1781 1792
Previously Organist of Wells Cathedral. Two very florid Double Chants by him, in E flat and F, are in a Collection edited by George Cleland, Organist of St. Mary's (Episcopal) Chapel, Bath, 1823.

JOSEPH CORFE 1792 1804
Born at Salisbury, 1740. Chorister in Salisbury Cathedral. Gentleman of the Chapel Royal, 1783. Succeeded R. Parry at Salisbury, 1792. Resigned in favour of his son, A. T. Corfe, 1804. Died July 29, 1820. Buried in the North-West Transept of Cathedral. Composer of Church Music, Glees, &c. Author of a treatise on Singing, &c.

ARTHUR THOMAS CORFE 1804 1863
Son of the preceding. Born at Salisbury, April 9, 1773. Chorister in Westminster Abbey. Pupil of Dr. Cooke and Clementi. Succeeded his father at Salisbury. Died suddenly whilst kneeling in prayer at his bedside, January 28, 1863. Buried in the Cathedral Cloisters. Composer of Church Music, Pianoforte pieces, &c. Author of a book on Harmony and Thorough Bass

JOHN ELLIOTT RICHARDSON 1863 1881
Born at Salisbury. Pupil of A. T. Corfe, and Assistant Organist at Salisbury. Succeeded his master, 1863. Resigned the appointment owing to ill-health, 1881. Afterwards became Organist of a Roman Catholic Church at Bognor. Composer of Church Music. Editor of the Salisbury Chant Book, a Collection of Sanctuses and Kyries, and a set of Voluntaries for the Organ.

* When Rosingrave was appointed, Stephen Jeffries (of Gloucester Cathedral), Vaughan Richardson, and John Freeman were also candidates for the office. Richardson was successful, however, in obtaining the post at Winchester Cathedral vacated by Rosingrave.

Bertram Luard Selby 1881 1883

Born at Ightham, Kent, February 12, 1853. Studied at the Leipzig Conservatorium under Reinecke and Jadassohn. Organist of St. Barnabas, Marylebone, and of Highgate School, 1876; Salisbury Cathedral, 1881; St. John's, Torquay, 1884; St. Barnabas, Pimlico, 1887. Composer of Operas, Church Music, Orchestral Music, Organ pieces, Pianoforte pieces, Songs, Chamber Music, &c.

Charles Frederick South ... ... 1883 ——

Born in London, February 6, 1850. Pupil of his brother, H. J. South, and George Cooper, occasionally deputising for the latter at St. Paul's Cathedral. Organist of Aske's Hospital, Hoxton, 1866; St. Augustine and St. Faith, E.C., 1868, resigning the latter post on his appointment to Salisbury. Conductor for a few years of the Sarum Choral Society. Composer of Church Music.

SOUTHWELL.

Before the Reformation the post of Organist at Southwell was held by one of the fifteen Vicars. This is confirmed by the mention of one, George Vincent, who was admitted Vicar Choral in 1505 and was Organist in 1519, the entry in records stating that in that year he was "presented" for frequent absence from the Choir, "so that the organs are not played." The new statutes, ordained by Queen Elizabeth in 1585, which are in force at the present day, required the appointment of a "Magister Puerorum" and "Rector Chori," one of whose duties was "Organa pulsanda."

It is to be regretted that, owing to the incomplete and illegible state of the record books at Southwell, no information can be furnished between that given above and the eighteenth century.

William Popely ... ... —— 1718

Died 1718. Buried in the South Transept of the Cathedral.
Two Anthems, "Not unto us" and "O be joyful," and a Psalm tune by him are included in an old book in the possession of Mr. J. S. Bumpus.

William Lee 1718 1754

Died 1754. Buried in the South Transept. His Single Chant in G is still to be found in various Collections.

Edmund Ayrton, Mus.B., Cantab., 1784; (?)Mus.D., Oxon., 1788 ... ... 1754 1764

Born at Ripon, 1734. Son of Edward Ayrton, *Chirurgeon*, of Ripon. Pupil of Nares. Succeeded William Lee as Organist at Southwell. Was also Auditor of the Cathedral. Gentleman of the Chapel Royal, 1764. Vicar Choral of St. Paul's Cathedral, 1767. Lay Vicar of Westminster Abbey, 1780. Master of the Choristers of the Chapel Royal, 1780-1805. Died at 24, James Street, Buckingham Gate, May 22, 1808. Buried in the North Cloister of Westminster Abbey. Composer of Church Music, Glees, &c. His degree exercise, the Anthem "Begin unto my God with timbrels," was sung at St. Paul's Cathedral at the Service of Thanksgiving for the close of the American Revolution, 1784.

"1756. Ap: 22. Mr. Ayrton to have leave to go to London for three months further instruction by Mr. Nares the Organist."

THOMAS SPOFFORTH 1764 1818

Born 1742. Uncle and Musical Instructor of Reginald Spofforth and of Samuel Spofforth. Retired on a pension, 1818. Died May 16, 1826. Buried in the South Transept of the Cathedral, to which he was a considerable benefactor. A Double Chant in F by him was inserted in Cleland's Bath Collection in 1823.

EDWARD HEATHCOTE 1818 1835

Previously Organist of Bakewell Church, Derbyshire, for the use of which he compiled a book of Words of Anthems. Died 1835. Buried in the South-East portion of the Cathedral Yard. Set to music the Ordination Hymn, "Come, Holy Ghost, Eternal God." Some of his Church Music in MS. is at Southwell, including a once popular Service in B flat.

1818. July 23. Mr. Spofforth allowed £25 per ann: for his long services. Ed. Heathcote Organist *vice* Mr. Spofforth, "to receive the ancient salary as Organist, as Rector Chori, and as one of the singing men, making together the annual sum of £30."

FREDERICK GUNTON 1835 1841

(See under Chester.)

CHAPPELL BATCHELOR 1841 1857

Born at Southwell, 1822. Chorister in Southwell Cathedral, 1830. King's Scholar of the Royal Academy of Music, 1838, under Potter, Goss, and others. Organist of Southwell Cathedral, 1841. Resigned 1857, and removed to Belper, afterwards to Derby.

HERBERT STEPHEN IRONS 1857 1872

Born at Canterbury, January 19, 1834, and Chorister in the Cathedral there, of which his father was a Lay Vicar. Pupil of Dr. Stephen Elvey at Oxford. Organist and Precentor of St. Columba's College, Rathfarnham, 1856. Organist of Southwell Cathedral, 1857. Assistant Organist of Chester Cathedral, 1873. Organist of St. Andrew's, Nottingham, 1876. Composer of Church Music, Organ pieces, &c.

CEDRIC BUCKNALL, Mus.B., Oxon., 1878 ... ... 1872 1876

Some years Assistant Organist to Professor W. H. Monk at King's College, London, and St. Matthias', Stoke Newington; Organist of St. Thomas's, Clapton, 1870; Organist of Southwell Cathedral, 1872. Resigned 1876, and since then Organist of All Saints', Clifton, and of the Clifton Victoria Rooms. Composer of Church Music, Part-songs, &c.

WILLIAM WEAVER RINGROSE, Mus.B., Oxon., 1870 1876 1879

Previously Organist of All Saints', Clifton, where he was succeeded by Cedric Bucknall. Shortly after leaving Southwell his mind gave way, and he died.*

* These are all the particulars I have been able to gather concerning him.

ARTHUR MARRIOTT 1879 1888

Son of Frederick Marriott, Lay Clerk, St. George's Chapel, Windsor. Pupil of Sir George Elvey. Resigned the post at Southwell, 1888, and went to Denver, America.

ROBERT WILLIAM LIDDLE ... ... 1888 ——

Born at Durham, March 14, 1864. Chorister in the Cathedral, and afterwards pupil of Dr. Armes. Organist of North Berwick Parish Church, 1886; Organist of Southwell Cathedral, 1888. Composer of Church Music.

TRURO.

SEE ESTABLISHED IN 1876.

NEW CATHEDRAL CONSECRATED IN 1887.

GEORGE ROBERTSON SINCLAIR 1881 1889

(See under Hereford.)

MARK JAMES MONK, Mus.D., Oxon., 1888 ... 1890 ——

Born at Hunmanby, March 16, 1858. Chorister in York Cathedral, and afterwards pupil of his namesake, Dr. E. G. Monk. Organist of several churches in York; St. John's, Ladywood, Birmingham, 1879; Ashby-de-la-Zouch Parish Church, 1880; Banbury Parish Church, 1883, leaving the latter on his appointment to Truro. Conductor of the Diocesan Festivals and of various choral bodies. Composer of Church Music, an Elegiac Ode, a Madrigal, pieces for Pianoforte and Organ, &c.

WAKEFIELD.

SEE ESTABLISHED IN 1888.

JOSEPH NAYLOR HARDY, Mus.B., Dunelm, 1895; F.R.C.O. ... ... 1886 ——

Pupil of J. Emmerson (his predecessor at Wakefield), Dr. Spark, Dr. Creser, and Dr. Corbett. Organist of the Roman Catholic Chapel, Wakefield, 1875; West Parade Chapel, Wakefield, 1878; Parish Church, Wakefield—now the Cathedral—1886. The Choirmaster of the Cathedral is Matthew Henry Peacock, M.A., Mus.D., Oxon.

WELLS.

RICHARD HUGO ... ... 1487 ——

The Dean and Chapter awarded him, "for his diligent labour and good service to the honour of God and St. Andrew, 26s. 8d. annually in augmentation of his annual pension from the proceeds of a vacant stall, for the term of his life."

RICHARD BRAMSTON (Deputy) ... ... 1507 ——

"Master Hugo, with the consent of the Chapter, promised to pay Richard Bramston, Vicar Choral, 40s. per annum to teach the Choristers to sing well and faithfully as Richard Hugo had done in time past, and that Richard Bramston would take care of and play at the Organs in the Great Choir, and also in the Lady Chapel."

JOHN CLANSAY ... ... 1508 ——

The Sub-Dean and Chapter ordered that John Clansay should have the Office of instructing and teaching the Choristers, "et Tabellarios ad cantandam et discantandam et singula alia facienda quæ ad hujus modi officium pertinent." He was also to play the Organ in the Great Choir as well as in the Lady Chapel behind the High Altar "temporibus congruis," as Richard Hugo had done.

His payment:—

(*a*) Four marcs from two vacant stalls.
(*b*) All the annual fines and perquisites which would belong to a vicar, not perpetuated, during the lifetime of Richard Hugo.
(*c*) A house of the annual value of 26/8.
(*d*) The payment of a deputy for Richard Hugo, as before 40/- ann. with power to appoint a fit deputy, should he become ill or too old.

[There is a blank in the Chapter Registers from 1513 to 1571.]

JOHN CLERK, Senr.... ... ... —— ——

Vicar and Organist. Was suspended for six months, in 1592, for refusing the Office of Escheator.

RICHARD BROWN ... ... 1614 ——

He was Organist in 1614. Vicar, Organist, and Master of the Choristers. A Richard Brown was appointed Organist of Worcester Cathedral in 1662.

JOHN OKER (or OKEOVER), Mus.B., Oxon., 1633 ... 1619 1639

He was Vicar, Organist, and Master of the Choristers. Organist of Gloucester Cathedral, 1640. The MS. Bass part-book belonging to Mr. J. S. Bumpus, before referred to, contains an Anthem by John Oker—"God shall send forth His mercy and truth."

During this period (in 1620) Dean Meredith gave £100 for a new organ, and promised a further sum of £100.

[Between 1644 and the Restoration the Chapter Records are again blank —"per Bella Civilia."]

In 1662 (after the Restoration) an agreement was drawn up between the Dean and Chapter and Robert Taunton, of Bristol, Organ Maker, to build "a fair, well-tuned, useful double-organ" in the Cathedral, for the sum of £800.

JOHN JACKSON 1674 1688

Admitted Organist and Vicar, his payment being £50 "for this year only." He was previously "Instructor in Music to the Choristers" at Ely Cathedral. An Anthem by him, "The Lord said unto my Lord," is included in the Tudway Collection, one in the Ely Collection, and two are to be found in Playford's "Cantica Sacra." There is also a Service in C in MS. at Wells, and Organ Parts to eight Anthems, &c., in a MS. in the Library of the Royal College of Music.

ROBERT HODGE 1688 1689

Vicar and Organist. Corrected and admonished for breaking windows, July 5, 1688. On August 7 of the same year £5 a quarter and the stall of Henstridge were appropriated to him, but only during the pleasure of the Dean and Chapter.

He was probably the Robert Hodge who afterwards became Organist of St. Patrick's Cathedral, Dublin.

JOHN GEORGE 1690 1712

Organist, at a salary of £5 a quarter, during the pleasure of the Dean and Chapter, and no longer. There is an entry in the Chapter books, "John George—pro modulandis organis—£20."

WILLIAM BRODERIP 1713 1726

Born 1683. Died 1726. A Service in D and an Anthem—"God is our hope and strength"—by him are contained in the Tudway Collection.

WILLIAM EVANS ... ... 1734 (?) 1741

Died September 22, 1740. Buried in the South Aisle of Cathedral Nave.

JOHN BRODERIP 1741 1774

Son (?) of William Broderip. He was also Organist of Shepton Mallett. Died 1785. Composer of Songs, Psalms, Glees, &c.

ROBERT PARRY 1774 1781

(See under Salisbury.)

DODD PERKINS 1781 1819

Died April 9, 1820. Buried in the "Palm Churchyard," Wells. Composer of Songs, Glees, &c. Two Chants by him are contained in Dr. Beckwith's Collection.

WILLIAM PERKINS 1819 1860

Son of the foregoing. He wrote a Double Chant in E natural, traditionally known at Wells as "Malibran's Chant," from the circumstance of that great singer joining in it at Wells Cathedral, August 22, 1830. Died November 11, 1860. Buried by the side of his father.

CHARLES WILLIAMS LAVINGTON 1860 1895

Born at Wells, February, 1819. Chorister in the Cathedral. Pupil of William Perkins, and afterwards of James Turle at Westminster Abbey. Assistant Organist of Wells Cathedral, and, in 1842, Acting Organist. Appointed to the full office on the death of William Perkins; also Organist of the Theological College. Died at Wells, October 27, 1895. Buried in the Cloister Churchyard.

PERCY CARTER BUCK, M.A., Mus.D., Oxon., 1897 1895 1899

Born at West Ham, 1871. Chorister in West Ham Parish Church. Student of the Guildhall School of Music. Afterwards won an Organ Scholarship at the Royal College of Music. Organist successively at Kingston-on-Thames and Worcester College, Oxford. Music master at Rugby School. Organist of Wells Cathedral, 1895. Organist of Bristol Cathedral, 1899. Composer of Church Music, an Organ Sonata, Vocal Trios, Songs, &c.

THOMAS HENRY DAVIS, B.A., Mus.B., Lond., 1889 1899 ——

Priest in Holy Orders.
Previously a Priest Vicar of the Cathedral.

WINCHESTER.

The Chapter books of Winchester do not distinguish by name the Organists from among the Lay Clerks, previous to the appointment of Christopher Gibbons in 1638. Hence the meagre information concerning the Organists before that year.

At the Restoration it appears that the Organist of Winchester Cathedral, although technically a Lay Clerk (see Preface, p. iv.), was an important officer of the Cathedral staff, being amply rewarded for his services, His salary was £57 5s., while that of the Precentor was only £34, a Minor Canon £30, and a Lay Clerk £13 10s.

JOHN HOLMES ... ... —— 1602

(See under Salisbury.)

(?)JOHN LANT .. .. —— (?)1615

Thomas Oliphant, in his "Musica Madrigalesca," p. 232, says: "I have a MS. book, about 70 years old, containing a number of Catches stated to have been collected by John Lant, Org. of Winchester Cathedral, d. 1615."

GEORGE KING ... ... —— ——

Father of William King (Organist of New College, Oxford).
At the Restoration he became Organist of Winchester College. Died 1665. Buried in the Cloisters of Winchester College.

CHRISTOPHER GIBBONS, Mus.D., Oxon. ... ... 1638 (?)1644

Organist, not Master of the Choristers.
(See under Westminster Abbey.)

JOHN SILVER 1661 1667

Previously Organist of King's College, Cambridge,

He had been Master of the Choristers of Winchester Cathedral since 1638, and was appointed Organist at the Restoration. From this time the offices of Master of the Choristers and Organist were combined.

The MS. parts of a Service by him in F are in the possession of Mr. J. S. Bumpus.

The Survey of Houses in the Cathedral Close, July, 1649, includes the following:—

"A Howse in the possession of one Mr. Silver, formerly Organist of the Cathedrall Church, and did hold the same in right of his place. The said Howse consistinge of three chambers and three small roomes, all above staires, valued at Forty Shillings p. ann. (&c.)"

From this it would appear that John Silver had also been Organist before the period of the Rebellion. Probably he undertook the duties of this office from the time Gibbons joined the Royalist Army until the Cathedral Services were suspended in the Autumn of 1645.

(See also under Cambridge—King's College.)

RANDALL (OT RANDOLPH) JEWITT, Mus.B., Dub. 1667 1675

Chorister in Chester Cathedral. Pupil of Dr. Orlando Gibbons. Organist of Christ Church and St. Patrick's Cathedrals, Dublin, 1631; and afterwards Vicar Choral of both these Cathedrals. Returned to England and became Organist of Chester Cathedral, 1643; Winchester Cathedral, 1667. Died July 4, 1675. Composer of Church Music.

JOHN READING 1675 1681

Lay Vicar of Lincoln Cathedral, 1667, and Master of the Choristers there, 1670.

Organist of Winchester Cathedral, 1675; Organist of Winchester College, 1681. Died at Winchester, 1692. Probably buried in the Cloisters of Winchester College. Composer of the Winchester College "Graces."*

From the following letter it would seem that, at this time, the Organist's duty as a singer in the choir was taken by another Lay Clerk, who objected, apparently, to sing gratuitously:—

"Reverend Sir,

"Excuse I pray my presumption in writeing to you, but it is oppression causes itt, in way of Appeall to you; I have faithfully performed my owne duty in the Church Service, and because I am unwilling to doe anothers I am suspended, and my pay withheld from mee. I humbly appeal to your worship, whither it is equitable that I should reade for the Organist his Corse, without consideration for the same; or why I should be imposed upon in the performance of this his duty; this is the true state of my condition; I submitt wholey to your decision in the case, and shall willingly obay your order herein; I confesse whilest Mr. Jewett lived and was organist, by your worshipp's Command and order I did willingly perform the service for him; but I humbly conceive now he is dead, that I am not bound to doe the same for his successor, If it please your worp to

* The words of the Grace "Dulce Domum" are said to have been written by a boy named Turner, whilst confined to the College during the holidays for some offence.—(See Kirby's "Annals of Winchester College.")

take this into your serious consideration and releive mee herein, I shall (as in bounden duty) approve myselfe
"Your most humble and dutifull Servant
"THO. WEBB.

"2 July, 1676
Winton

"These
To the Reverend Deane
of Winchester at his house
in New King Street neere
Kingsgat in Holborne
London
post payed."—

["Cathedral Documents," edited by the Very Rev. R. W. Stephens (Dean) and the Rev. F. T. Madge (Minor Canon)].

There is no record as to how this curious point was settled at that time, but it is certain that the duties of the Organist as a singer in the choir have now long ceased to be recognised.

DANIEL ROSINGRAVE 1682 1692

(See under Dublin—Christ Church Cathedral.)

VAUGHAN RICHARDSON 1692 1729

Pupil of Blow. Died 1729. Composer of Church Music, Odes, Cantatas, Songs, &c. His Anthem, "O how amiable," is still in frequent use in all "choirs and places where they sing."

Mr. J. S. Bumpus possesses a volume of music, entirely in Richardson's autograph, containing a Service in C, fourteen Anthems, a Song for the King (1697), a Song for St. Cecilia's Day, and six Sonatas for Strings.

JOHN BISHOP 1729 1737

Born 1665. Pupil of Daniel Rosingrave. Lay Vicar of King's College, Cambridge, 1687; also Organist of the same from Michaelmas to Christmas of the same year. Organist of Winchester College, 1695; Lay Clerk of the Cathedral, 1696; afterwards succeeding Vaughan Richardson as Organist of the Cathedral.* Died at Winchester, December 19, 1737. Buried in the Cloisters of the College Chapel.

Bishop's epitaph in Cloisters of Winchester College:—

"H. S. E.
Johannes Bishop
Hujus Collegii
Nec non Ecclesiæ Cathedralis Winton, Organista
Vir
Singulari Probitate,
Integerrima Vita,
Moribus innocuis,
Musicæque Scientiæ bene peritus;
Qui
Postquam huic Collegio
Per XLII. annos sedulo inserviisset,
Ad cœlestem chorum placide migravit,
Decimo Nono Die Decembris,
Anno {Dom. 1737.
{Ætat. 72.

* Bishop's rival for the post of Organist at Winchester Cathedral was James Kent, who was esteemed a better player, but the "age and amiable disposition" of the former, coupled with the sympathy felt for some family misfortune he had suffered, induced the Dean and Chapter to give him the appointment.

Composer of Church Music, a Collection of Airs for two Flutes, daily Grace for Winchester College, Hymn "Te de profundis, summe Rex," &c. Some MS. Compositions by him are in the British Museum. His fine Service in D (with Benedictus) is unpublished. Some of his Anthems were edited by Rev. Sir W. H. Cope.

JAMES KENT... ... ... 1737 1774

Son of a glazier. Born at Winchester, March 13, 1700. Chorister in Winchester Cathedral, and afterwards in the Chapel Royal. Organist of Finedon Parish Church,* 1717; Trinity College, Cambridge, 1731; Winchester Cathedral and College, 1737. Resigned these last two appointments, 1774. Died at Winchester, May 6, 1776. Buried in the North Transept of the Cathedral. Composer of a number of Services and Anthems, &c.

"A few years before his death he presented some of his compositions to Trinity College, Cambridge, for which he received the thanks of that body, from the Master, informing him at the same time that the College had voted him a piece of plate, value ten pounds, and desiring to know in what form it should be presented. Mr. Kent chose a tankard."—(From the "Succinct Account" in Arnold's "Cathedral Music.")

The following paragraph occurs in Bishop Huntingford's (of Hereford) account of James Kent, written for Joseph Corfe's edition of the second volume of Kent's Anthems, published in 1796. (The autograph of this account is in the possession of Mr. J. S. Bumpus):—

"As an Organist he was conscientiously diligent, not only in punctual attendance at times of Choral Prayers, but also in the more laborious and indispensably requisite part of an Organist's duty, the teaching of the boys. His manner of playing was neither indecorously rapid, nor heavily slow; but such as became the sanctity of the Church and the solemnity of the Service. He was reputed to be one of the best players of Dr. Croft's music in the kingdom."

PETER FUSSELL 1774 1802

Pupil of James Kent, eventually succeeding him in the two appointments at Winchester. Taught Charles Dibdin (Senr.) his notes at Winchester College. Died July, 1802. Buried in the North Transept of the Cathedral. Composer of Church Music. His Cantate Service in A was once popular.

GEORGE WILLIAM CHARD, Mus.D., Cantab., 1812 1802 1849

Born at Winchester, 1765. Chorister in St. Paul's Cathedral. Lay Clerk and Assistant-Organist of Winchester Cathedral, 1787. Organist of the Cathedral, and of the College, 1802. Also for some years Organist of St. Maurice with St. Mary Kalendar Church, Winchester. Died at Winchester, May 23, 1849. Buried in the Cloisters of Winchester College Chapel. Composer of Church Music, Glees, &c.†

An "Offertorio" by him was performed at the Hereford Festival of 1825. Dr. Chard (like Dr. Buck, of Norwich) gained some considerable reputation as a trainer of boys' voices.

There is a story extant that he was very fond of hunting, and frequently neglected his pupils for this pastime, when his wife used to have to invent all sorts of excuses for his non-appearance at lessons.

* An organ stool preserved at Finedon Church has the initials "J. K." and the date "1717" carved upon it.

† A number of Services and Anthems by Dr. Chard, in his autograph, are in the possession of Mr. J. S. Bumpus.

BENJAMIN LONG was Deputy-Organist in 1834.

SAMUEL SEBASTIAN WESLEY, Mus.D., Oxon. .. 1849 1865
(See under Exeter.)

GEORGE BENJAMIN ARNOLD, Mus.D., Oxon., 1861 F.R.C.O. ... ... 1865 ——

Born at Petworth, December 22, 1832. Pupil of Dr. S. S. Wesley. Organist of St. Columba's College, Rathfarnham, 1853; St. Mary's, Torquay, 1856; New College, Oxford, 1860; succeeding his master at Winchester Cathedral, 1865. Conductor of Dr. Arnold's Choir. Composer of Oratorios, Cantatas, Church Music, Part-songs, Songs, Pianoforte pieces, &c. His Cantata, "Sennacherib," was produced at the Gloucester Festival, 1883.

WORCESTER.

According to the Registers there appear to have been, at times, two Organists of Worcester Cathedral, one being "Organist of the little organ." Where such cases of dual appointment occur in the list given below the two names have been bracketed together.

—— DANIELL ... ... —— ——

Was Organist about 1448.

"MASTER" R. GREENE ... ... —— ——

Organist, about thirty years after Daniell. His stipend was forty shillings per annum.

JOHN HAMPTON ... ... —— ——

Organist sometime during the Reign of Henry VII.

DANIEL BOYCE, about 1527 ... ... —— ——

JOHN TOMKINS, about 1590 ... ... —— ——

Probably a brother of the Rev. Thomas Tomkins, of Gloucester, and uncle of Thomas Tomkins, Mus.B., mentioned below.

NATHANIEL PATRICK ... ... —— ——

Organist in 1597. Composer of "Songs of sundry natures," printed by Este in 1597.

THOMAS TOMKINS, Mus.B., Oxon., 1607 ... ... —— (?)1644

Son of the Rev. Thomas Tomkins, Minor Canon of Gloucester, and brother of John Tomkins, Mus.B., Organist of St. Paul's. Born 1586. Chorister in Magdalen College, Oxford, and afterwards successively Clerk and Usher there. Pupil of Bird. Gentleman and Organist of the Chapel

Royal, 1621; afterwards Organist of Worcester. Died 1656. Composer of "Musica Deo Sacra et Ecclesiæ Anglicanæ; or, Musick dedicated to the Honor and Service of God,"* and other Church Music, Madrigals, &c. In 1625, 40 shillings was paid to him "for composing of many songes against the coronation of Kinge Charles."

RICHARD BROWN 1662 1664

Died 1664. Buried in the North Aisle of the Cathedral Nave. A Richard Brown was Organist of Wells Cathedral in 1614.

RICHARD (or WILLIAM) DAVIES ... ... (?) 1664 1712

Probably a relative of Hugh Davies, of Hereford.

CHARLES HOPKINS ... ... —— ——

{—— RICHARDSON ... ... —— ——

{WILLIAM DAVIES, Organist of the little organ until 1724.

R. CHERINGTON 1690 1700

In October, 1697, he was ordered to do penance in the Cathedral for quarrelling and fighting with a Lay Clerk.

—— SMITH ... ... 1700 ——

{JOHN HODDINOTT 1724 1731

Died 1731. Buried in the North Cloister of the Cathedral.

{JOHN ABBOTT (probably Organist of the little organ).

WILLIAM HAYES, Mus.D., Oxon., 1749 ... ... 1731 1734

Born at Hanbury, Worcestershire, December, 1706. Chorister in Gloucester Cathedral, and afterwards pupil of William Hine. Organist of St. Mary's, Shrewsbury, 1729; Worcester Cathedral, 1731; Magdalen College, Oxford, 1734. Conductor of the Worcester Festival of 1734. University Professor of Music, Oxford, 1742. Conductor of the Gloucester Festival of 1763. Died at Oxford, July 27, 1777. Buried in the Churchyard of St. Peter-in-the-East, Oxford. Composer of Church Music, Cantatas, Odes, &c. Author of "Remarks on Mr. Avison's Essay on Musical Expression."

"After a paralytic stroke, which he bore with Christian resignation for nearly three years, in a tottering state, more deranged in health than in his faculties, he resigned his breath to Him who had bestowed it, in July, 1777, in his 70th year; being called from hence by the Lord and Giver of Life, to join the Heavenly Choir above, amid the noble army of Martyrs, Saints, and Angels, with good men made perfect."—(From a short account of the Author attached to a volume of his Cathedral Music, edited by his son, Dr. Philip Hayes).

JOHN MERRIFIELD ... ... (?) 1734 1748

Died 1748. Buried in the North Cloister of the Cathedral.

* This interesting work consists of five Services and ninety-eight Anthems. In the Preface are included directions for counting time and for the pitch to which organs should be tuned.

Elias Isaac ... ... (?)1748 1793

Born, July 14, 1734.* Pupil of Dr. Greene. Conductor for some years of the Worcester Festivals. Died 1793. Buried in the North Cloister of the Cathedral. At his funeral the choir sang as an Anthem Greene's "Lord, let me know mine end."

Thomas Pitt 1793 1806

Chorister in Worcester Cathedral, and afterwards Pupil-Assistant to Isaac, succeeding him as Organist of the Cathedral and Conductor of the Worcester Festivals. Resigned 1806. Composer of Church Music. Author of "A selection of Sacred Music, principally from the Works of Handel, inscribed by permission to the Hon. and Rev. the Dean and Chapter of the Cathedral Church of Worcester."

It is related that on one occasion a Lay Clerk of the Cathedral, named Griffiths, took offence at Pitt's accompaniment to one of his solos, and being a man of rather eccentric manners, he surprised the choir and congregation by slamming his book and shouting "Pitt's wrong, Pitt's wrong!"

Jeremiah Clarke, Mus.B., Oxon., 1799 ... ... 1806 1807

Chorister in Worcester Cathedral. Violinist at the Three Choirs and other Festivals. Succeeded Pitt as Cathedral Organist and Conductor of the Worcester Festivals. Died (?) 1807. Composer of Glees, Songs, Harpsichord Sonatas, &c.

William Kenge 1807 1813

Conductor of the Worcester Festivals of 1809 and 1812.

Charles Erlin Jackson Clarke 1814 1844

(See under Durham.)

William Done, Mus.D., Cantuar., 1894 ... ... 1844 1895

Born at Worcester, October 4, 1815. Chorister in Worcester Cathedral. Pupil-Assistant to C. E. J. Clarke, whom he eventually succeeded as Cathedral Organist. The degree of Mus.D. was conferred on him by the Archbishop of Canterbury upon the celebration of his Jubilee as Cathedral Organist, in 1894. Conductor of the Worcester Festivals from 1845 to 1887, and of the Worcester Philharmonic Society. Died August 17, 1895. Composer of Church Music.

During Dr. Done's Organistship great improvements were effected in the Cathedral Services. A large voluntary choir was formed, and Oratorios were performed on special occasions.

Hugh Blair, M.A., Mus.B., Cantab., 1887 ... 1895 1897

Born at Worcester, May 26, 1864. Pupil of Dr. Done, and afterwards of Professor Macfarren and Dr. Garrett. Organ Scholar at Christ's College, Cambridge, 1883. Assistant-Organist of Worcester Cathedral, 1886; Acting Organist, 1889; succeeding to the full office on the death of Dr. Done, 1895. Conductor of the Worcester Festivals, 1893 and 1896. Resigned 1897. Composer of Cantatas, Anthems, Services, Part-songs, Violin pieces, &c.

* This is the date given by Dr. Rimbault, in his notes to "Annals of the Three Choirs." But if both this and the year of his appointment as Organist of the Cathedral were correct, he would have commenced the duties of the latter office at the early age of fourteen!

IVOR ALGERNON ATKINS, Mus.B., Oxon., 1892; F.R.C.O. ... ... 1897 ——

Son of Frederick Atkins, Mus.B. Born at Cardiff, November 29, 1869. Chorister in Cardiff Parish Church. Pupil of G. R. Sinclair and Assistant Organist to him at Truro and Hereford Cathedrals. Organist of Ludlow Parish Church, 1893; Worcester Cathedral, 1897. Composer of Church Music, &c.

YORK.

JOHN THORNE ... ... —— 1573

He was probably Organist. According to Drake's "Eboracum" he lies "buried in the middle aisle, from the West Door." His inscription has been quoted by Drake ("Eboracum"), Hawkins ("History of Music"), and others, and runs thus:—

"Here lyeth Thorne, musician most perfect in his art,
In Logick's Lore who did excell; all vice who set apart:
Whose Lief and conversation did all men's Love allure,
And now doth reign above the Skies in joys most firm and pure.
Who dyed Decemb. 7, 1573."

There is a Motet, "Stella cœli extirpavit," by him in Hawkins's "History of Music," and his name is included in the Catalogue of Great Musicians in Morley's "Introduction to Practicall Musicke" (1597).

JOHN WYRNAL ... ... —— ——

Buried under the Window of the Clock (rose window), in the South Transept. The following is the inscription on his tomb:—

"Musicus et logicus Wyrnal hic jacet ecce Johannes
Organa namque quasi fecerat ille loqui."

Translated thus in Hawkins's "History":—

"Musician and Logician both,
John Wyrnal lieth here;
Who made the organs erst to speak
As if, or as it were."

And in Drake's "Eboracum":—

"Here lies John Wyrnal, so well skilled in the Art of Music and speech, that he made even the Organ speak."

—— KIRBY (or KIRKBY) ... ... —— ——

Also buried under the Window of the Clock (Drake)—

"Hic jacet egregius cantor Kirkbius in urna,
Organa qui scite tangeret unus erat.
Edidit insignes cantus modulamine dulci,
Hujus erat templi gloria, splendor, honor.
Magna hujus fuerat probitas, sapientia, virtus,
Consilio enituit, moribus, ingenio."

Translation: "Here lie the ashes of Kirby, an excellent Chanter and incomparable Organist. He sang extraordinary songs to charming tunes. He was the boast, glory, and honour of this Church. Great were his probity, wisdom, and virtue; and his understanding, morality, and genius remarkable."

JOHN HUTCHINSON ... ... 1633 ——

Doubtless a relative of Richard Hutchinson, of Durham. There are three Anthems by John Hutchinson in the Durham Cathedral Library. The Very Rev. A. P. Purey-Cust, Dean of York, has in his possession some MS. notes by Dr. Naylor upon former Organists of York Minster, from which he has very kindly favoured me with extracts. Speaking of John Hutchinson, Dr. Naylor says: "Canon Raine once shewed me a copy of Morley's 'Introduction' (1597), and in it was the name—J. Hutchinson—written in a bold hand, and the Canon said that Hutchinson was a former Organist of York Minster."

J. CHARLES ... ... 1662 ——

Vol. III. of "The Cathedral Magazine of Divine Harmony" (York Minster Library Collection) contains an Anthem for four voices, "Out of the deep," composed by "Mr. Charles, late Organist at York." According to Dr. Naylor's notes upon this Anthem, "There are several serious errors in the print, and if rectified the Anthem might be considered a fair composition." Also, "From a note beneath the Table of Contents of the above volume the date of its publication was probably about 1777-8." Is it not possible, therefore, that this Anthem is by Charles *Quarles*, Organist from 1722-1727? (See below.)

THOMAS WANLESS, Mus.B., Cantab., 1698 .. 1691 ——

Probably son of John Wanless(e), of Lincoln. In the Chapter books he is described as "in musicis expertium." He published at York a collection of Words of Anthems sung in the Cathedral. Composer of the "York Litany," of which there are various versions extant. An Anthem by him is in the Tudway Collection.

CHARLES MURGATROYD (or MURGETROYD) was Organist in 1715. (See under Lincoln.)

CHARLES QUARLES, Mus.B., Cantab., 1698 ... 1722 1727

Probably son of Charles Quarles, the builder of the Organs at Pembroke and Christ Colleges, Cambridge, in 1707.

Organist of Trinity College, Cambridge, 1688. A "Lesson for the Harpsichord" by him was published by Goodison in 1788

(?) EDWARD SALISBURY 1727 1734

Resigned his post at York. Afterwards (1737) Organist of Trinity College, Cambridge.

JAMES NARES, Mus.D., Cantab., 1757 ... ... 1734 1756

Born at Stanwell, 1715. Chorister in the Chapel Royal. Pupil of Dr. Pepusch. Assistant Organist of St. George's Chapel, Windsor. Organist of York Minster in succession to Edward Salisbury. Resigned at York and was appointed Organist, Master of the Children, and Composer of the Chapel Royal. Died in London, February 10, 1783. Buried in St. Margaret's, Westminster. Composer of an Ode, Church Music, Organ pieces, Harpsichord Lessons, Glees, &c. Author of two treatises on Singing and one on the Harpsichord or Organ. Arranger of Six Choruses of Handel for the Organ or Harpsichord.

He was an excellent trainer of boys' voices, and some of his Anthems are said to have been written to display the fine voices of his young pupils.

I am indebted to Mr. J. S. Bumpus for the following interesting anecdote concerning Nares:—

On the resignation of Salisbury in 1734, Nares was chosen to succeed him as Organist of York Minster, being then only nineteen. It is related, on undoubted authority, that when the old musician first saw his intended successor, he said rather angrily: "What! is that child to succeed me?" which being mentioned to the organist-elect, he took an early opportunity, on a difficult service being appointed, to play it throughout half a note below the pitch, which brought it into a very remote key, and went through it without the slightest error. Being asked why he did so, he said that he "only wished to show Mr. Salisbury what a *child* could do."

JOHN CAMIDGE 1756 1803

Born about 1734. Chorister in York Cathedral. Pupil of Dr. Greene and Handel. Organist of Doncaster Parish Church, 1755. Succeeded Nares at York. Died at York, April 25, 1803. Buried in St. Olave's Churchyard, York. Composer of Church Music, "Six Easy Lessons for the Harpsichord," Glees, Songs, "The Duke of York's March," &c.

MATTHEW CAMIDGE 1803 1844

Son of the preceding. Born at York, 1764. Chorister in the Chapel Royal. Pupil of Nares. Assistant Organist to his father at York, and afterwards Organist. Died October 23, 1844. Buried in St. Olave's Churchyard. Composer of Church Music, Sonatas, Marches for the Pianoforte, &c. Compiler of a Collection of Tunes, set to Sandy's Version of the Psalms, and Author of a "Method of Instruction in Music by Questions and Answers," &c.

JOHN CAMIDGE, Mus.D., Cantab., 1819; et Cantuar., 1855 ... ... 1844 1859

Son of the preceding and grandson of the John Camidge before mentioned. Born at York, 1790. Pupil of his father. Was Acting Organist for his father some years before being appointed his successor. Died September 21, 1859, having latterly been afflicted with paralysis. Composer of Church Music, Glees, &c.

The large organ, by Hill, was built under his direction, the previous instrument having perished when the Choir of the Minster was destroyed by fire at the hands of a maniac, named Jonathan Martin, in 1829.

Dr. Camidge was first seized with paralysis on November 28, 1848, whilst playing the Evening Service, and never afterwards touched the organ.

At the farewell Service for the Right Rev. Canon Charles E. Camidge, D.D., after his consecration as Bishop of Bathurst, at York Minster, on October 19, 1887, the music included compositions from five generations of the Camidge family, relatives of the Bishop. Such a circumstance is probably unique in history. The processional hymn was to a tune adapted from a short Anthem by John Camidge, Organist of York Minster, 1756-1803. The Psalms and Canticles were sung to Chants composed by Matthew Camidge, the son of the latter. The Anthem, "Sing unto the Lord," was by Dr. Camidge, son of Matthew Camidge. The Kyrie, Creed, Sanctus, and Gloria were by John Camidge, grandson of Dr. Camidge, and the present Organist of Beverley Minster; and during the Offertory was sung "Be merciful after Thy power," by Thomas S. Camidge, son of Dr. Camidge, his Deputy at the Minster, and father of Mr. J. Camidge, of Beverley.—(*See Musical Times*, November, 1887.)

EDWIN GEORGE MONK, Mus.D., Oxon., 1856; F.R.A.S. 1859 1883

Born at Frome, December 13, 1819. Pupil of Henry and George Field, John Hullah, Henry Phillips, and afterwards of Professor Macfarren. Organist successively of Midsomer-Norton Parish Church, and Christ Church, Frome. Organist and Precentor of St. Columba's College, Navan, Ireland, 1844. Organist and Music Master of St. Peter's College, Radley, 1848. Organist of York Minster, 1859. Retired from the latter post, 1883, and removed to Radley. Composer of two Odes, Church Music, Part-songs, &c. Editor of the "Anglican Chant Book," &c. Compiler of the libretti of two Oratorios set to music by his friend Professor Macfarren. Author of "A Descriptive Account of the York Minster Organ" (Novello, 1863).

Dr. Monk has also devoted considerable attention to the study of Astronomy, and is a Fellow of the Royal Astronomical Society.

JOHN NAYLOR, Mus.D., Oxon., 1872 ... ... 1883 1897

Born at Stanningley, June 8, 1838. Chorister in Leeds Parish Church, and afterwards Assistant Organist there. Organist of St. Mary's, Scarborough, 1856; All Saints', Scarborough, 1873; York Cathedral, 1883. Resigned at York, owing to ill-health, 1897. Died May 15, 1897, during a voyage to Australia. Composer of Church Cantatas, Services, Anthems, Part-songs, &c.

THOMAS TERTIUS NOBLE ... ... 1898 ——

Born at Bath, May 5, 1867. Organist, at the age of fourteen, of All Saints', Colchester, 1881. Pupil of Edwin Nunn, and afterwards student of the Royal College of Music, 1885. Organist of St. John's, Wilton Road, London, 1889, and afterwards Assistant Organist of Trinity College, Cambridge. Organist of Ely Cathedral, 1892, which post he resigned on his appointment to York. Composer of Church Music, Organ pieces, Songs, Comic Operas, Incidental Music to Cambridge "Plays," &c.

COLLEGIATE CHURCHES AND CHAPELS, &c.

CAMBRIDGE—KING'S COLLEGE.

EDWARD GIBBONS, Mus.B., Cantab. et Oxon. ... 1592 (?)1599

(See under Bristol.)

JOHN TOMKINS, Mus.B., Cantab. ... ... 1606 { 1619 or 1621

His stipend on appointment was 50s. a quarter as Organist and 11s. 8d. for instructing the Choristers. The stipend as Organist was afterwards augmented to 58s. 4d.

According to the records his payment as Organist ceased in 1619; but his name appears from time to time in the list of resident members of the College who were entitled to allowances for Commons, until 1621.

(See under St. Paul's Cathedral.)

MATTHEW BARTON 1622 1624

His stipend on appointment was 50s. a quarter; afterwards augmented to 58s. 4d.

GILES TOMKINS 1624 1626

His stipend on appointment was 50s. a quarter; afterwards augmented to 58s. 4d. At Christmas, 1626, he received 30s. as "nuper Organistæ," his successor, George Marshall, at the time receiving 10s. "pro pulsandis organis."

(See under Salisbury.)

—— MARSHALL 1626 1627

He was appointed on the recommendation of the Earl of Sheffield, as appears from a letter dated September 29, 1626. Soon afterwards, however, he was granted permission to travel abroad, and was furnished with a protection, under the College Charter, against a press for the wars.

JOHN SILVER ... ... —— 1627

At Michaelmas, 1627, Mr. Silver, Organist, received 30s. "pro expensis in itinere de Winton."

(See under Winchester.)

HENRY LOOSEMORE, Mus.B., Cantab., 1640 ... 1627 1670

His stipend on appointment was £2 10s. a quarter; at Christmas, 1628, it was £3; at Lady Day, 1629, £3 6s. 8d.; and at Lady Day, 1634, £5. At Christmas, 1627, he received £5 in payment for a new organ book.

He was *not* appointed Organist of Exeter Cathedral after the Restoration, as has frequently been stated, but continued as Organist of King's College, Cambridge, during the whole of the period from 1627 until his death at Cambridge in 1670, his services and those of the Lay Clerks being retained by the College throughout the time of the Commonwealth. Further evidence bearing upon this point has been supplied by the following extract from a valuable paper on Organs and Organ building at Cambridge in 1606, by T. Brocklebank (sometime Bursar and Vice-Provost of King's College, Cambridge), which appeared in the *Ecclesiologist* for 1859:—

"The year after the Restoration the College set about reviving the Choral Service, which had been grievously interrupted by the troubles of the times, and we find Mr. Henry Loosemore, the Organist, lending his Chamber Organ for use in the Chapel, 35s. being charged for its removal thither from his room by Lancelot Pease. It did not, however, remain there long."

Compositions by him are included in the Tudway, Ely, and other Collections. His pathetic Litany in D minor is published in Dr. Jebb's "Choral Responses and Litanies" (1847), and is still in frequent use in Lichfield Cathedral.

THOMAS TUDWAY, Mus.D., Cantab., 1705 ... ... 1670 1726

Born about 1650. Is said to have been a Chorister in the Chapel Royal and afterwards a Lay Vicar of St. George's Chapel, Windsor. Organist of King's College, Cambridge, 1670; also Organist to the University and of Pembroke Hall. University Professor of Music, 1705. Composer and Organist Extraordinary to Queen Anne, 1705. Deprived of his appointments owing to some remarks which he made being considered disloyal to the Queen, 1706, but re-instated in all these posts the following year.* Eventually resigned them in 1726, and spent the latter portion of his life in forming, at the instigation of Lord Harley, the valuable collection of English Music known as the "Tudway" Collection (British Museum, Harleian MSS., 7337-7342). Died 1730. Composer of Church Music, Songs, &c.

Tudway was an inveterate punster, and part of the offence which deprived him of his appointments was a remark complaining of the paucity of the patronage of the Chancellor, the Duke of Somerset: "The Chancellor rides us all, without a bit in our mouths."

ROBERT FULLER, Mus.B., Cantab., 1724 ... ... 1727 1742

Also Organist to the University, 1731. Died 1743. Buried in All Saints' Church.

JOHN RANDALL, Mus.D., Cantab., 1756 ... ... 1743 1799

Born 1715. Chorister in the Chapel Royal. Organist of King's College, Cambridge, 1743; Trinity College, 1777; also Organist to the University and Pembroke Hall. University Professor of Music, 1755. Died March 18, 1799. Buried in St. Benet's Churchyard, Cambridge. Composer of Church Music, Songs, &c. One or two of his Chants are well known at the present day.

JOHN PRATT... ... ... 1799 1855

Son of Jonas Pratt, a music-dealer. Born at Cambridge, 1772. Chorister in King's College, and afterwards pupil of Dr. Randall. Succeeded Randall as Organist of King's College and to the University, 1799. Organist of St. Peter's College, 1813. Died at Cambridge, March 9, 1855. Buried in the Cemetery, Mill Road. Composer of Church Music. Compiler of a Collection of Anthems in Score, selected from the works of Handel, Haydn, Mozart, and others.

A Service by Pratt, in E flat, in triple time throughout, is still sung at Ely.

* John Bishop (see under Winchester) officiated as Organist during the vacancy.

WILLIAM AMPS, M.A., Cantab. 1855 1876

Organist also of Peterhouse and Christ's College, Cambridge. Conductor of the University Musical Society. Resigned the appointment at King's College, 1876. Composer of Pianoforte Sonatas, Part-songs, &c.

ARTHUR HENRY MANN, Mus.D., Oxon., 1882; F.R.C.O. ... ... 1876 ——

Born at Norwich, May 16, 1850. Chorister in Norwich Cathedral, and Assistant Organist there to Dr. Z. Buck. Organist of St. Peter's, Wolverhampton, 1870; Tettenhall Parish Church, 1871; Beverley Minster, 1875; King's College, Cambridge, 1876. Organist to the University, 1897. Composer of Church Music, Organ Music, Part-songs, &c. Editor of Tallis's Motet for forty voices. One of the Compilers of the Music Catalogue of the Fitzwilliam Museum, Cambridge. Musical Editor of Church of England Hymnal, &c.

CAMBRIDGE—ST. JOHN'S COLLEGE.

THOMAS WILLIAMS

was Organist in 1680. There is an Anthem by him, "Arise, arise," in the Ely Collection.

WILLIAM TIREMAN, Mus.B., Cantab. Feb., 1777, March, 1777

(See under Trinity College.)

JONATHAN SHARPE ... ... April, 1777 1799

Probably a relative of Carter Sharpe, Organist of Peterborough Cathedral.

JOHN CLARKE-WHITFELD, Mus.D., Dub., Cantab. et Oxon. 1799 1820

(See under Hereford.)

WILLIAM BEALE 1820 1821

(See under Trinity College.)

SAMUEL MATTHEWS, Mus.B., Cantab. ... 1821 (or 22) 1832

(See under Trinity College.)

THOMAS ATTWOOD WALMISLEY, M.A., Mus.D., Cantab. 1833 1856

(See under Trinity College.)

ALFRED BENNETT (Junr.) ... ... June, 1856, Dec., 1856

Only son of Alfred Bennett, Mus.B., Oxon., Organist of New College, Oxford. Alfred Bennett, Junr., afterwards became Organist of St. John's Church, Calcutta.

George Mursell Garrett, M.A., Cantab., 1878; Mus.D., Cantab., 1867; F.R.C.O. 1857 1897

Born at Winchester, June 8, 1834. Chorister in New College, Oxford. Pupil of Dr. S. S. Wesley. Organist of St. Thomas's, Winchester, 1848; Holy Trinity, Winchester, 1852; Madras Cathedral, 1854; St. John's College, Cambridge, 1857. Organist to the University, 1873. M.A., *propter merita*, 1878. University Lecturer in Harmony and Counterpoint, 1883. Conductor of St. John's College Musical Society. Died April 8, 1897. Buried in the Cambridge Cemetery, Mill Road. Composer of Cantatas, Church Music, Organ pieces, Pianoforte pieces, Part-songs, Songs, &c. Lecturer on Musical Subjects, Editor of a Collection of Chants, &c.

Edward Thomas Sweeting, Mus.D., Oxon. ... 1897 ——

Born September 16, 1863. Scholar of the National Training School for Music. Organist of St. Mary's, West Kensington, 1874. Music Master of Rossall School, 1882. Organist of St. John's College, Cambridge, 1897. Composer of a Choral Ballad for Men's voices, "The Burial of Dundee"; a Festal March for Orchestra, Madrigals, Part-songs, Songs, pieces for Violin and Pianoforte, &c.

CAMBRIDGE—TRINITY COLLEGE.

John Hilton ... ... 1594 ——

(See under Lincoln.)

George Mason ... ... 1612 (?)1629

Composed, with John Earsden, "The Ayres that were sung and played at Brougham Castle in Westmoreland, in the King's Entertainment, given by the right honourable the Earl of Cumberland, and his right noble sonne the Lord Clifford."

Robert Ramsey, Mus.B., Cantab., 1616 ... ... 1628 1664

Was required to compose for his degree a "Canticum" to be performed at St. Mary's Church. A Service in F by him is in the Tudway Collection. There are also Services, Anthems, &c., at the British Museum, Ely, and Peterhouse, Cambridge.

George Loosemore, Mus.D., Cantab., 1665 ... 1660 1682

Probably a son of Henry Loosemore, Organist of King's College, and a Chorister there under his father. Anthems by him are to be found in the Tudway and Ely Collections.

Robert Wildbore 1682 1688

Charles Quarles, Mus.B., Cantab. 1688 1709

(See under York.)

JOHN BOWMAN ... ... 1709 (?) 1730

THOMAS EBLYN 1730 1731

JAMES KENT 1731 1737

(See under Winchester.)

EDWARD SALISBURY 1737 1741

(See under York.)

WILLIAM TIREMAN, Mus.B., Cantab., 1757 ... 1741 1777

Organist of Doncaster Parish Church, 1739; Trinity College, Cambridge, 1741. Also Organist to the University; of St. John's College, Cambridge, from February to March, 1777. Died March 16, 1777. Buried in All Saints' Church, Cambridge.

JOHN RANDALL, Mus.D., Cantab. 1777 1799

(See under King's College.)

JOHN CLARKE-WHITFELD, Mus.D., Dub., Cantab. et Oxon. 1799 1820

(See under Hereford.)

WILLIAM BEALE 1820 1821

Born at Landrake, Cornwall, January 1, 1784. Chorister in Westminster Abbey. Pupil of Drs. Arnold and Cooke. Gentleman of the Chapel Royal, 1816. Organist, successively, of Wandsworth Parish Church and St. John's, Clapham Rise. Organist of Trinity and St. John's Colleges, Cambridge, 1820. Afterwards returned to London, where he died, May 3, 1854. Composer of Glees, Madrigals, and one or two pieces of Church Music. His Anthem, "Bow down Thine ear," has been edited by Dr. A. H. Mann.

SAMUEL MATTHEWS, Mus.B., Cantab., 1828 ... 1821 1832

Born 1769. Chorister in Westminster Abbey. Lay-Clerk of Winchester Cathedral. Organist of Trinity and St. John's Colleges, Cambridge, 1821. Died December 9, 1832. Buried in St. Botolph's Churchyard, Cambridge. Composer of a Service in D. Arranged and published four Anthems from the works of Haydn, Mozart, and others.

THOMAS ATTWOOD WALMISLEY, M.A., Cantab., 1841; Mus.D., Cantab., 1848 ... ... 1833 1856

Born at Westminster, January 21, 1814. Pupil of his father, Thomas Forbes Walmisley, and of his godfather, Thomas Attwood. Organist of Croydon Church, 1830; Trinity and St. John's Colleges, Cambridge, 1833. University Professor of Music, 1836, while he was still in residence for his B.A. degree. It is said that about this time he was playing the organ at as many as eight services every Sunday—twice at each of the following places: King's College, Trinity College, St. John's College, and the University Church. Died at Caroline Place, Hastings, January 17, 1856. Buried in Fairlight Churchyard. Composer of Odes, Church Music, Organ pieces, Songs, Duets for Pianoforte and Oboe, &c. His Cathedral music was edited by his father, T. Forbes Walmisley.

It is said that his death was hastened by an unwise indulgence in lethal remedies, taken as a sedative to an active brain and over-sensitive mind.

Inscription on the gravestone of Walmisley:—

"Here lies the body of
Thomas Attwood Walmisley,
M.A. and Mus.D.,
Professor of Music
in the University of Cambridge,
Born Jan. 21st, 1814. Died Jan. 17th, 1856.
He fell asleep in the humble hope that when Christ, Who is our Life, shall appear, then shall we also appear with Him in glory."

There is a memorial brass to him in the Ante-Chapel of Trinity College.

JOHN LARKIN HOPKINS, Mus.D., Cantab. ... 1856 1874

(See under Rochester.)

CHARLES VILLIERS STANFORD, D.C.L., Durham; M.A., Cantab., 1877; Mus.D., Oxon., 1883; et Cantab., 1888; F.R.C.O. 1874 1892

Born at Dublin, September 30, 1852. Pupil of Arthur O'Leary and Sir Robert Stewart, and afterwards of Reinecke and F. Kiel. Matriculated at Cambridge University, and, in 1873, succeeded Dr. J. L. Hopkins as Organist of Trinity College, Cambridge. For some years Conductor of the Cambridge Amateur Vocal Guild and Cambridge University Musical Society. Professor of Composition and Conductor of the Orchestra at the Royal College of Music since its opening in 1883. Conductor of the Bach Choir, 1885. University Professor of Music at Cambridge, 1887. Resigned the post of Organist of Trinity College, Cambridge, 1892, and removed to London. Elected Corresponding Member of the Société des Compositeurs de Musique, Paris, 1892. Conductor of Leeds Philharmonic Society, 1897. Composer of Oratorios, Operas, Cantatas, Odes, Incidental Music to Plays, Church Music, Orchestral Music, Chamber Music, Organ pieces, Songs, Pianoforte pieces, &c. Editor of Irish Melodies. Writer and Lecturer on Music, &c.

ALAN GRAY, LL.M., Cantab., 1883; Mus.D., Cantab., 1889 ... ... 1892 ——

Born at York, December 23, 1855. Studied for the legal profession. Pupil (for music) of Dr. E. G. Monk. Organist and Music Master of Wellington College, 1883. Organist of Trinity College, Cambridge, 1892. Conductor of Cambridge University Musical Society. Composer of Cantatas, Odes, Church Music, Orchestral Music, Chamber Music, Sonatas for Organ, Songs, &c.

ETON COLLEGE.

It is impossible to give a complete and reliable succession of the Organists of Eton College, owing to the fact that for two hundred years or more previous to 1867 the choir was supplied by that of St. George's Chapel, Windsor, and the post of Organist was often held by either the Organist or one of the Lay Clerks of the latter. In 1867 a separate Choral Establishment and Organist were instituted at Eton, the holder of the latter office being designated Precentor.

Much of the information given below is the result of a long and laborious search through the College account books, for which I am greatly indebted to Mr. Richard Cope, Clerk to the College.

JOHN MUNDY (MUNDAY, or MUNDIE), Mus.D., Oxon. ... ... circa 1575

(See under St. George's Chapel, Windsor.)

WILLIAM ELLIS, Mus.B., Oxon. ... ... —— ——

(See under St. John's College, Oxford.)

LEONARD WOODSON ... ... 1615 1641 (or later).

The accounts for 1642-1646 are missing.

There is a Te Deum in D minor by him in Barnard's Collection, and two Anthems—"Arise, O Lord God," and "Hear, O Lord, hear my prayer"—are included in a MS. collection of Church Music in the Library of the Royal College of Music.

The words of the first-named Anthem are given in Clifford's "Divine Service and Anthems," 1664 edition.

CHARLES PEARSE ... ... 1648 1653 (or later).

From 1654 till 1660 an Organist's salary was paid but no name is given.

BENJAMIN ROGERS, Mus.D., Oxon. ... ...(?)1661 (?)1664

His name appears in the accounts, but he is not mentioned as Organist. In fact, from this time until 1701, the word Organist is not to be found in the books.

(See under Magdalen College, Oxford.)

BENJAMIN LAMB ... ... circa 1687

He also held the office of Verger of St. George's Chapel, Windsor.

Composer of Church Music, Organ pieces, Songs, &c. His Single Chant in F is included in most of the Collections of the present day.

JOHN WALTER ... ... circa 1690

He may have been Organist, but probably he was merely a Lay Clerk. One of the musical instructors of John Weldon. Composer of Church Music.

FRANCIS PIGOTT (Junr.) ... ...(?)1733 1756

His name first appears as Organist in 1733.

(See under St. George's Chapel, Windsor.)

EDWARD WEBB 1756 1788
(See under St. George's Chapel, Windsor.)

STEPHEN HEATHER 1788 1831
Born 1748. Lay Clerk of St. George's Chapel, Windsor, and Organist of Eton College. Died at Windsor, November 14, 1831.

JOHN MITCHELL 1831 1867
Born at Eton, 1809. Chorister, and afterwards Lay Clerk of St. George's Chapel, Windsor, and Organist of Eton College. Resigned the latter post on the establishment of a separate Choir and Organist, 1867. Died at Windsor, January 6, 1892.
Mitchell sang at the Coronations of George IV., William IV., and Queen Victoria, and also at the Jubilee Service in Westminster Abbey, June 21, 1887. After the latter event Her Majesty the Queen presented him with an engraved portrait of herself as a recognition of his long musical services.

LEIGHTON GEORGE HAYNE, Mus.D., Oxon., 1860 1867 1871
Born at Exeter, February 28, 1836. Organist of Queen's College, Oxford, 1857; Precentor ditto, 1860. Took Holy Orders, 1861. Coryphæus of Oxford University, 1863. Vicar of Helston, 1866. Precentor of Eton, 1867. Rector of Mistley, 1871. Died at Bradfield (Essex), March 3, 1883. Composer of Psalm Tunes, &c. Editor (with the Rev. H. W. Sargeant) of "The Merton Tune Book."
The organ was his special hobby. He had a large instrument of five manuals built in the music room of Eton College. This was eventually divided between the churches of Mistley and Bradfield.

CHARLES DONALD MACLEAN, M.A., Oxon., 1875; Mus.D., Oxon., 1865 ... ... 1872 1875
Born at Cambridge, March 27, 1843. Pupil of Ferdinand Hiller at Cologne. Organist of Exeter College, Oxford, 1862. Organist and Director of the Music at Eton College, 1872. Resigned the post at Eton and was for some years resident in India. Now living in London. Composer of an Oratorio, "Noah," a Cantata, "Sulmala," a Requiem Mass, Church Music, Orchestral Music, Chamber Music, Songs, Pianoforte pieces, &c.

SIR JOSEPH BARNBY, F.R.C.O. 1875 1892
Born at York, August 12, 1838. Chorister in York Minster. Student of the Royal Academy of Music. Organist of Mitcham Parish Church for a short period, after which he returned to York for four years. Then Organist successively of St. Michael's, Queenhithe; St. James the Less, Westminster; and (in 1863) St. Andrew's, Wells Street, London. Musical Adviser to Messrs. Novello & Co. Conducted a performance of Bach's Passion Music ("St. Matthew") at Westminster Abbey, April 6 (Maundy Thursday), 1871. Director of the music at St. Anne's, Soho, 1871. Founded "Mr. Joseph Barnby's Choir" in 1867, which afterwards gave its performances under the title of "The Oratorio Concerts," and eventually amalgamated with M. Gounod's Choir as The (Royal) Albert Hall Choral Society. Precentor of Eton College, 1875-1892. Conductor of the Concerts of the Royal Academy of Music, 1886-1888. Principal of the Guildhall School of Music, 1892. Conductor of the Cardiff Musical Festivals, 1892 and 1895. Knighted in 1892. Died suddenly in London, January 28, 1896. Composer of a Sacred Idyll, "Rebekah," a setting of Psalm 97, Church Music, Part-songs, Trios, Songs, Carols, Organ pieces, &c. Musical Editor of the Hymnary, &c.

CHARLES HARFORD LLOYD, M.A.; Mus.D., Oxon. 1892 ——
(See under Gloucester.)

LONDON—CHAPEL ROYAL (FIRST AT WHITEHALL; AFTERWARDS AT ST. JAMES'S).

The Chapel Royal has generally possessed, until comparatively recently, two or more organists at a time, the duties of the office being divided according to certain arrangements.

In the "Orders for the Attendance of the Gentlemen of his Majestes Chapell," about the year 1604, occur the following paragraphs concerning the attendance of the organists:—

"(8.) If ther be above two Organistes at once, two shall allwaies attend: if ther be but two in all, then they shall wayte by course, one after another, weekly or monethly, as they shall agree betwixt them selves, givinge notice to the Subdeane and the Clark of the Check how they do dispose of their waytinge, that therby it may be knowne who is at all tymes to be expected for the service, and they shalbe subject to such orders, and to such checks, in the same manner as the other gentlemen are.

"(9.) The check for absence from morning prayers, holy dayes, festivall tymes, and sermon dayes, shalbe 4d., from evening prayer uppon such dayes and their festivall eves 3d., from eveninge prayer 2d.

"(10.) The check for late cominge, viz., after the first Gloria Patri 1d., after the first lesson 2d., after the second as for absent from the whole service."—("The Old Cheque Book of the Chapel Royal." Edited by E. F. Rimbault.)

The office of *Composer* to the Chapel Royal was created in 1699, Dr. Blow being its first holder.* It has generally, though not always, been held by one of the Organists of the Chapel. The holder of the office is expected to compose music for the Services on State or other occasions when required by the Sovereign. A second Composer's post was established in 1715. John Weldon was the first appointed second Composer, his initial undertaking being a setting of the Sanctus and Gloria in E flat.

CHRISTOPHER TYE, Mus.D., Cantab. et Oxon.... 1562 1580
The first *Lay* Organist.
(See under Ely.)

THOMAS TALLIS (or TALLYS) ... ... before 1575 1585
Often called the Father of English Church Music. Born about 1520. Is supposed to have been a Chorister in the Chapel Royal. Organist of Waltham Abbey for some years, until its dissolution, 1540. Gentleman of the Chapel Royal, and afterwards Organist of the same. Held letters patent, jointly with Bird, for the exclusive right to print music. Died, November 23, 1585. Buried in Greenwich Parish Church. Composer of a large number of works

* His salary as Composer was £40 per annum.

for the Church, some with Latin and others with English words. Known at the present day chiefly by his harmonies to the old Plain-song Responses, called "Tallis's Responses."

It is said that Tallis was in attendance upon Queen Elizabeth at Greenwich Palace at the time when he died. There was an epitaph to him engraved upon a brass plate in the chancel of the old church of Greenwich, where he was buried. The church was pulled down during the last century, when all trace of the brass plate was lost.

The epitaph occurs, however, in Strype's continuation of Stow's "Survey of London," and is as follows:—

"Enterred here doth ly a worthy wyght,
Who for long tyme in musick bore the bell;
His name to shew was Thomas Tallis hyght,
In honest vertuous lyff he dyd excell.

He served long tyme in Chappel with grete prayse,
Fower sovereygnes reignes (a thing not often seene),
I mean King Henry and Prince Edward's dayes,
Quene Marie, and Elizabeth our Quene.

He maryed was, though children he had none,
And lyv'd in love full three and thirty yeres
With loyal spowse, whos name yclept was Jone,
Who here entom'b, him company now bears.

As he dyd lyve, so also dyd he dy,
In myld and quyet sort, O happy man,
To God ful oft for mercy did he cry,
Wherefore he lyves, let Deth do what he can."

WILLIAM BIRD 1585 1623

(See under Lincoln.)

WILLIAM BLITHEMAN, Mus.B., Cantab., 1586 ... 1585 1591

Master of the Choristers, Christ Church Cathedral, Oxford, 1564. Organist of the Chapel Royal, 1585. Died 1591. Buried in St. Nicholas Olave Church, Queenhithe. Composer of Church Music and pieces for the Organ, Virginals, &c.

JOHN BULL, Mus.D., Cantab. et Oxon. ... ... 1591 (?)1613

(See under Hereford.)

WILLIAM RANDALL (or RANDOLL) ... ... —— (?)1621

Organist in 1592 (according to the Chapel Royal Cheque Book). He was previously a Chorister in Exeter Cathedral. Composer of Church Music.

ARTHUR COCK (or COCKE), Mus.B., Oxon. ... —— 1604

(See under Exeter.)

ORLANDO GIBBONS, Mus.B., Cantab., 1606; Mus.D., Oxon., 1622 ... ... 1604 1625

Son of William Gibbons, one of the "Wayts" of Cambridge.

Born at Cambridge, 1583. Chorister in King's College, Cambridge, under his brother, Edward Gibbons. Organist of the Chapel Royal, 1604. Organist of Westminster Abbey, 1623. Died at Canterbury, June 5, 1625, whilst undertaking the commission of Charles I. to direct the music for the reception of Henrietta Maria. Buried in the Nave of Canterbury Cathedral. Celebrated composer of Church Music, Madrigals, pieces for Virginals, Fantasias for Viols, &c.

Inscription to Orlando Gibbons on the wall of the North Aisle at Canterbury:—

"Orlando Gibbons, Cantabridgiæ inter Musas et Musicam
nato, sacræ R. Capellæ Organistæ, Sphærarum
Harmoniæ digitorum; pulsu æmulo cantionum
complurium quæque eum non canunt minus quam
Canuntor Canditori; viro integerrimo et cujus
vita cum arte suavissimus moribus concordissime
certavit ad nupt: C. R. cum M. P. Doroberii
accito ictuque heu sanguinis crudo et crudeli
fato extincto, choroque cælesti transcripto
die Pentecostes A. D. N. MDCXXV. Elizabetha
conjux semptemque ex eo liberorum parens,
tanti vix doloris superstes merentissimo mærentissima posuit."

Dart's translation:—

"To Orlando Gibbons of Cambridge, born among
the muses and music; Organist of the Royal Chapel;
emulating by the touch of his fingers the harmony
of the spheres; composer of many hymns which
sound his praise no less than that of his Maker;
a man of integrity whose manner of life and
sweetness of temper vy'd with that of his art:
being sent for to Dover to attend the nuptials of
King Charles and Mary; he died of the small pox,* and
was conveyed to the Heavenly choir on Whitsun
Day, anno 1625. Elizabeth his wife, who bore
him seven children, little able to survive such a
loss, to her most deserving Husband hath, with
tears, erected this monument."

This inscription is surmounted by a bust of the eminent musician.

EDMUND HOOPER ... ... —— (?)1621

Is said to have succeeded Randall as Organist.
(See under Westminster Abbey.)

THOMAS TOMKINS, Mus.B., Oxon. 1621 1656

(See under Worcester.)

THOMAS WARWICK ... ... 1625 ——

Father of Sir Philip Warwick, Secretary to the Treasury in the reign of Charles II. Was Lutenist to Charles I. Gentleman and Organist of the Chapel Royal, 1625. Organist of Westminster Abbey, 1642. Composer of Church Music, and a Song in forty parts, which is said to have been performed before Charles I.

During his appointment as Organist of the Chapel Royal, he had (on March 29, 1630) to forfeit a month's salary "because he presumed to play verses on the organ at service tyme, being formerly inhibited by the Deane from doinge the same, by reason of his insufficiency for that solemn service."

WILLIAM CHILD, Mus.D., Oxon., 1663 ... ... 1632 1697

Born at Bristol, 1606. Pupil of Elway Bevin. Appointed Lay Clerk and Organist of St. George's Chapel, Windsor, 1632; Organist of the Chapel Royal, 1632. During the Civil Wars be devoted himself to composition, and at the Restoration he was re-appointed Organist of

* Dart's translation is rather free. He renders *ictu sanguinis crudo* "small-pox" (!!), and other writers have copied him.

St. George's Chapel, Windsor, and made Private Musician to Charles II. and Chanter of the King's Chapel. As Senior Gentleman, or "Father" of the Chapel Royal he walked first in the procession at the Coronation of James II. The Choir of St. George's Chapel, Windsor, was re-paved at his expense.* Died March 23, 1697, aged ninety. Buried in the North Choir Aisle of St. George's Chapel. Composer of Church Music, Catches, Airs, &c.

His Service in D was a favourite of Charles I. It is more than usually intricate for music of that period, and was supposed to have been written as a "teaser" for his choir, who had previously ridiculed the simplicity of his music.

In the Registers of St. George's Chapel, Windsor, occurs the following entry:—

"Wm. Child, buried in woollen, March 26th, 1697."

EPITAPH ON DR. CHILD, at St. George's Chapel, Windsor:—

"Heare lyes y bodye of Will. Childe, Doctor of Musick, one of y organists of y Chapple Royale at Whitehall, & of His Majestie's Free Chapel at Windsor 65 years. He was born in Bristol, and dyed heare y 23rd of March, 169$\frac{6}{7}$, in y 91st yeare of his age. He paved the body of the Quire."

"Go, happy soul, and in the seats above,
"Sing endless hymns of thy great Maker's love.
"How fit, in Heavenlie Choirs to bear thy part,
"Before well practised in y sacred art.
"Whilst hearing us sometimes y Choir divine
"Will sure descend, and in our concert join.
"So much y musick thou to us hast given,
"Has made our earth to represent their Heaven."†

CHRISTOPHER GIBBONS, Mus.D., Oxon.... ... 1660 1676

Chief Organist at the Restoration.

(See under Westminster Abbey.)

Joint Organists.

EDWARD LOWE 1660 1682

(See under Oxford.)

HENRY LAWES 1660 1662

Born at Dinton, Wiltshire, 1596. Pupil of Coperario. Epistoler to the Chapel Royal, 1626; Gentleman, ditto, the same year. Clerk of the Cheque, Musician in Ordinary and Organist to His Majesty at the Restoration. Died October 21, 1662. Buried in the Cloisters, Westminster Abbey. Composer of Church Music, Masques, Songs, &c.

JOHN BLOW, Mus.D., Cantuar. 1676 1708

Master of the Children, 1674. Organist, 1676. Composer, 1699. Blow was the first Composer to the Chapel Royal, on the creation of that office.

(See under Westminster Abbey.)

HENRY PURCELL 1682 1695

(See under Westminster Abbey.)

* "While he was at St. George's, the salaries of the officers were very much in arrears, and Child, not expecting ever to see his, which amounted to some £500, said to one of the Canons that he would be glad to take £5 and some bottles of wine for his arrears. The Canons accepted this offer, and had sealed articles drawn up confirming the bargain. When James II. came to the throne, the arrears in the official salaries were paid off; but Dr. Child had lost all claim, owing to his bargain. The Canons, however, released him, on condition of his promising to pave the Choir of the Chapel, which he accordingly did, and it is recorded on his tombstone."—("Dictionary of National Biography.")

† These lines were set as a Glee by Robert Hudson, Mus.B., Almoner of St. Paul's, 1773-1793.

FRANCIS PIGOTT, Mus.B., Cantab. 1697 1704
(See under Magdalen College, Oxford.)

WILLIAM CROFT, Mus.D., Oxon.... 1704 1727
Organist, 1704. Composer and Master of the Children, 1708.*
(See under Westminster Abbey.)

JEREMIAH CLARK 1704 1707
Joint Organist with Croft.
(See under St. Paul's.)

Joint Organists. Croft was appointed full Organist on Jeremiah Clark's death (1707).

JOHN WELDON 1708 1736
Organist, 1708. Composer, 1715. (A second Composer's appointment was created and Weldon was the first to hold it.)
Born at Chichester, January 19, 1676. Pupil of John Walter at Eton College, and of Henry Purcell. Organist of New College, Oxford, 1694. Gentleman Extraordinary of the Chapel Royal, 1701; Organist, ditto, 1708. Organist of St. Bride's, Fleet Street. Composer (in the second place) to the Chapel Royal, 1715. Organist of St. Martin's-in-the-Fields, 1726. Died May 7, 1736. Buried in the Churchyard of St. Paul's, Covent Garden. Composer of Church Music, Operas, Songs, Airs for two Flutes and a Bass, &c.

MAURICE GREENE, Mus.D., Cantab. 1727 1755
Organist and Composer.
(See under St. Paul's.)

JONATHAN MARTIN 1736 1737
Organist.
Born 1715. Chorister in the Chapel Royal. Pupil of Thomas Rosingrave. Sometime Deputy-Organist of St. George's, Hanover Square. Organist of the Chapel Royal, 1736. Died in London (of consumption), April 4, 1737. Buried in the Cloisters of Westminster Abbey.

JOHN TRAVERS 1737 1758
Organist.
Born about 1703. Chorister in St. George's Chapel, Windsor. Pupil of Dr. Greene and Dr. Pepusch. Organist of St. Paul's, Covent Garden, 1726, and afterwards of Fulham Parish Church. Organist of the Chapel Royal, 1737. Died 1758. Composer of Church Music, Songs, Organ pieces, &c.

JAMES NARES, Mus.D., Cantab. 1756 1783
Organist and Composer, 1756. Master of the Children, 1757-1780.
(See under York.)

WILLIAM BOYCE, Mus.D., Cantab., 1749 ... ... 1758 1779
Composer, 1736. Organist, 1758.
Born in London, 1710. Chorister in St. Paul's Cathedral. Pupil of Dr. Greene and Dr. Pepusch. Organist of Oxford Chapel, 1734; St. Michael's, Cornhill, 1736. Composer to the Chapel Royal, 1736. Organist of All Hallows' the Great and Less, Thames Street, 1749. Master of the Royal Band of Music, 1755. Organist of the Chapel Royal, 1758. Died at

* At a salary of £80 more per annum—"to teach them to read, write, and to cast accompts, and to play upon the organs, and to compose music."

Kensington, February 7, 1779. Buried in St. Paul's Cathedral. Composer of Church Music, Masques, Odes, Sonatas, Concertos, and other Instrumental Music, Songs, Duets, &c.

Compiler of Boyce's well-known Collection of Cathedral Music, which was commenced by Dr. Greene, but upon the failure of the latter's health the collected material was handed over by him to Dr. Boyce, with the request that he (Dr. Boyce) would complete it.

THOMAS SANDERS DUPUIS, Mus.D., Oxon., 1790 1779 1796

Organist and Composer.

Born, in London, of an old Huguenot family, November 5, 1733. Chorister in the Chapel Royal. Pupil of Gates and Travers. Organist of Charlotte Street Chapel, 1773. Organist and Composer to the Chapel Royal, 1779. Died, through an overdose of opium, at King's Row, Park Lane, London, July 17, 1796. Buried in the West Cloister, Westminster Abbey. Composer of Church Music, Organ pieces, Pianoforte pieces, Songs, &c.

SAMUEL ARNOLD, Mus.D., Oxon. 1783 1802

Organist and Composer.

(See under Westminster Abbey.)

CHARLES KNYVETT 1796 1822

Organist.

Born February 22, 1752. Gentleman of the Chapel Royal, 1786. Organised, with S. Harrison, the Vocal Concerts, 1791. Organist of the Chapel Royal, 1796. Died in London, January 19, 1822. Composer of Glees, Catches, Rounds, &c.

JOHN STAFFORD SMITH 1802 1836

Organist, 1802. Master of the Children, 1805-1817.

Son of Martin Smith, Organist of Gloucester Cathedral. Born at Gloucester, 1750. Pupil of his father, and afterwards of Dr. Boyce. Gentleman of the Chapel Royal, 1784. Organist at the Gloucester Festival of 1790. Lay Clerk of Westminster Abbey, 1794. Organist of the Chapel Royal, 1802; Master of the Children and "Lutenist," ditto, 1805 until 1817. Died September 21, 1836. Composer of Church Music, Glees, &c. Editor of "Musica Antiqua," Songs, &c.

Smith greatly assisted Hawkins in the compilation of his "History of Music," by lending him old and rare MSS., of which he possessed a large and interesting collection. His extensive and valuable Musical Library was sold by auction in 1844.

SIR GEORGE THOMAS SMART 1822 1867

Organist, 1822. Composer, 1838.

Born in London, May 10, 1776. Chorister in the Chapel Royal. Pupil of Dupuis and Ayrton. Organist of St. James's Chapel, Hampstead Road, 1791. Knighted at Dublin, 1811. Conductor of the Philharmonic Society, 1813-1844. Organist of the Chapel Royal, 1822; Composer to the same, 1838. Conductor of the principal Musical Festivals of the time. Died at 12, Bedford Square, London, February 23, 1867. Buried in the catacombs, Kensal Green Cemetery. Composer of Church Music, Glees, Sonatinas for the Pianoforte. Editor of a Collection of Madrigals, &c.

THOMAS ATTWOOD 1836 1838

Composer, 1796. Organist, 1836.

(See under St. Paul's.)

JOHN BERNARD SALE 1838 1856

Organist.

Born at Windsor, 1779. Chorister in St. George's Chapel, Windsor, and in Eton College. Lay Vicar of Westminster Abbey, 1800. Gentleman of the Chapel Royal, 1803. Organist of St. Margaret's, Westminster, 1809. Instructor in Music to H.M. the Queen. Organist of the Chapel Royal, 1838. Died in London, September 16, 1856. Editor of "Psalms and Hymns for the Service of the Church," Glees, Songs, &c.

GEORGE COOPER (Junr.) 1867 1876

Organist.

Son of George Cooper (Senr.), Assistant Organist of St. Paul's and Organist of St. Sepulchre's, Holborn. Born in London, July 7, 1820. Organist of St. Benet's, Paul's Wharf, 1833; St. Anne and St. Agnes', 1836; St. Sepulchre's, Holborn, 1843; Christ's Hospital, 1845; Chapel Royal, 1867. Assistant Organist for a time at St. Paul's Cathedral. Died in London, October 2, 1876. Buried in Kensal Green Cemetery. Composer of Part-songs, Songs, Psalm Tunes, Chants, &c. Compiler of "The Organist's Assistant" and "The Organist's Manual."

CHARLES SHERWOOD JEKYLL 1876 1891

Organist and Composer.

Born at Westminster, November 29, 1842. Chorister in Westminster Abbey. Pupil of James Coward and Sir G. A. Macfarren. Organist of St. Paul's, Kensington, 1857; Assistant Organist of Westminster Abbey, 1860-1875; Organist of Acton Parish Church, 1860; St. George's, Hanover Square, 1861; Organist and Composer to the Chapel Royal, 1876. Retired 1891. Composer of Church Music, Part-songs, Songs, Organ pieces, Pianoforte pieces, &c.

WILLIAM CRESER, Mus.D., Oxon., 1880; F.R.C.O. 1891 ——

Organist and Composer.

Born at York, 1844. Chorister in York Cathedral. Pupil of Sir G. A. Macfarren. Organist successively of Holy Trinity, Micklegate, York; St. Paul's, York; St. Andrew's, Grinton; St. Martin's, Scarborough, 1875; Leeds Parish Church, 1881. Organist and Composer to the Chapel Royal, 1891. Conductor of the Western Madrigal Society, 1896. Composer of an Oratorio, "Micaiah," an Operetta, "Naxine," Cantatas, Church Music, Orchestral Music, Organ pieces, Chamber Music, &c.

LONDON—TEMPLE CHURCH.

Cathedral Service was first established here on the Restoration of the Church and removal of the organ from the West Gallery to its present position, in 1842. For the sake of completeness, however, a record is given of the Organists from 1688, when Father Smith's organ was finally accepted by the Benchers.* This record is based upon a list of the Organists given in Mr. Edmund Macrory's interesting little book, entitled "A Few Notes on the Temple Organ," where may also be found a long Agreement between the Hon. Societies of the Inner and Middle Temple and the first mentioned Organist, Francis Pigott.

FRANCIS PIGOTT, Mus.B., Cantab. 1688 1704
(See under Magdalen College, Oxford.)

J. PIGOTT ... ... 1704 ——
Son of the preceding.
According to Hawkins' History of Music he came into a large fortune upon the death of a relative—Dr. John Pelling, Rector of St. Anne, Westminster (Soho)—and either retired or performed his duties by deputy. Died 1726.

CHARLES JOHN STANLEY, Mus.B., Oxon., 1729 ... 1734 1786
The famous blind Organist.
Born in London, January 17, 1713. Became blind from an accident when about two years old. Pupil of John Reading and Dr. Greene. Organist of All Hallows', Bread Street, 1724; St. Andrew's, Holborn, 1726; and Temple Church, 1734. Succeeded Dr. Boyce as Master of the Royal Band of Music, 1779. Died in London, May 19, 1786. Composer of three Oratorios, Cantatas, Songs, Concertos, &c., for Strings, Organ Voluntaries, Concertos for Harpsichord or Organ, &c.

JAMES VINCENT† 1737 1749
Died 1749.

JOHN JONES† 1749 1796
(See under St. Paul's.)

RICHARD JOHN SAMUEL STEVENS ... ... 1786 (?)1837
(The well known Glee Composer).
Born in London, March 27, 1757. Chorister in St. Paul's Cathedral. Organist of the Temple Church, 1786; Charterhouse, 1796. Gresham Professor of Music, 1801. Died at Peckham, September 23, 1837. Composer of Glees, Songs, &c. Compiler of a selection of Sacred Music.

MISS EMILY DOWDING 1796 1814

GEORGE PRICE 1814 1826
Died 1826.

* The circumstances of the competition between the two organ builders, "Father Smith" and Renatus Harris, for supplying the Temple Organ at this period, are too well known to need a description here.
† Colleagues of John Stanley.

George Warne 1826 1843

Born 1792. He was blind. Retired from the post, 1843. Died at Bath, October 29, 1868. Composer of a "Set of Psalm Tunes, as sung at the Temple Church, London" (1838), several Songs, and Piano pieces.

Edward John Hopkins, Mus.D., Cantuar., 1882; F.R.C.O. 1843 1898

Brother of John Hopkins, of Rochester Cathedral, and cousin of Dr. J. L. Hopkins, of Rochester and Trinity College, Cambridge. Born at Westminster, June 30, 1818. Chorister in the Chapel Royal. Pupil of Thomas Forbes Walmisley (the father of Dr. T. A. Walmisley). Organist of Mitcham Parish Church, 1834; St. Peter's, Islington, 1838; St. Luke's, Berwick Street, 1841; Temple Church, 1843. Retired from the latter post, 1898. One of the Founders of the (Royal) College of Organists. Granted the honorary degree of Mus.D. by the Archbishop of Canterbury, 1882. A testimonial was presented to him on attaining his Jubilee as an Organist in 1884, and also on his completion of fifty years office as Organist to the Temple Church in 1893. He has been for many years Professor of the Organ at the Royal Normal College for the Blind, Norwood. Composer of Church Music, Organ pieces, Madrigals, Songs, Part-songs, &c. Arranger of Organ Music. Editor of Madrigals, Organ pieces, Hymnals, Chant Books, &c. Joint Author, with Dr. E. F. Rimbault, of "The Organ: its History and Construction"; and Author of a similar work to be issued by Messrs. Novello. Lecturer on various musical subjects.

Henry Walford Davies, Mus.D., Cantab., 1898 1898 ——

Born at Oswestry, September 6, 1869. Chorister in St. George's Chapel, Windsor. Pupil of Sir Walter Parratt. Student of the Royal College of Music. Assistant Organist of St. George's Chapel, Windsor; also Organist of Park Chapel, Windsor. Organist of St. Anne's, Soho, 1890; Christ Church, Hampstead, 1891; Temple Church, 1898. Associate and Professor of the Royal College of Music. Composer of Cantatas, Church Music, Orchestral and Chamber Music, Songs, &c.

LONDON—WESTMINSTER ABBEY.

John Howe ... ... 1549 ——

"Probably a monk, and the person called 'Father Howe,' whose name occurs in the old parish accounts of Lambeth, St. Mary-at-Hill, St. Helen's, &c., as 'mendyng,' and otherwise attending to the 'orgayns.'"—(Dr. E. F. Rimbault, in *Notes and Queries*, Sept. 8, 1866.)

Master Whitt (or White?) ... ... 1560 ——

John Taylor ... ... 1562 ——

Robert White, B.A., Mus.B., Cantab. ... 1570 ——

(See under Ely.)

Henry Leeve ... ... 1575 ——

EDMUND HOOPER ... { Master of the Choristers 1588 / Organist ... ... 1606 } 1621

Supposed to be the first regular appointment of Organist at the Abbey.

Born at North Halberton, Devon, and said to have been a Chorister in Exeter Cathedral. Died July 14, 1621. Buried in the Abbey Cloisters. Also Gentleman and Organist of the Chapel Royal. Composer of Church Music.

His Patent (for life) from the Dean and Chapter as Organist of Westminster Abbey bears the date May 9, 1606, one having previously been taken out by him as Master of the Choristers on December 3, 1588.

According to the Abbey records he was occasionally employed in "mending the organs" and "pricking new song-books."

JOHN PARSONS 1621 1623

His salary was £16 per annum as Organist and £36 13s. 4d. for "teaching and finding the children." Died July, 1623. Buried in the Abbey Cloisters. A Burial Service by him is included in Ed. Lowe's "Review" of his "Short Directions for the performance of the Cathedral Service."

Camden's "Remaines concerning Britain" (1657) contains the following epitaph upon Parsons* :—

"Death passing by and hearing Parsons play
Stood much amazèd at his depth of skill,
And said, 'This artist must with me away,'
For death bereaves us of the better still;
But let the quire, while he keeps time, sing on,
For Parsons rests, his service being done."

ORLANDO GIBBONS, Mus.B., Cantab.; Mus.D., Oxon. 1623 1625

(See under Chapel Royal.)

THOMAS DAY 1625 1632

In 1612 he was one of the musicians to Prince Henry, and when Charles I. came to the throne he served him in a similar capacity. Master of the Children of the Chapel Royal, 1637. Died about 1654.

RICHARD PORTMAN 1633 1642

Pupil of Orlando Gibbons, and succeeded Thomas Day as Organist. He is said to have lived some time in France with the then Dean of Westminster, The Very Rev. Dr. Williams, who was a patron of music and musicians. Composer of Church Music. One of the composers of Services in Clifford's Collection.

THOMAS WARWICK 1642 1644

(See under Chapel Royal.)

CHRISTOPHER GIBBONS, Mus.D., Oxon. { Per Literas Regias, 1664 } 1660 1665

Son of Orlando Gibbons. Born 1615. Chorister in the Chapel Royal. Pupil of his uncle, Edward Gibbons, at Exeter. Organist of Winchester Cathedral until about 1644, when he joined the Royalist Army. At the Restoration he became Organist of Westminster Abbey and the Chapel

* Hawkins assigns this epitaph to *Robert* Parsons, but it more probably refers to *John*.

Royal. Died October 20, 1676. Buried in the Abbey Cloisters. Composer of Church Music, an Act Song (performed for his Degree), Music to a Masque, &c.

According to Wood, he was "a grand debauchee. He would often sleep at Morning Prayer when he was to play the organ."

It is said that he carried the £1,000 lent to the King by his uncle Edward. (See under Bristol.)

The Royal Letter to the University of Oxford, directing them to confer the degree of Doctor of Music on Christopher Gibbons, is as follows:—

"Whereas the bearer, Christopher Gibbons, one of the Organists of our Royal Chapel, hath from his youth, served our royal Father and ourselves, and hath so well improved himself in musick as well in our judgement as the judgement of all men well skilled in the science, as that he may worthily receive the honor and degree of Doctor therein. We in consideration of his merit and fitness thereunto, have thought fit by these our Letters to recommend him unto you, and to signify our gracious pleasure to you that he be forthwith admitted and created Doctor in Music."

Albertus Bryan (Brian or Bryne) 1666 1669

(See under St. Paul's.)

John Blow, Mus.D., Cantuar (circa 1675) 1669 1680

Born in Westminster, 1648. Chorister in the Chapel Royal. Pupil of Hingston (Organist to Oliver Cromwell) and Dr. Christopher Gibbons. Organist of Westminster Abbey, 1669. Gentleman of the Chapel Royal, 1673. Master of the Children of the Chapel Royal, 1674. Organist of the Chapel Royal, 1676. Resigned the organistship of Westminster Abbey in favour of his pupil, Henry Purcell, 1680. Member of the Royal Band of James II., 1685. Almoner and Master of the Choristers of St. Paul's Cathedral, 1687-1693. Re-appointed Organist of Westminster Abbey on the death of Purcell, 1695. (See below.) Composer of the Chapel Royal (the first appointed to that office), 1699. Died October 1, 1708. Buried in North Aisle of the Choir of the Abbey, where a tablet is erected to his memory. On his tombstone is engraved an open book, showing the "Gloria Patri" from his Service in Gamut. Composer of Church Music (much of which unfortunately has never been published), an "Ode for St. Cecilia's Day," an "Elegy on Queen Mary," Lessons for the Harpsichord, &c.

When the late Emperor of Brazil visited Westminster Abbey some years ago, the first thing he asked Dean Stanley to show him was Dr. Blow's monument.

In the epistle dedicatory to his "Amphion Anglicus" (a collection of songs) to the Princess Ann of Denmark, the author (Blow) informs her Royal Highness that he was preparing to publish his Church Services and Divine Compositions. It seems, however, that he did not live to carry out this design. From some verses prefixed to this Collection, it appears that a Canon composed by Blow had been much admired at Rome:—

"His *Gloria Patri* long ago reach'd Rome;
Sung and rever'd too in S. Peter's dome;
A Canon will outlive her jubilees to come."

This is the Canon in his Service in Gamut already referred to. That it should be sung at Rome may seem strange, yet it is true; as some compositions of Blow and Purcell had been sent to Cardinal Howard, at his particular request, from Dr. Ralph Battell, Sub-dean of the Chapel Royal. The Canon also was printed separately in the editions of Playford's "Introduction" subsequent to the year 1700.

HENRY PURCELL 1680 1695

Son of Henry Purcell, a Gentleman of the Chapel Royal. Chorister in the Chapel Royal. Pupil of his predecessor at Westminster Abbey, Dr. Blow, who retired from the post in his favour. Previously held the appointment of Copyist to the Abbey (1676-1678). Organist of the Chapel Royal, 1682. Appointed one of the Composers to the King, 1683. Appointed with Dr. Blow to play on Father Smith's organ at the Temple Church, during the latter's competition with Harris for supplying an organ there, 1684. Again Copyist to the Abbey, 1688. In 1689, engaged in a dispute with the Dean and Chapter of Westminster concerning certain monies that he had received for admission to the organ loft of spectators of the Coronation of William and Mary, and which he considered as a perquisite arising from his office as Organist. Died November 21, 1695. Buried in the North Aisle of the Choir of the Abbey. Composer of Church Music, a large number of Operas and other Dramatic pieces, Odes, Sonatas for Strings, Lessons for the Harpsichord, Songs, &c.

The following is the inscription on Purcell's gravestone:—

"Plaudite, felices superi, tanto hospite; nostris
Præfuerat, vestris additur ille choris:
Invida nec vobis Purcellum terra reposcat,
Questa decus sedi deliciasque breves.
Tam cito decessisse, modos cui singula debet
Musa, prophana suos, religiosa suos,
Vivit, Io et vivat, dum vicina organa spirant,
Dumque colet numeris turba canora Deum."

Translated thus:—

"Applaud so great a guest, celestial pow'rs,
Who now resides with you, but once was ours;
Yet let invidious earth no more reclaim
Her short-lived fav'rite and her chiefest fame;
Complaining that so prematurely died
Good-nature's pleasure and devotion's pride.
Died? No, he lives, while yonder organs sound
And sacred echoes to the choir rebound."

On a pillar near to the grave is a tablet with this inscription:—

"Here lyes | HENRY PURCELL, Esq. | Who left this Life | And is gone to that Blessed Place | Where only his Harmony | can be exceeded. Obijt 21 mo die Novembris | Anno Ætatis suæ 37mo. | Annoq. Domini 1695."

The following are the concluding lines of an Ode, written by Henry Hall (Senr.), a fellow pupil of Purcell under Dr. Blow, and afterwards Organist successively of Exeter and Hereford Cathedrals, "To the memory of my Dear Friend, Mr. Henry Purcell":—

"Hail! And for ever hail, Harmonious shade,
I lov'd thee living, and admire thee Dead.
Apollo's harp at once our souls did strike;
We learnt together, but not learnt alike:
Though equal care our Master might bestow,
Yet only Purcell e're shall equal Blow:
For thou by Heaven for wondrous things design'd
Left'st thy companion lagging far behind.
Sometimes a Hero in an age appears,
But once a Purcell in a Thousand Years."—

See "Purcell" ("The Great Musicians" Series), by W. H. Cummings.

JOHN BLOW, Mus.D., Cantuar. (Re-appointed) ... 1695 1708

(See above.)

WILLIAM CROFT, MUS.D., OXON., 1713 ... ... 1708 1727

Born at Nether Eatington, 1677. Chorister in the Chapel Royal and pupil of Dr. Blow. Organist of St. Anne's, Westminster (Soho), 1700-1711. Joint Organist of the Chapel Royal with Jeremiah Clark, 1704. Sole Organist (on the death of Clark), 1707. Master of the Chapel Royal Children and Composer to the Chapel Royal (in succession to Blow), 1708. Tuner of the Regals, 1716. Died at Bath, August 14, 1727. Buried in the North Aisle of the Choir of Westminster Abbey. Composer of Church Music, Songs, Sonatas, Instrumental Act Music, &c.

His monument bears a Latin inscription, of which the following is a translation, taken from Dr. W. A. Barrett's "English Church Composers":—

"Near to this place lies interred William Croft, Doctor in Music, Organist of the Royal Chapel and of this Collegiate Church. His harmony he derived from that excellent artist in modulation, who lies on the other side of him.* In his celebrated works, which for the most part he consecrated to God, he made a diligent progress; nor was it by the solemnity of the numbers alone, but by the force of his ingenuity and the sweetness of his manners, and even his countenance, that he excellently recommended them. Having resided among mortals for fifty years, behaving with the utmost candour (not more conspicuous for any other office of humanity than a friendship and love truly paternal to all whom he had instructed), he departed to the heavenly choir on the fourteenth day of August, 1727, that, being near, he might add his own Hallelujah to the Concert of Angels. 'Awake up my glory, awake lute and harp, I myself will awake right early!'"

JOHN ROBINSON 1727 1762

Born 1682. Chorister in the Chapel Royal, and pupil of Blow. Organist of St. Lawrence, Jewry, 1710; St. Magnus, London Bridge, 1713, retaining both these appointments until his death. Deputy-Organist at Westminster Abbey for some years before succeeding Dr. Croft in the full office. Died April 30, 1762. Buried in the North Aisle of the Choir of the Abbey, in the same grave as Dr. Croft. His Double Chant in E flat, said to have been the favourite of George III., is still very popular.

Boyce, in the biographical notes to his "Cathedral Music," describes Robinson as "a most excellent performer on the organ."

From the following memorandum, in a MS. book at the Abbey, it appears that during Robinson's time the organ was removed from its ancient position in the North Choir Aisle to the Screen:—

"The new organ built by Mr. Shrider and Mr. Jordan was opened on the 1st August, 1730, by Mr. Robinson; the anthem, Purcell's 'O give thanks.'"

BENJAMIN COOKE, MUS.D., {Cantab., 1775 / et Oxon., 1782} ... 1762 1793

Son of Benjamin Cooke, a musicseller in New Street, Covent Garden. Born in London, 1734. Pupil of Dr. Pepusch. Appointed Deputy-Organist to Robinson at Westminster Abbey at the age of twelve. Conductor of Academy of Ancient Music, 1752. Lay Vicar of Westminster Abbey, 1758; Master of the Choristers, 1759; Organist, 1762. Organist of St. Martin-in-the-Fields, 1782. Died at Dorset Court, Cannon Row, Westminster, September 14, 1793. Buried in the West Cloister. Composer of Church Music, Glees, &c.

His Evening Service in G was composed for the re-opening of the Abbey Organ after the addition of the Pedal Organ (by Avery). There is a tablet to his memory on the wall of the West Cloister of the Abbey, on which is engraved his fine Canon, three in one by augmentation, which he intended to be sung as an appendix to Bird's "Non nobis."

* Dr. Blow.

SAMUEL ARNOLD, Mus.D., Oxon. 1773 ... ... 1793* 1802

Born in London, August 10, 1740. Chorister in the Chapel Royal. Composer to Covent Garden Theatre, 1773, afterwards Proprietor of Marylebone Gardens and Director of the music there. Organist and Composer of the Chapel Royal, 1783. Conductor of the Academy of Ancient Music, 1789. Organist (not Master of the Choristers) of Westminster Abbey, 1793.* Died October 22, 1802. Buried in the North Aisle of the Choir of the Abbey. Composer of Church Music, Oratorios, Operas, Burlettas, &c. Editor of the "Arnold Edition" of Handel's works; also of "Cathedral Music" in continuation of Boyce.

MURAL TABLET TO DR. ARNOLD.

To the beloved and respected Memory of SAMUEL ARNOLD, Doctor of Music. Born July 30, O.S., 1740. Died Oct. 22, 1802. Aged 62 years and two months. And is interred near this spot. This tablet is erected by his affectionate widow.

Here lies of genius, probity, and worth
All that belongs to nature and to earth.
The hand that freely felt and warmly gave
The heart that pity stretched to help and save
The form that late a glowing spirit warmed
Whose spirit fled to Him, Who spirit gave,
Now smiles triumphant o'er the feeble grave
That could not chain it here, and joins to raise
With Heaven's own choir the song of prayer and praise.

Oh Shade revered! Our nation's loss and pride
(For mute was harmony when ARNOLD died).
"Oh let thy 'still-loved son' inscribe thy stone
"And with a 'mother's sorrow' mix his own."

[These lines are by Arnold's son, S. J. Arnold (d. 1852), the dramatic author and some time lessee of the English Opera House, now the Lyceum.]

ROBERT COOKE 1802 1814

Son of Dr. B. Cooke. Born 1768. Organist of St. Martin-in-the-Fields (in succession to his father), 1793. Organist of Westminster Abbey, 1802. Master of the Choristers, 1806. Committed suicide, owing to a love affair, by drowning himself in the Thames, August 22, 1814. Buried in the same grave as his father in the West Cloister. Composer of Church Music.

GEORGE EBENEZER WILLIAMS 1814 1819

Born 1783. Chorister in St. Paul's Cathedral. For some time Assistant Organist at the Temple and (to Dr. Arnold) at Westminster Abbey. Organist of the Philanthropic Chapel, St. George's Road, 1805. Died April 17, 1819. Buried in the South Cloister. Composer of Chants, Sanctuses, &c. Author of "An Introduction to the Art of Playing on the Pianoforte," "Exercises for the Pianoforte," &c.

THOMAS GREATOREX 1819 1831

(See under Carlisle.)

JAMES TURLE 1831 1882

Born at Taunton, March 5, 1802. Chorister in Wells Cathedral. Pupil of J. J. Goss and G. E. Williams. Appointed Deputy-Organist at Westminster

* The year of his appointment is wrongly given as 1789 on his tombstone in the Abbey.

Abbey, 1819. Organist of Christ Church, Southwark, 1819; St. James's, Bermondsey, 1829. Music Master to the School for the Indigent Blind, 1829. Succeeded Greatorex as Organist of Westminster Abbey, 1831. Retired from active duties of the post, 1875. Died in London, June 28, 1882. Buried in Norwood Cemetery. Composer of Church Music, Glees, &c. Joint Author, with E. Taylor, of "The Art of Singing at Sight." Editor of Willbye's First Set of Madrigals; Single and Double Chants, composed for the use of the Choral Service of Westminster Abbey. Joint Editor, with Dr. J. F. (now Sir Frederick) Bridge, of the Westminster Abbey Chant Book, &c. Compiler of Hymn and Chant Books, &c.

On the day of Turle's retirement, September 19, 1875, his Service in D was sung at Westminster Abbey.

There is a memorial tablet to him in the West Cloister, and a window in the North Aisle of the Choir.

Sir Frederick Bridge, Knt., Mus.D., Oxon., 1874; F.R.C.O. ... ... 1882 ——

Born at Oldbury, Worcestershire, December 5, 1844. Chorister in Rochester Cathedral. Pupil of John Hopkins, Sir J. Goss, and Sir George Elvey. Organist of Shorne Church, 1861; Parish Church, Strood, 1862; Holy Trinity, Windsor, 1865; Manchester Cathedral, 1869; Lecturer on Musical Composition, Owens College, Manchester, 1872. Appointed Permanent Deputy-Organist, Westminster Abbey, 1875, succeeding Turle in the full office, 1882. Conductor for some years of the Highbury Philharmonic and Western Madrigal Societies. Director of the Music at the Royal Jubilee Thanksgiving Service in Westminster Abbey, June 21, 1887. Appointed Gresham Professor of Music, 1890. Conductor of the Purcell Commemoration Festival in Westminster Abbey, November 21, 1895. Conductor of Royal Choral Society, 1896. Knighted in 1897. Professor of Counterpoint and Composition at the Royal College of Music. Lecturer. Composer of Oratorios, Cantatas, Church Music, Organ Music, Madrigals, Part-songs, Songs, &c. Author of works on Counterpoint, Double Counterpoint and Canon, Organ Accompaniment, Musical Gestures, &c. Editor of various works.

The present Assistant Organist is Walter Galpin Alcock, Mus.B., Dunelm., F.R.C.O., appointed in 1889.

OXFORD—MAGDALEN COLLEGE.

(For Christ Church College, Oxford, *see* under Cathedrals, p. 65.)

In Bloxam's "Registers of Magdalen College" will be found a complete list of the Instructors of the Choristers and Organists of the College from the year 1483. It should be remembered, however, that at this early period the office of Organist was not the department of a single individual, but of several of the musical staff of the College Chapel in turn.

Robert Perrot ... ... 1530 ——

Instructor of the Choristers and Organist.

A descendant of an ancient Pembrokeshire family. Born at Hackness, Yorks. Was Instructor of the Choristers, 1510-1535. According to Wood's "Fasti" he supplicated in 1615 for the degree of Mus.B., and the request was to be granted on the condition that he composed a Mass and one Song.

Whether he actually obtained the degree is not recorded. At one time he was Principal of Trinity Hall, and in 1534 Receiver-General of the Archdeaconry of Buckingham. He died in 1550 and was buried in St. Peter's Church.*

JOHN SHEPPARD, (?) Mus.B., Oxon.† ... ... 1542 ——

Instructor of the Choristers and probably also Organist. Fellow, 1549-1551. Chorister in St. Paul's Cathedral under Thomas Mulliner. He appears to have supplicated, as a "student of music for the space of twenty years," for the degree of Mus.D., but it is not known whether he was admitted. Admonished three times by his College for offences "contra formam statuti." One of these was entrapping and carrying away a chorister without the King's license for so doing. His music, some of which is preserved in MS., is mentioned by Hawkins, Burney, and Morley ("Introduction"). The words of some of his Anthems appeared in Clifford's Collection. An Anthem by him, "I give you a new Commandment," was printed in "The Parish Choir" (1848).

RICHARD NICHOLSON, Mus.B., Oxon., 1595-6 ... 1595 1639

Instructor of the Choristers, and probably also Organist. Afterwards became the first University Professor of Music (or rather *Choragus*) under the endowment of Dr. William Heather. Died 1639. Composer of Madrigals, &c. Contributor to "The Triumphs of Oriana." Died 1639. In 1637 Nicholson appears to have had an assistant named Courteis or Curtis.

ARTHUR PHILLIPS, Mus.B., Oxon. ... ... 1639 ——

(See under Bristol.)

THEODORE COLEBY (or COLBY) 1661 1664

(See under Exeter.)

BENJAMIN ROGERS, Mus.B., Cantab., 1658; Mus.D., Oxon., 1669 ... ... 1664 1685-6

"Informator Choristarum" and Organist.

Born at Windsor, 1614. Chorister in St. George's Chapel, Windsor, and afterwards Lay Clerk there. Organist of Christ Church Cathedral, Dublin, 1639. Returned to England owing to the Rebellion and was again Lay Clerk of Windsor until 1644, when the Choir was disbanded. After the Restoration he became Organist of Eton College and, for the third time, Lay Clerk of Windsor, also Assistant Organist there to Dr. Child. Organist and "Informator Choristarum" of Magdalen College, Oxford, 1664, at a salary of £60 per annum and rooms in the College.‡ Was dismissed by the College, 1685-6, but was allowed a pension of £30, and lived in comparative obscurity at Oxford until his death in June, 1698. Buried at St. Peter-le-Bailey, Oxford. Composer of much

* For further information concerning Perrot, see Bloxam's *Magdalen Registers*.

† According to Grove's "Dictionary of Music and Musicians."

‡ There was considerable opposition to this at first, in consequence of the salary being larger than had been given to any previous organist at the College. But it was explained that it "was little enough for a man of that quality, and at a time when organists were scarce. Nor had any man there to object against it."—(See Bloxam.)

Church Music, Glees, and the Hymn "Te Deum Patrem colimus," which is sung annually on May 1st at early morning on the Magdalen Tower. Some of his Anthems are in MS. at Magdalen and New Colleges.*

One cause of his dismissal was "his troublesome behaviour in the Chapel, where usually he would talk so loud in the organ loft, that he offended the company, and would not leave it off, though he hath been sent to by the President not to make such a scandalous noise there. There were frequent complaints of him from the Clerks, to whom, especially the Chanter, he used to be very cross, in not playing Services as they were willing and able to sing, but out of a thwarting humour would play nothing but Canterbury Tune, wherein he minded not the honour of the College, but his own ease and laziness."—(See Bloxam.)

FRANCIS PIGOTT, Mus.B., Cantab., 1698 ... ... 1685-6 1687

According to Dr. Clerk's MS. (see Bloxam) he appears to have been previously Organist of St. John's College, and to have "offered his service in Dr. Rogers's place for £40 per annum, and the reversion of £20 more after the decease of Dr. Rogers." Organist of the Temple Church, London, 1688. Gentleman of the Chapel Royal, 1695. Organist of the Chapel Royal, 1697. Died 1704. Composer of Church Music, Airs for the Harpsichord, &c.

DANIEL PURCELL 1688 1695

Brother of the great Henry Purcell (Organist of Westminster Abbey). Born in London about 1660. Nothing is known of his early career. Organist of Magdalen College, Oxford, 1688. Resigned this post, and went to London, 1695. Organist of St. Andrew's, Holborn, 1713. Died 1717. Composer of Church Music, Operas, Masques, Odes, Songs, Sonatas, "A Lamentation for the Death of Mr. Henry Purcell," &c.

Burney says: "He was a wicked punster, and no less wicked composer." His right to the second title is doubtful, but that to the first is recorded in "Joe Miller," from which the following is a specimen of his "wonderful replies":—

"Dr. Sewel and two or three more gentlemen, walking towards Hampstead on a summer's day, were met by the famous Daniel Purcell, the punster, who was very importunate with them to know upon what account they were going thither. The Doctor merrily answered him 'To make hay,' 'Very well,' replied the other, 'you'll be there at a very convenient season, the country wants *rakes*.'"—(See Bloxam.)

THOMAS HECHT 1695 1734

Son of Andrew Hecht, Organist of Lincoln Cathedral. Was admitted Organist of Lincoln in succession to his father, but declined office. Appointed Organist of Magdalen College, Oxford, 1695. Matriculated 1714. Died April 5, 1734. Buried in St. Ebbe's Churchyard.

He left £120 towards the enlargement of the College organ. According to his will he was cousin to Edward Thom(p)son, Organist of Salisbury Cathedral.

MATTHEW PHILLIPS was Organist for about three months during the vacancy. Doubtless he was the Matthew Phillips to whom Hecht bequeathed one of his spinets.—(See his Will in Bloxam.)

---

* Mr. J. S. Bumpus has in his possession a volume containing the whole of Dr. Benjamin Rogers's compositions for the Church, scored in the autograph of Dr. Phil. Hayes and transcribed from the books of Magdalen and New Colleges.

WILLIAM HAYES, Mus.D., Oxon.... ... ... 1734 1777

(See under Worcester.)

PHILIP HAYES, Mus.D., Oxon., 1777 ... ... 1777 ——

Son of the foregoing. Born at Shrewsbury, 1738. Chorister in the Chapel Royal. Pupil of his father. (Is said to have been Organist of Christ Church Cathedral, Oxford, 1763-1765, and to have been displaced by Thomas Norris.) Gentleman of the Chapel Royal, 1767. Organist of New College, 1776. Organist of Magdalen College, and University Professor of Music, 1777. Organist of St. John's College, Oxford, 1790. Died suddenly, in London, March 19, 1797. Buried in St. Paul's Cathedral. Composer of an Oratorio, "Prophecy," Odes, a Masque, Church Music, Glees, Songs, Concertos for Organ or Harpsichord, &c. Author of "Memoirs of Prince William Henry, Duke of Gloucester."

Dr. Philip Hayes was extremely corpulent, and was supposed to be the largest man in England. His unusual bulk earned for him the name of "Phil. Chaise."* Being of a very conceited and overbearing disposition, he made himself unpopular to his brother musicians on more than one occasion.

"When the Grand Commemoration of Handel, which took place in May, 1784, was in contemplation, two very pompous gentlemen, Dr. Hayes of Oxford and Dr. Miller of Doncaster, came to Town to give their gratuitous assistance as conductors by beating time. After several meetings and some bickerings, it was at length agreed that Dr. Hayes should conduct the first act, and Dr. Miller the second. When the time of performance had arrived, and Mr. Cramer, the leader, had just tapt his bow, (the signal for being ready,) and looked round to catch the eyes of the performers, he saw to his astonishment a tall gigantic figure with an immense powdered toupée, full dressed, with a bag and sword, and a huge roll of parchment in his hand. 'Who is that gentleman?' said Mr. Cramer. 'Dr. Hayes,' was the reply. 'What is he going to do?' 'To beat time.' 'Be so kind,' said Mr. Cramer, 'to tell the gentleman, that when he has sat down I will begin.' The Doctor, who never anticipated such a *set down* as this, took his seat, and Mr. Cramer did begin."—(Parke's "Musical Memoirs," Vol. I., p. 39.)

WALTER VICARY, Mus.B., Oxon., 1805 ... ... 1797 1845

Born 1770. Chorister in the Chapel Royal. Assistant Organist to Dr. P. Hayes at Magdalen College; Organist, ditto, 1797. Lay Chaplain of New College, Oxford, 1812-1844. Lay Clerk of St. John's College, Oxford, 1816-1828. Organist to the University, 1830. Died at Oxford, January 5, 1845. Buried in Holywell Churchyard. Composer of Church Music, Songs, &c.

---

* At a time when the facilities of coach travelling were not very great, it was common to see upon the chimney piece of the public room of an inn, an announcement of "the want of a companion in a chaise." Dr. Philip Hayes, of Oxford (whose unwieldly person rendered his travelling in one of the "six insides" of the time a matter of considerable inconvenience), contemplating a journey to London, accepted the first companionship that offered at the Star; and, to avoid the toil of a walk from his house in Holywell, it was arranged that he should be taken up there. On the morning appointed, the enquirer for a companion jumped into the chaise—luggage all right—and, dashing up to the Doctor's door, he saw a figure little less than the great Daniel Lambert, supported by a servant on either side, slowly advancing from the wall. In amazement, he hastily lowered the front glass, roaring out, "Post-Boy—Hoy, is that the gentleman we are to take up?" "Ees, sir; that be Dr. Phil. Hayes." "Fill chaise, by ——," replied the traveller, "he shan't come in here; drive on, drive on," thus leaving the poor Doctor to get on his journey as well as he could.

BENJAMIN BLYTH, M.A., Oxon. 1845 1859

Son of Benjamin Blyth, Mus.D., Oxon. Born 1824. Chorister in Magdalen College. Matriculated at the College, 1841. Clerk, 1842-1845. Organist, 1845. "A.D. 1845, Jan. 26to. In locum Gualteri Vicary (Choristarum Informatoris atque Organistæ) suffectus est Benjaminus Blyth, hujus Collegii Clericus, et in arte musicâ peritissimus."—(See Bloxam.) Died at Whitchurch, Oxon., 1883. Composer of the Music to "Sicut Lilium," sung before the Vacation at Magdalen College School. His uncle, Mr. Blyth (of the firm Blyth and Sons, Organ Builders), is mentioned in the Registers as the tuner and repairer of the old College organ.

(SIR) JOHN STAINER, M.A. and Mus.D., Oxon.; D.C.L. and Mus.D., Dunelm.; F.R.C.O. ... 1859 1872

(See under London—St. Paul's Cathedral.)

(SIR) WALTER PARRATT, Mus.D., Oxon.; F.R.C.O. 1872 1882

(See under St. George's Chapel, Windsor.)

JOHN VARLEY ROBERTS, Mus.D., Oxon., 1876; F.R.C.O. ... ... 1882 ——

Born at Stanningley, near Leeds, September 25, 1841. Organist (when twelve years old) of St. John's, Farsley. Organist of St. Bartholomew's, Armley, 1862; Halifax Parish Church, 1868; Magdalen College, Oxford, 1882; St. Giles's, Oxford, 1885-1893. Conductor of the Oxford Choral and Philharmonic Society, 1885-1893. Founder and first Conductor of the University Glee and Madrigal Society. Lecturer in Harmony and Counterpoint for the University Professor of Music. One of the Examiners for University Musical Degrees. Composer of Church Music, Organ pieces, Songs, Part-songs, &c. Editor of the "Parish Church Chant Book," &c.

OXFORD—NEW COLLEGE.

WILLIAM MEREDITH ... ... —— 1637

Died January 5, 1637. On his tombstone in the Cloisters he is described as "Vir pius et facultate sua peritissimus." The following epitaph also upon him is from Wood's "Hist. et Antiq. Univ. Oxon.":—

"Here lyes one blowne out of breath,
Who liv'd a merry life, and dyed a merry death."

ROBERT PICKHAVER ... ... (?)1660 1664

(See under Winchester College.)

WILLIAM KING,* B.A., Oxon. 1664 1680

Son of George King (Organist of Winchester Cathedral). Clerk of Magdalen College, 1648-1652. Chaplain of Magdalen College, 1652-1654. Died November 17, 1680. Buried in New College Cloisters. Composer of a complete Service in B flat, containing a setting of the Litany still sung at Lichfield Cathedral. It was published by John Bishop, of Cheltenham, half-a-century ago. Composer also of Anthems, Songs, &c.

Inscription on his gravestone: "Hoc sub lapide obdormiscit quicquid mortale reliquum est Gulielmi King, istius Collegii nuperrime Organistæ, cujus in Musicâ singularis eminentia ipsum angelorum consortii participem fecit die mensis Nov. 17, 1680, ætat 57."

RICHARD GOODSON (Senr.), Mus.B., Oxon. ... 1682 1694

(See under Oxford—Christ Church Cathedral.)

JOHN WELDON 1694 1702

(See under Chapel Royal.)

SIMON CHILD ... ... —— ——

A MS. book of Anthems in score, by Weldon and others, in S. Child's autograph, formerly belonging to Archdeacon Heathcote (who was a Fellow of New College), is now in the possession of Mr. J. S. Bumpus. On the fly-leaf of this book are some notes by Archdeacon Heathcote relating to former Organists of the College, one of which says that Child was succeeded by Richard Church. On the same fly-leaf is scribbled in pencil, "Simon Child, Ejus Liber. 1716." This interesting book contains several *unpublished* Anthems by Weldon.

RICHARD CHURCH 1732 1776

(See under Oxford—Christ Church Cathedral.)

PHILIP HAYES, Mus.D., Oxon. 1776 1797

(See under Magdalen College.)

ISAAC PRING, Mus.B., Oxon., 1799 ... ... 1797 1799

Brother of Dr. Joseph Pring, of Bangor. Born at Kensington, 1777. Chorister in St. Paul's Cathedral. Pupil of Dr. Philip Hayes, and afterwards succeeded him as Organist. Died of consumption, at Oxford, October 18, 1799. Composer of Church Music.

WILLIAM WOODCOCK, Mus.B., Oxon., 1806 ... 1799 1825

Born at Canterbury, 1754. Chorister in Canterbury Cathedral. Assistant Organist of the Cathedral and St. John's College, Oxford, 1778-1784. Lay-Clerk of the Cathedral, and of Magdalen, New, and St. John's Colleges, resigning the two latter appointments on becoming Organist of New College. Died at Oxford, 1825. Composer of Church Music.

* "When appointed to preside over the *new* organ at New College, the salary of his office was raised to £50 per annum, and the following agreement was made with him by Dr. Woodward, the Warden, viz.: That he should play the organ upon Surplice Days and Litany Days only, unless he should be by some of the House desired at any other time."—(MS., Elvey.)

ALFRED BENNETT, Mus.B., Oxon., 1825 ... ... 1825 1830

Son of Thomas Bennett and brother of H. Bennett, of Chichester Cathedral. Born 1805. Pupil of his father. Organist of New College, Oxford, and of the University Church, 1825. Died September 12, 1830, from injuries sustained by a fall from the stage-coach "Aurora," whilst on his way to the Worcester Musical Festival. Buried in the Cloisters of New College. Composer of Church Music. Editor, with (Dr.) William Marshall, of a Collection of Chants. Author of "Instructions for the Spanish Guitar," "Vocalist's Guide," &c.

STEPHEN ELVEY, Mus.D., Oxon., 1838 ... ... 1830 1860

Brother of Sir George Elvey, Organist of Windsor. Born at Canterbury, June, 1805. Chorister in Canterbury Cathedral, and pupil of Skeats (Senr.). Organist of New College, 1830; University Church, 1845; St. John's College, 1846. University Choragus, 1848. Died at Oxford, October 6, 1860. Composer of Church Music. Editor of the work known as "Elvey's Psalter." His Evening Service, in continuation of Croft's Morning Service in A, is well known.

I am indebted to Mr. J. S. Bumpus for the following particulars concerning Dr. Stephen Elvey:—

Very early in life Dr. Stephen Elvey lost his right leg by an accidental shot, but with a wooden substitute he was enabled to manage the pedals. Notwithstanding this disadvantage, few performers could give greater effect to Handel's choruses in Wykeham's beautiful chapel.

His love for Handel's music was only exceeded by the way in which he interpreted that music to others. At the opening of the Crystal Palace, at Sydenham, in 1854, after listening to the "Hallelujah" Chorus, he turned to a friend, saying, with tears in his eyes: "What will this be like in Heaven?"

Mr. Bumpus has in his possession a Kyrie, Credo, and Sanctus in E flat, and Magnificat and Nunc dimittis in F, by Stephen Elvey (*all unpublished*). The Kyrie is adapted from Handel's Minuet in "Berenice."

GEORGE BENJAMIN ARNOLD, Mus.D., Oxon.; F.R.C.O. 1860 1865

(See under Winchester.)

JAMES TAYLOR, Mus.B., Oxon., 1873; Mus.D., Oxon., *honoris causâ*, 1894 ... ... 1865 ——

Born at Gloucester, 1833. Pupil of G. W. Morgan. Organist of St. Mary-le-Crypt, Gloucester, 1850. Organist of New College, Oxford, 1865. Composer of Church Music, Organ pieces, Pianoforte pieces, Songs, &c.

OXFORD—ST. JOHN'S COLLEGE.

Very little information can be obtained of the early Organists of St. John's College, owing to the fact that the College records were many years ago destroyed by damp.

JOHN FRITH, Mus.B., Oxon., 1626 ... ... —— ——

"He was required to compose a piece in seven parts for his degree."—("Degrees in Music," by C. F. Abdy Williams.)

A Service in G by him is included in an old MS. Organ book in the possession of Mr. J. S. Bumpus, who is of opinion that the book once belonged to St. John's College.

ROBERT LUGG (or LUGGE), Mus.B., Oxon., 1638 ... —— ——

His degree exercise was a Canticum in five parts, which was required to be sung in the music school.—(See "Degrees in Music.")

A Service in G and three Anthems by Robert Lugg are included in the Organ book above mentioned.

According to the "Oxoniensis Alumni" he "changed his religion for that of Rome, and went beyond the seas."

WILLIAM ELLIS, Mus.B., Oxon., 1639 ... ... —— (?)1646

(?)Re-appointed ... ... circa 1660 1674

Previously Organist of Eton College. On being deprived of his appointment at St. John's College, Oxford, during the Rebellion, he established weekly meetings for the practice of music at his house in Oxford, which were attended by some of the most notable musicians of the period. A detailed account of these gatherings may be found in Hearne's "Life of Anthony Wood," or in Hawkins's "History of Music."

At the Restoration it is supposed that Ellis was re-appointed Organist of St. John's College. Died 1674. Some Rounds and Canons by him are included in Hilton's Collection, "Catch who catch can" (1652).

The MS. Organ book above mentioned contains three Anthems by William Ellis. Two of these, "Almighty God" and "This is the record of John," were evidently composed for the Feast of the patron Saint of the College—St. John the Baptist's Day.

FRANCIS PIGOTT, Mus.B., Cantab. ... ... —— ——

(See under Magdalen College, Oxford.)

Nothing is known of the Organists of St. John's College during this period. Probably the Choral Service was suspended.

THOMAS NORRIS, Mus.B., Oxon.... ... ... 1765 1790

(See under Oxford [Christ Church] Cathedral.)

PHILIP HAYES, Mus.D., Oxon. 1790 1797

(See under Magdalen College, Oxford.)

WILLIAM CROTCH, Mus.D., Oxon. 1797 1807

(See under Oxford [Christ Church] Cathedral.)

WILLIAM CROSS 1807 1825

(See under Oxford [Christ Church] Cathedral.)

WILLIAM MARSHALL, Mus.D., Oxon. 1825 1846
(See under Oxford [Christ Church] Cathedral.)

STEPHEN ELVEY, Mus.D., Oxon.... ... ... 1846 1860
(See under New College, Oxford.)

THOMAS GRIZZELLE 1860 1868

ROBERT PORTER 1868 1875
Born 1839. Organist of St. Paul's, Oxford, at the age of 14. Afterwards Assistant Organist to Dr. S. Elvey. Succeeded his father as Organist of St. Martin's ("Carfax"), 1857. Organist of St. John's College, 1868. Was also Assistant Organist of New College. Died of consumption, January, 1875. Buried on January 13 in Holywell Cemetery.

WILLIAM THOMAS HOWELL ALLCHIN, Mus.B., Oxon., 1869 ... . 1875 1883
Born 1843. Conductor of the Oxford Choral Society, 1869. Organist of St. John's College, Oxford, 1875. Local Examiner for R.A.M., 1881. Died at Oxford, January 8, 1883. Composer of a Sacred Cantata, "The Rebellion of Korah," Songs, &c.

FREDERICK ILIFFE, M.A., Mus.D., Oxon., 1879 ... 1883 ——
Born at Smeeton-Westerby, Leicestershire, February 21, 1847. Organist successively of St. Wilfred's, Kibworth, and St. Barnabas', Oxford. Organist of St. John's College, Oxford, 1883. Conductor of the Queen's College (Eglesfield) Musical Society, 1883. Composer of an Oratorio, "The Visions of St. John the Divine," Cantatas, Church Music, Orchestral Music, Organ pieces, Pianoforte pieces, &c. Author of a critical analysis of Bach's "Das Wohltemperirte Clavier" (Novello & Co., 1896).

RATHFARNHAM—ST. COLUMBA'S COLLEGE.

Founded in 1843 at Stackallan, the mansion of Lord Boyne, near Navan. Removed to Rathfarnham, near Dublin, 1849. The first public school established upon strictly Church principles in Ireland.

EDWIN GEORGE MONK, Mus.D., Oxon., F.R.A.S. 1844 1846
(See under York.)

JOHN BAPTISTE CALKIN, F.R.C.O. 1846 1852
Born in London, March 16, 1827. Pupil of his father, James Calkin. Organist and Precentor of St. Columba's College, Navan (afterwards Rathfarnham), 1846; Organist of Woburn Chapel, London, 1853; Camden Road Chapel, 1863; St. Thomas's Church, Camden Town, 1870-1884. Professor at the Guildhall School of Music. Composer of Church Music, Chamber Music, Part-songs, Songs, Organ pieces, Pianoforte pieces, &c.

GEORGE BENJAMIN ARNOLD, Mus.D., Oxon., F.R.C.O. 1853 1856
(See under Winchester Cathedral.)

HERBERT STEPHEN IRONS 1856 1857
(See under Southwell.)

ALEXANDER SAMUEL COOPER, F.R.C.O.... ... 1857 1859
Born in London, April 30, 1835. Organist of St. Columba's College, Rathfarnham, 1857. Afterwards Organist successively of St. John's, Putney, and St. Paul's, Covent Garden. Composer of Church Music, Part-songs, Songs, &c. Editor of "Parochial Psalter" and "Parochial Chant Book."

EDWARD MURLESSE CLARKE 1859 1862
Born 1827. Organist of St. Columba's College, Rathfarnham, 1862. Afterwards Inspector of Choral Union, 1863-1882, for the Diocese of Canterbury. Died at Ringmore, Devon, March 15, 1887.

FREDERICK CAMBRIDGE, Mus.B., Dunelm., 1893 ... 1862 1865
Born at South Runcton, Norfolk, March 29, 1841. Chorister in Norwich Cathedral. Pupil of Dr. Z. Buck, and afterwards of Molique. Organist of St. Columba's College, Rathfarnham, 1862; St. Mary's, Leicester, 1866; Parish Church, Croydon, 1868. Conductor of the Croydon Vocal Union, &c. Composer of Church Music, Glees, Organ pieces, Pianoforte pieces, &c.

THEODORE EDWARD AYLWARD ... ... May, 1866, Dec., 1866
(See under Chichester.)

FREDERICK WILLIAM HOGAN, M.A., Dub. ... 1866 1868
Born at Reichill, Armagh, August 23, 1845. Pupil of Robert Turle, at Armagh, and Dr. J. C. Marks, at Cork. Choirmaster to the Llandaff Diocesan Choir Union, 1866. Organist of St. Columba's College, Rathfarnham, in November of the same year. Took Holy Orders, and held several Curacies from 1870. Vicar of All Saints', Eglantine, Co. Down, 1883. Composer of Church Music, &c.

GEORGE HARDACRE 1869 1870
Present Organist of the Parish Church, Daventry.

W. KEELING 1870 1871

J. HEIGHTON... ... ... May, 1871, July, 1871

R. NASH ... ... Aug., 1871 1872

E. HARDING, B.A., Oxon.... ... ... 1872 1872
A nephew of Dr. Pusey.
Afterwards became a Master at the Priory School, Bath.

CHARLES LEE WILLIAMS, Mus.B., Oxon., F.R.C.O. 1872 1875
(See under Gloucester.)

E. C. OWSTON 1875 1877

WALTER LANGLEY APPLEFORD, M.A., Dub. Feb., 1877, Apr., 1877
One of the Masters. Took duty for two months, until Mr. Hyde succeeded him in April. Now Chaplain of Ripley Hospital, Lancaster.

C. F. HYDE 1877 1886

Pupil of Sir F. Ouseley, at St. Michael's College, Tenbury. Organist of St. Paul's, Old Charlton, Kent, and afterwards of St. Columba's College, Rathfarnham. Died 1894, at Giggleswick School, where he was Music-master.

HARRY CRANE PERRIN, Mus.B., Dub.; F.R.C.O. 1886 1888

(See under Canterbury.)

DONALD WALLACE LOTT 1888 1890

Son of J. B. Lott, Mus.B., the present Organist of Lichfield Cathedral. Born at Canterbury, March 18, 1868. Pupil of his father, H. Walters, Mus.B., and Sir Robert Stewart. Organist of the Chapel of St. John's Hospital, Lichfield, 1885; Assistant Organist of Lichfield Cathedral, 1885; Organist of St. Columba's College, Rathfarnham, 1888; Organist and Music Master of St. Chad's College, Denstone, 1890; Organist of the Parish Church, Lancaster, 1892; Holy Trinity, Broadstairs, 1893; Holy Trinity, Swansea, 1895-1898. Composer of College Grace (MS.). Lecturer on Music.

JOSHUA N. BRYANT, B.A., Dunelm. 1890 1891

Born, June 4, 1864. Pupil of Sir Robert Stewart. Organist of King Alfred's School, Wantage, and afterwards of St. Columba's College, Rathfarnham. Now Organist and Choirmaster to the Countess of Craven.

MYLES CECIL BERKELEY, M.A., Cantab. ... 1892 1894

Born at Secunderabad, August 7, 1866. Chorister in Manchester Cathedral. Student at the Royal Academy of Music, under T. Westlake, F. Walker, F. Davenport, and H. Rose. Afterwards pupil of Drs. A. H. Mann and C. Wood, at Cambridge. Since 1894 Precentor and Organist of Forest School, Walthamstow.

FREDERIC WILLIAM ATTWOOD ... ... 1894 ——

Born at Onderton, near Tewkesbury, August 9, 1869. Pupil of Drs. C. J. Frost and J. V. Roberts. Successively Organist of Bow Parish Church, London; Assistant Organist of St. Peter's, Brockley; and Organist and Choirmaster at "The Philberds," Maidenhead. Organist of St. Columba's College, Rathfarnham, 1894.

TENBURY—ST. MICHAEL'S COLLEGE.

Founded in 1856 by the Rev. Sir Frederick A. Gore Ouseley, Bart., mainly for the education of boys in music.

JOHN CAPEL HANBURY, M.A., Oxon, 1859 ... ... 1856 (?)1857

Subsequently took Holy Orders and became Curate of Pipe and Lyde, and Second Classical Master of Hereford Cathedral School, 1858. Divinity Lecturer and Chaplain of Wadham College, Oxford, 1872. Rector successively of Lower Bromley, Essex, 1880; and Bourton-on-the-Water, Gloucestershire, 1884. Hereford Chaplain at Wiesbaden, 1888.

(SIR) JOHN STAINER, M.A., and Mus.D., Oxon.; D.C.L., and Mus.D., Dunelm; F.R.C.O. ... 1857 1859

(See under London—St. Paul's Cathedral.)

LANGDON COLBORNE., Mus.B., Cantab.; Mus.D., Cantuar. 1860 1874

(See under Hereford.)

ALFRED ALEXANDER 1874 1877

Born at Rochester, May 6, 1844. Chorister in Rochester Cathedral. Pupil of and Assistant to John Hopkins. Organist of Shorne Church (in succession to Sir F. Bridge), 1862; Strood Parish Church, 1865. Subsequently Organist to the Earl of Mar and Kellie. Organist successively of St. Michael's College, Tenbury, 1874; Wigan Parish Church, 1877; American Church, Nice, 1891; and St. Andrew's, Southport. Composer of Cantatas, Church Music, Chamber Music, Organ pieces, Songs, Part-songs, &c.

WILLIAM CLAXTON, M.A., Oxon., 1895; Mus.B., Oxon., 1882 ... ... 1877 1886

Subsequently took Holy Orders and became Curate of Hartley Wintney, 1887; Curate of Woolston, Hants, 1893; and Vicar of Navestock, Essex, 1897. Composer of Church Music, Part-songs, Songs, &c.

WALTER J. LANCASTER, Mus.B., Vict.; F.R.C.O. 1886 1889

Born 1860. Chorister in St. George's Chapel, Windsor (for six months only). Pupil of T. E. Jones, Dr. Longhurst, and Dr. E. J. Hopkins. Organist of Dover Parish Church, 1878; All Saints', Kingston-on-Thames, 1883. Organist and Music Master of St. Michael's College, Tenbury, 1886. Organist of the Parish Church, Bolton, 1889. Composer of Church Music, Songs, &c.

ALLAN PATERSON, Mus.B., Dub., 1895; F.R.C.O. 1889 1893

Born August 3, 1865. Assistant Organist of Hereford Cathedral, 1884; Organist of St. Michael's College, Tenbury, 1889; Priory Church, Malvern, 1893; Govan Parish Church, 1895; St. Paul's Church, Cannes, 1898-1899. Composer of Church Music, &c.

JAMES LYON... ... ... 1893 1896

Born October 25, 1872. Pupil of Drs. T. W. Dodds and Herbert Botting. Sub-Organist of Bangor Cathedral, 1892. Organist of St. Michael's College, Tenbury, 1893; St. Mark's, Surbiton, 1896. Organist and Music Master of Warwick School, 1897. Composer of Church Music, Organ Music, Songs, Pianoforte pieces, Violin pieces, &c.

During the latter part of 1893 Mr. C. H. MOODY, the present Organist of Holy Trinity Church, Coventry, shared the duty with Mr. Lyon.

EDGAR C. BROADHURST ... ... 1896 ——

Born at Lympstone, Devon, June 10, 1876. Chorister in Hereford Cathedral. Pupil of G. R. Sinclair, and Assistant Organist of Hereford Cathedral. For some time Accompanist to the Hereford Choral and Orchestral Societies and to the Hereford Festival Choir. Organist of St. Michael's College, Tenbury, 1896.

WINCHESTER COLLEGE.

In William of Wykeham's Statutes of 1400 there is no provision for an Organist, and for more than a century one of the Lay Clerks appears to have taken the duty. The first mention of a regular Organist occurs in 1542, when, according to the Bursar's book,

ROBERT MOSE

held the appointment at a salary of £5 per annum. This seems to have continued to be the amount of the Organist's salary until the time of John Reading.

—— HAWKYNS was Organist in 1548.
His name appears in the Computus Roll for that year.

THOMAS WEELKES ... ... —— ——
(See under Chichester.)

WILLIAM EMES ... ... —— 1637
Succeeded Weelkes. Died 1637.

GEORGE KING ... ...(?)1661 1665
Organist at the Restoration.
(See under Winchester Cathedral.)

ROBERT PICKHAVER 1665 1678
Previously Organist of New College, Oxford. In 1665 "he received £4 9s. 6d. in payment for an instrument of music called 'le harpselen' (the harpsichord ?)"—(Kirby's "Annals of Winchester College.") Died 1678.
Two Anthems by him, "Consider and hear me" and "Sing unto the Lord," are included in the MS. Organ book in the possession of Mr. J. S. Bumpus, mentioned on p. 125.

—— GEFFRYS (JEFFRIES ?) 1678 1681

JOHN READING 1681 1692
(See under Winchester Cathedral.)
During Reading's time the salary was increased from £5 to £50 per annum.

JEREMIAH CLARK ... . 1692 (?)1695
(See under London—St. Paul's Cathedral.)

JOHN BISHOP 1695 1737
(See under Winchester Cathedral.)

JAMES KENT 1737 1774
(See under Winchester Cathedral.)

PETER FUSSELL 1774 1802
(See under Winchester Cathedral.)

George William Chard, Mus.D., Cantab. ... 1802 1849
(See under Winchester Cathedral.)

Samuel Sebastian Wesley, Mus.D., Oxon. ... 1849 1865
(See under Gloucester.)

William Hutt ... ... 1865 ——

Born August 25, 1843. Chorister in Westminster Abbey. Pupil of James Turle, James Coward, and Professor G. A. Macfarren. Organist successively of St. Michael's, Queenhithe; Berkeley Chapel, Mayfair; and the Parish Church, Mitcham. Organist and Music Master of Winchester College, 1865.

WINDSOR—ST. GEORGE'S CHAPEL (ROYAL).

John Marbeck (or Merbeck), Mus.B., Oxon., 1550 —— (?)1585

Born 1523. Chorister in St. George's Chapel, Windsor, 1531. Condemned to the stake, for his adherence to the Protestant faith, about 1544, but escaped through the intervention of Gardiner, Bishop of Winchester. Died about 1585. Adapter of the ancient Plain-Song to the English Service, published in 1550 as "The booke of Common Praier Noted." Composer of Church Music. Author of a Concordance, "The Lives of the Holy Sainctes, Prophets, Patriachs, and others, contained in Holy Scripture," 1574, &c.

In the dedication, to Edward VI., of his "Concordance," he describes himself as "destitute bothe of learnyng and eloquence, yea, and suche a one as in maner never tasted the swetnes of learned Letters, but altogether brought up in your highnes College at Wyndsore in the study of musike and plaiyng on organs, wherin I consumed vainly the greatest part of my life." According to the "Injunctions newly given by the Kinges Mats Commissioners for the reformation of certain abuses" (4 Edward VI., October 26, 1550), George Thexton was evidently a Joint Organist with Marbeck at that time:—

"And whereas we understand that *John Merbeck* and *George Thexton*, hath of your graunt, ffees appointed them severally for playing upon organs. We take ordre that the sayd John and George shall enjoy their severall offices during their Lyves, if they continue in that Colledge, in as large and ample maner as if organ plaing had still continued in the Church."—(Ashmolean MS., No. 1123, f. 38b-41b.)

Richard Farrant ... ... 1564 (?)1585

Master of the Choristers and probably a Joint Organist with Marbeck.

Born about 1530. Gentleman of the Chapel Royal until 1564. Master of the Choristers and probably Organist of St. George's Chapel, Windsor, 1564. Re-appointed a Gentleman of the Chapel Royal, 1569. Died at Windsor, November 30, 1585. Composer of Church Music. The well-known Anthem, "Lord, for Thy tender mercies' sake," attributed to R. Farrant, is more probably the work of John Hilton.

Farrant had an allowance of £81 6s. 8d. as Master of the Choristers of St. George's Chapel, for their board and education. He resided in a house within the Castle, called *Old Commons*.

JOHN MUNDY (MUNDAY, or MUNDIE), Mus.D., Oxon., 1624 ... ... 1586 1630

Is said to have succeeded Marbeck as Organist. Pupil of his father, William Mundy, and for some time Organist of Eton College. Organist of St. George's Chapel, Windsor, 1586. Died 1630. Buried in the Cloisters, St. George's Chapel. Composer of Church Music, Madrigals, "Songs and Psalms," &c.

NATHANIEL GILES (or GYLES), Mus.D., Oxon., 1622 1595 (?)1633

Son of Thomas Giles, Organist of St. Paul's Cathedral. Born about 1550. Chorister in Magdalen College, Oxford, and afterwards Clerk of the same. Organist and Master of the Choristers of St. George's Chapel, Windsor, 1595. Master of the Children of the Chapel Royal, 1597. Died January 24, 1633. Buried in St. George's Chapel, Windsor. Composer of Church Music, Madrigals, &c.

The Dean and Canons of St. George's Chapel, Windsor, by Deed dated 1st October, 1595, nominate Nathaniel Gyles, B.M., to be Clerk in the Chapel, and one of the Players on the Organs there, and also to be Master, Instructor, Tutor, and Creansor, or Governor of the ten Choristers, agreeing to give him an annuity of £81 6s. 8d. and a dwelling-house within the castle, called the *Old Commons*, wherein John Mundie did lately inhabit, with all appurtenances, as one Richard Farrante enjoyed the same. The stipend to be paid monthly by the Treasurer, over and beside all other gifts, rewards, or benevolence that may be given to the Choristers for singing of Ballads, Plays, or the like: also such reasonable leave of absence as the statutes allow, except when Her Majesty shall be present, or an Installation or Funeral of any noble person shall be solemnized,—on condition that the said Nathaniel Gyles shall procure meet and apt Choristers within the space of three months after avoidance, (Her Majesty's Commission for the taking of children being allowed unto him,) and that he shall instruct them in Singing, Pricksong, and Descant, and bring up such as be apt to the Instrument; and that he shall find them sufficient meat and drink, apparel, bedding and lodging at his own costs within the *New Commons* lately appointed for them; and that he shall find a sufficient deputy during the times of sickness and absence."—(Ashmolean MS., No. 1125, 33).

"Nathaniel Giles, Dr. of mewsicke died ye 24th of Janewary & was bewryed the 29th of the same munneth, 1633."—(Extract from the Registers of St. George's Chapel.)

WILLIAM CHILD, Mus.D., Oxon.... ... ... 1632 1697

(See under Chapel Royal.)

[The Choral Service and Organ were suppressed from 1644 until the Restoration.]

JOHN GOLDWIN (or GOLDING) 1697 1719

Born 1670. Pupil of Dr. Child. Organist of St. George's Chapel, Windsor, 1697; Master of the Choristers there, 1703. Died at Windsor, November 7, 1719. Composer of a Service in F, a few Anthems, and some "Lessons" for the Harpsichord (MS.).

FRANCIS PIGOTT (Junr.) ... ... —— 1756

Probably grandson of Francis Pigott (Senr.), and son of J. Pigott (Organists of the Temple Church). The year of his appointment to St. George's Chapel is not known.

EDWARD WEBB 1756 1788

Died 1788, through loss of blood, after undergoing an operation for the removal of a wen from the nostril. Buried in the Cloisters.

THEODORE AYLWARD, Mus.D., Oxon., 1791 ... 1788 1801

Born 1730. Organist of Oxford Chapel, London, W., about 1760; St. Lawrence, Jewry, 1762; St. Michael's, Cornhill, 1768; St. George's Chapel, Windsor, 1788. Was also Private Organist to Queen Charlotte. Gresham Professor of Music, 1771. Died in London, February 27, 1801. Buried in St. George's Chapel, Windsor. Composer of Church Music (in MS.), Musical Dramas, pieces for the Harpsichord, Glees, Songs, &c.

Epitaph (by the poet Hayley) on Dr. Aylward, in the Rutland Chapel, North Aisle of St. George's Chapel:—

"Aylward, adieu! my pleasing, gentle friend,
Regret and honour on thy grave attend:
Thy rapid hand harmonious skill possest,
And moral harmony enriched thy breast;
For heaven most freely to thy life assign'd
Benevolence, the music of the mind;
Mild as thy nature all thy mortal scene,
Thy death was easy, and thy life serene."

WILLIAM SEXTON 1801 1824

Born 1764. Chorister in St. George's Chapel, Windsor, and in Eton College. Pupil of Edward Webb. For some years Assistant Organist of St. George's Chapel. Organist, Sub-Precentor, and Master of the Choristers, 1801. Died 1824. Composer of Church Music, Glees, Songs, &c.

KARL FRIEDRICH HORN 1824 1830

Born at Nordhausen, Saxony, 1762. Pupil of Schröter. Came to London as valet to the Marquis of Stafford, 1782. Afterwards became a teacher of music, and was Music Master to Queen Charlotte until 1811. Organist of St. George's Chapel, Windsor, 1824. Died August 5, 1830. Composer of Sonatas for the Pianoforte, Twelve Themes with variations for the Pianoforte, with an accompaniment for the Flute or Violin. Author of a Treatise on Thorough Bass. Collaborated with Samuel Wesley in the preparation of an English edition of J. S. Bach's "Wohltemperirte Clavier," which was published in 1810-12.

His son, Charles Edward Horn, was a celebrated Singer and Composer, whose songs "Cherry Ripe" and "I know a bank" have taken a place among our national ballads.

HIGHMORE SKEATS (Junr.) 1830 1835

Born at Canterbury, 1786. Presumably a pupil of his father, whom he succeeded as Organist of Ely Cathedral, 1804. Organist of St. George's Chapel, Windsor, 1830. Died at Windsor, February 24, 1835. Buried in the Cloisters of St. George's Chapel. Composer of Church Music.

SIR GEORGE JOB ELVEY, Knt., Mus.D., Oxon., 1840 1835 1882

Born at Canterbury, March 27, 1816. Chorister in Canterbury Cathedral. Pupil of Highmore Skeats (Senr.); also of his brother, Stephen Elvey, and afterwards, at the Royal Academy of Music, of Cipriani Potter and Dr. Crotch. Lay Clerk of Christ Church Cathedral, Oxford, 1833. Organist of St. George's Chapel, Windsor, 1835. Private Organist to Her Majesty, 1837.

Knighted 1871. Conductor of the Windsor Glee and Madrigal Society and of the Windsor and Eton Choral Society. Retired from the post at Windsor, 1882. Died at Windlesham, Surrey, December 9, 1893. Buried outside the West Front of St. George's Chapel, Windsor. Composer of Oratorios, Odes, Church Music, Glees, Part-songs, Music for Orchestra, Organ, Pianoforte, Violin, Songs, &c.

SIR WALTER PARRATT, Knt., Mus.D., Oxon., 1894; F.R.C.O. ... ... 1882 ——

Born at Huddersfield, February 10, 1841. Pupil of his father, Thomas Parratt (Organist of Huddersfield Parish Church), and George Cooper. Appointed Organist of Armitage Bridge Church, 1852; St. Paul's, Huddersfield, 1854; Witley Court (Private Organist to Earl Dudley), 1861; Wigan Parish Church, 1868; Magdalen College, Oxford, 1872; St. George's Chapel, Windsor, 1882. Conductor of the Windsor and Eton Madrigal Society, 1882. Sometime Conductor of the Windsor and Eton Choral Society. Founder and Conductor of the Windsor and Eton Orchestral Society. Professor of the Organ at the Royal College of Music, 1883. Knighted 1892. Master of the Music to Her Majesty the Queen, 1893. Composer of Music to "Agamemnon," "Story of Orestes," "Elegy to Patroclus," Church Music, Organ pieces, Songs, Pianoforte pieces, &c. Lecturer and Writer on Music.

INDEX OF ORGANISTS' NAMES.

When more than one page number is given against an Organist's name, that in the larger type indicates where the biographical notes concerning that Organist are to be found.

A.

PAGE

Abbott, John 90
"Adam the Organist" 61
Alcock, John 45
Alcock, Walter G. 118
Alexander, Alfred.. 129
Allchin, William Thomas Howell 126
Allen, John 12
Allen, Hugh Percy .. 31, 75
Allinson (or Allanson), Thomas.. 48
Amner, John 30
Amott, John 37
Amps, William 98
Angel, Alfred 34
Appilby, Thomas.. 47
Appleford, Walter Langley .. 127
Armes, Philip 17, 28
Arnold, George Benjamin 89, 124, 126
Arnold, Samuel 109, 117
Atkins, Ivor Algernon .. 92
Atkins, Robert Augustus .. 75
Atkinson, Frederick Cook .. 64
Attwood, Frederick William .. 128
Attwood, Thomas .. 55, 109
Ayleward, Richard 62
Aylward, Theodore 133
Aylward, Theodore Edward 18, 52, 127
Ayrton, Edmund 80
Ayrton, Thomas 70
Ayrton, William 70
Ayrton, William Francis Worrall 70

B.

Badham, John 41
Bailey, Edward 14, 75
Bailey, John 14
Baker, Edmund 14
Baker, Henry 61
Banks, Ralph 73
Barcrofte, George.. 29
Barcrofte, Thomas 29
Barnby, Sir Joseph 103
Barnes, Robert 1
Barrett, John 77
Barton, Matthew.. 96
Barneys, Thomas.. 12
Batchelor, Chappell 81

PAGE

Bates, Frank 64
Bates, George 71
Bateson, Thomas.. .. 12, 21
Batten, Adrian 53
Beale, George Galloway.. .. 52
Beale, William 98, 100
Beckwith, John Charles 63
Beckwith, John Christmas .. 63
Bedsmore, Thomas 46
Bennett, Alfred (Senr.) 124
Bennett, Alfred (Junr.) 98
Bennett, George John 50
Bennett, Henry R. 17
Bennett, Thomas.. 17
Berkeley, Myles Cecil 128
Bettridge, Samuel 1
Betts, Edward 59
Bevin, Elway 6
Bishop, John 87, 130
Bishop, William 77
Black, George 14
Blair, Hugh 91
Blitheman, William 105
Blow, John .. 107, 114, 115
Blundell, Roper 71
Blyth, Benjamin 122
Bolton, Thomas 2
Bond, John Henry 70
Booth, John Stocks 74
Booth, Richard 58
Bowers, Robert 72
Bowman, John 100
Boyce, Daniel 89
Boyce, William 108
Boys, William 47
Bramston, Richard 83
Brewer, Alfred Herbert 39
Bridge, John Frederick (Sir Frederick) 60, 118
Bridge, Joseph Cox 15
Brimley (or Brimlei), John .. 26
Brind, Richard 54
Broadhurst, Edgar C. 129
Broadway, Edward 19
Broadway, Richard 25
Broderip, John 84
Broderip, William 84
Brooksbank, Hugh 52

	PAGE
Brown, Richard	83, 90
Brown, William	46
Browne, William	24
Browne, William (Senr.) ..	27
Browne, William (Junr.)	27
Bryan (Brian or Bryne), Albertus	53, 114
Bryant, Joshua R.	128
Buck, Percy Carter	7, 85
Buck, Zechariah	63
Bucknall, Cedric	81
Bull, John	40, 105
Bullis, Thomas	30
Burstall, Frederick Hampton ..	50
Butler, Thomas	47
Byrcheley, John	12
Byrd (or Bird), William ..	47, 105

C.

Calah, John	69
Calkin, John Baptiste	126
Cambridge, Frederick	127
Camidge, John	94
Camidge, Matthew	94
Camidge, Dr. John	94
Campyon, William	16
Capell, Thomas	17
Carr, George	51
Carter, William	58
Chard, George William ..	88, 131
Charles, J...	93
Cheese, Griffith James	60
Cherington, R.	90
Cherry, Richard	26
Child, Simon	123
Child, William	106, 132
Chipp, Edmund Thomas ..	31
Chomley, Richard	8
Church, Richard	66, 123
Clack, Richard	42
Clansay, John	83
Clark, Jeremiah ..	54, 108, 130
Clarke, Charles E. J. ..	28, 91
Clarke, Edward Murlesse ..	127
Clarke, James Hamilton Siree ..	51
Clarke, Jeremiah	91
Clarke-Whitfeld, John	1, 42, 98, 100
Claxton, Robert	30
Claxton, William	129
Clerk, John	83
Cobbold, William..	61
Cock (or Cocke), Arthur ..	32, 105
Codner, D. John D.	77
Cogan, Philip	25
Colborne, Langdon ..	43, 129
Coleby (or Colby), Theodore	33, 119
Collinson, Thomas Henry ..	28
Combes, George	7
Cooke, Benjamin	116
Cooke, Robert	117
Cooper, Alexander Samuel ..	127
Cooper, George (Junr.) ..	56, 110
Cooper, James	63
Corfe, Joseph	79
Corfe, Arthur Thomas	79
Corfe, Charles William	67
Corfe, John Davis..	7
Cotton, Humphry	63
Coyle, Miles	42
Creser, William	110
Croft, William	108, 116
Cross, William	67, 125
Crotch, William	67, 125
Crow, Edwin John	71
Crowe, James	47

D.

Daniell, —	89
Dare, Charles James	42
Davies, Henry Walford	112
Davies (or Davis), Hugh.. ..	41
Davies, Richard (or William) ..	90
Davies, William	90
Davies, William	13
Davis, Thomas Henry	85
Davy, John	46
Day, Thomas	113
De La Maine, Henry	19
Demonticall, John	13
Dobinson, Abraham	11
Dodson, —	27
Done, Michael	12
Done, William	91
Dowding, Emily	111
Doyle, Langrishe	1, 22
Dupuis, Thomas Sanders ..	109

E.

Ebdon, Thomas	28
Eblyn, Thomas	100
Edge, Edward	59
Elbonn, John	30
Elliott, Thomas	76
Ellis, William	102, 125
Elvey, Sir George Job	133
Elvey, Stephen	124, 126
Emes, William	130
Este, Michael	44
Evans, William	84

F.

Fairfax, Robert	74
Farrant, Richard	131
Farrant, John	29, 41, 78
Fermor, John	21
Ferrabosco, John	30

PAGE
Ferrer, — 3
Fidow, John 41
Finell, Thomas 22, 24
Ford, Henry Edmund 11
Foster, John 27
Fox, William 29
Frith, John 125
Fuller, Robert 97
Fussell, Peter 88, 130

G.

Gaffe, George 74
Galway, Richard 1
Garland, Thomas 63
Garrett, George Mursell 99
Garton, Frederick S. 77
Geffrys, — 130
George, John 84
Gerard, J. 75
Gerard, Alexander 75
Gerard, — 75
Gibbes, Thomas 8
Gibbons, Edward 6, 32, 96
Gibbons, Ellis 78
Gibbons, Orlando 105, 113
Gibbons, Christopher .. 85, 107, 113
Gibbs, — 41
Gibbs, Thomas 63
Gibbs, Richard 62
Gilbert, John 47
Giles (or Gyles), Thomas .. 53
Giles, Nathaniel 132
Gladstone, Francis Edward 18, 52, 64
Godfrey, Thomas 21, 24
Godwin, Matthew 8, 32
Goldwin (or Golding), John .. 132
Goodson, Richard (Senr.) 65, 123
Goodson, Richard (Junr.) .. 66
Goss, Sir John 56
Gray, Alan 101
Greatorex, Thomas .. 11, 117
Greene, Maurice 54, 108
Greene, R... 89
Greggs, William 27
Grizzelle, Thomas 126
Gunn, Barnabas 36
Gunton, Frederick .. 15, 81

H.

Hall, Henry (Senr.) .. 33, 41
Hall, Henry (Junr.) 41
Hall, Richard 17
Hampton, John 89
Hanbury, John Capel 128
Hardacre, George 127
Harding, E. 127
Hardy, Joseph Naylor 82
Harris, Joseph John 60

PAGE
Harwood, Basil 31, 67
Hasted, John 49
Hawkins, James (Senr.) 30
Hawkins, James (Junr.) 68
Hawkins, John 70
Hawkshaw, John (Senr.) 21, 24
Hawkshaw, John (Junr.) .. 1, 24
Hawkyns, — 130
Hayden, William 75
Hayes, Philip .. 66, 121, 123, 125
Hayes, William 90, 121
Haylett, Thomas 14
Hayne, Leighton George .. 103
Hayter, Aaron Upjohn 42
Hayward, Robert 20
Heath, John 72
Heathcote, Edward 81
Heather, Stephen 103
Hecht (or Hight), Andrew .. 48
Hecht, Thomas 48, 120
Heighton, J. 127
Henman, Richard 33
Henshaw, William 28
Henstridge, Daniel .. 9, 35, 72
Herbit, William 24
Hesletine, James 27
Higgins, Edward 7
Hill, Thomas 11
Hilton, John 47, 99
Hinde, Henry 44
Hine, William 36
Hoddinott, John 90
Hodge, John 40
Hodge, Robert 24, 84
Hodge, William 57
Hodge, William (Junr.) 1
Hogan, Frederick William .. 127
Holland, James 58
Hollister, Thomas 19
Holmes, George 49
Holmes, John 78, 85
Hooper, Edmund 106, 113
Hopkins, Charles 90
Hopkins, Edward John 112
Hopkins, John Larkin .. 73, 101
Hopkins, John 73
Horan, John 23
Horn, Karl Friedrich 133
Horncastle, Frederick William .. 1
Hosier, Philip 34
Howe, John 11
Howe, Thomas 11
Howe, Joseph 72
Howe, Richard 73
Howe, John 112
Hughes, Thomas 75
Hugo, Richard 83
Hunt, John 43

PAGE
Huntley, George Frederick .. 61
Husbands, Charles 65
Husbands, William 65
Hutchinson, John 93
Hutchinson, Richard 27
Hutt, William 131
Hyde, C. F. 128

I.

Iliffe, Frederick 126
Ingleton, John 46
Ingham, Richard 11
Inglott, William 62
Ions, William Jamson 61
Irons, Herbert Stephen .. 81, 127
Isaac, Elias 91
Isaac(ke), Peter 21, 79
Isaac, William 24

J.

Jackson, John 84
Jackson, William 33
Janes, Robert 31
Jarred (or Gerard), Richard .. 3
Jefferies, John Edward 61
Jeffries (or Jefferies), Stephen .. 35
Jekyll, Charles Sherwood .. 110
Jewitt, Randall (or Randolph) 12, 21, 24, 86
Jones, Dr. John 1
Jones, John 75
Jones, John 55, 111
Jones, Thomas 12
Jones, Thomas Evance 10
Juglott, William 41

K.

Kay (Key, or Keys), William .. 13
Kay (or Keys), — 75
Keeling, W. 127
Keeton, Haydn 69
Kelway, Thomas 16
Kemp, Joseph 7
Kempton, Thomas 30
Kenge, William 91
Kent, James 88, 130
Keys, William 58, 75
King, George 85, 130
King, William 123
Kingston, Thomas 47
Kirby (or Kirkby), — 92
Knight, Thomas 69
Knyvett, Charles 109

L.

Lamb, Benjamin 102
Lamb, — (Senr.) 44
Lamb, — (Junr.) 44
Lamb, George 44
Lancaster, Laurence 70
Lancaster, Walter J. 129
Langdon, Richard .. 1, 31, 33
Lant, Bartholomew 65
Lant, John 85
Larkin, Edmund 69
Lavington, Charles Williams .. 84
Lawes, Henry 107
Leche, — 75
Lee, William 80
Leeve, Henry 112
Leigh, John 58
Lichfield, Robert 34
Liddle, Robert William 82
Litster, Thomas 70
Lloyd, Charles Harford .. 39, 67, 104
Lloyd, Thomas 3
Lloyd, Llewelyn 75
Long, Benjamin 89
Longdon, Richard 69
Longhurst, William Henry 10
Loosemore, Henry .. 32, 96
Loosemore, George 99
Lott, John Browning 46
Lott, Donald Wallace 128
Love, William 18
Lowe, Edward 65, 107
Lowe, Thomas 35
Lugg (or Lugge), Robert .. 125
Lyon, James 129

M.

Maclean, Charles Donald .. 103
Macpherson, Charles 57
Maddox, Matthew 77
Mann, Arthur Henry 98
Marbeck (or Merbeck), John .. 131
Marchant, Charles George .. 26
Marks, James Christopher .. 19
Marks, Thomas Osborne.. .. 2
Marriott, Arthur 82
Marshall, — 96
Marshall, William .. 67, 126
Martin, Sir George Clement .. 56
Martin, Jonathan 108
Mason, George 99
Mason, Thomas 40
Masterman, Robert 27
Mathews, John 25
Matthews, Samuel .. 98, 100
Meredith, William 122
Merrifield, John 90
Middlebrook, William 49
Mineard, Samuel 7
Mitchell, John 103
Monk, Edwin George .. 95, 126
Monk, Mark James 82

PAGE
Mordant, R. 76
Mordant, Henry 76
Morgan, Thomas 21
Morgan, Tom Westlake 5
Morley, James 7
Morley, Thomas 53
Morris, Herbert C. 77
Mose, Robert 130
Mudd, John 68
Mudd, — 48
Mundy (Munday, or Mundie), John 102, 132
Murgatroyd (or Murgetroyd), Charles 49 93
Murphy, Samuel 22, 25
Murphy, William 26
Mutlow, William 37

N.

Nares, James 93, 108
Nash, R. 127
Naylor, John 95
Newbold, Richard 12
Nicholson, Richard 119
Nixon, — 51
Noble, Thomas Tertius .. 31, 95
Norman, John 76
Norris, Thomas 66, 125

O.

Olive, Edmund 3
Oker (or Okeover), John .. 35, 83
Orme, Edward 14
Ouseley, Sir Frederick 67
Owston, E. C. 127

P.

Paddon, James 34
Parratt, Sir Walter .. 122, 134
Parry, Robert 79, 84
Parsons, John 113
Pasmore, Peter 33
Paterson, Allan 129
Patrick, Nathaniel 89
Peach, Charles 72
Pearse, Charles 102
Pepir, Leonard 47
Perkins, Dodd 84
Perkins, William 84
Perrin, Harry Crane .. 10, 128
Perrot, Robert 118
Perry, William 42
Phillips, Arthur 6, 119
Phillips, Matthew 120
Philpott, Matthew 77
Pick, Charles 11
Pickhaver, Robert .. 122, 130

PAGE
Pigott, Francis .. 108, 111, 120, 125
Pigott, Francis (Junr.) .. 102, 132
Pigott, J. 111
Pitt, Thomas 91
Pleasants, Thomas 63
Plomer, Francis 8
Plomley, James 71
Popely, William 80
Porter, Robert 126
Porter, Samuel 9
Portman, Richard 113
Pratt, John 97
Preston, Thomas (Senr.) 70
Preston, Thomas (Junr.) 70
Price, George 111
Priest, Nathaniel 3, 7
Pring, Isaac 123
Pring, Joseph 3
Pring, James Sharpe 4
Propert, William Peregrine .. 77
Purcell, Daniel 120
Purcell, Henry 107, 115
Pyne, James Kendrick .. 18, 60

Q.

Quarles, Charles 93, 99

R.

Ramsey, Robert 99
Randall, John 97, 100
Randall (or Randoll), William .. 105
Rathbone, John 3
Rathbone, Thomas 3
Raylton, William 9
Raynor, Lloyd 49
Read, Frederick John 18
Reading, John 16
Reading, John 86, 130
Redford, John 52
Rese (or Rees), — 51
Richardson, Arthur 77
Richardson, — 90
Richardson, Alfred Madeley .. 57
Richardson, John Elliott 79
Richardson, Vaughan 87
Ringrose, William Weaver .. 81
Riseley, George 7
Roberts, — 24
Roberts, John Varley 122
Roberts, Robert 5
Roberts, Thomas 2
Robinson, Francis James 23, 25
Robinson, John 23, 25
Robinson, John 116
Roche, James 19
Rodgers, James 69
Rogers, Benjamin .. 21, 102, 119

	PAGE
Rogers, James	31
Rogers, Roland	5
Rooke, Edward	7
Rosingrave, Daniel	22, 24, 35, 79, 87
Rosingrave, Ralph	22, 25

S.

Sale, John Bernard	110
Salisbury, Edward	93, 100
Sandys, Michael	25
Selby, —	9
Selby, Bertram Luard	80
Senny, John	6
Sexton, William	133
Sharpe, Carter	68
Sharpe, Jonathan	98
Shaw, —	70
Shaw, Alexander	27
Sheppard, John	119
Shrubsole, William	3
Silver, John	86, 96
Silvester, John	33
Sinclair, George Robertson	43, 82
Skeats, Highmore (Senr.)	9, 31
Skeats, Highmore (Junr.)	31, 133
Skelton, George	49
Smart, Sir George Thomas	109
Smith, —	3
Smith, —	90
Smith, —	58
Smith, Elias	34
Smith, George Townshend	43
Smith, Martin	36
Smith, John Stafford	109
Smyth, William	19
Smyth, William	27
Smyth, Edward	27
Sorrell, William	70
South, Charles Frederick	80
Spain, John	72
Speechly, John	69
Spence, Charles	75
Spofforth, Thomas	81
Spofforth, Samuel	46, 69
Stainer, Sir John	56, 122, 129
Standish, David	68
Standish, Roger	68
Standish, William	68
Stanford, Charles Villiers	101
Stanley, Charles John	111
Stephens, James Brealsford	19
Stephens, John	79
Stevens, Richard John Samuel	111
Stevenson, Robert	12
Stewart, Charles Henry Hylton	18
Stewart, Sir Robert Prescott	23, 26
Stimpson, James	11
Stonard, William	65
Storey, Richard	68
Stringer, Peter	12, 58
Stringer, John	13
Sudlow, William	60
Swarbrick (or Schwarbrook), Henry	41
Sweeting, Edward Thomas	99

T.

Tallis (or Tallys), Thomas	104
Targett, James	17
Taverner, John	65
Taylor, James	124
Taylor, John	112
Tetlow, Edward	58
Thexton, George	131
Thompson, Edward	79
Thorne, Edward Henry	17
Thorne, John	92
Tiller, Richard	68
Tireman, William	98, 100
Tomkins, Giles	78, 96
Tomkins, John	53, 96
Tomkins, John	89
Tomkins, Richard	76
Tomkins, Thomas	89, 106
Tomson (or Thomson), Edmund	41
Toole, William	1, 19
Travers, John	108
Tremaine, Thomas	17
Tucker, Edward	78
Tudway, Thomas	97
Turle, James	117
Turle, Robert	2
Turner, William	58
Tye, Christopher	29, 104

V.

Vicar Choral, A	2
Vicary, Walter	121
Vincent, George	80
Vincent, James	111

W.

Wainwright, John	59
Wainwright, Robert	59
Wainwright, Richard	59
Walkeley, Anthony	79
Walmisley, Thomas Attwood	98, 100
Walond, William	17
Walsh, George	22, 25
Walsh, Henry	25
Walter, John	102
Wanlass, —	70
Wanless(e), John	48
Wanless(e), Thomas	93
Warne, George	112
Warren, William	22, 25
Warrock (or Warwick), Thomas	40
Warryn, Walter	76

	PAGE
Warwick, Thomas ..	106, 113
Wasbrough, Rice	7
Wasbrough, John	7
Webb, Bartholomew	16
Webb, Edward	103, 133
Webb, Robert	35
Weelkes, Thomas ..	16, 130
Weldon, John	108, 123
Wesley, Samuel Sebastian	34, 37, 43, 89, 131
White, Edmund	13
White, John	33
White, Matthew	65
White, Robert	29, 112
White, William Henry	26
White (or Whyte), —	12
Whitt (or White), —	112
Wildbore, Robert..	99
Wilkes, John Bernard	51
Williams, Charles Lee ..	39, 52, 127
Williams, George Ebenezer ..	117
Williams, Henry	77
Williams, John	72
Williams, Thomas	98
Willis (or Wilkes), Anthony ..	24
Wilson, Archibald Wayet ..	76
Wilson, —	70
Wise, Michael	76
Wise, Samuel	49
Woffington, John	1
Wood, Daniel Joseph ..	18, 34
Wood, David	30
Woodcock, William	123
Woodson, Leonard	102
Woodward, Richard	22
Wootton, Nicholas	8
Worrall, Benjamin	13
Wren, Charles	35, 72
Wren, Robert	8
Wrench, Berkeley	34
Wright, George	68
Wyrnal, John	92

Y.

Young, John Matthew Wilson ..	50